THE (BOOKS) OF FIRST & SECOND
TIMOTHY, TITUS,
AND PHILEMON

GOALS TO GODLINESS

Advancing the Ministries of the Gospel

AMG Publishers

God's Word to you is our highest calling.

TWENTY-FIRST CENTURY
BIBLICAL COMMENTARY SERIES®

THE BOOKS OF FIRST & SECOND TIMOTHY, TITUS, AND PHILEMON

GOALS TO GODLINESS

CHARLES
RAY

GENERAL EDITORS

MAL COUCH &
ED HINDSON

The Books of First and Second Timothy, Titus, & Philemon: Goals to Godliness
By Charles Ray
Twenty-First Century Biblical Commentary Series®
Copyright © 2007 by Scofield Ministries
Published by AMG Publishers
6815 Shallowford Road
Chattanooga, TN 37421

ISBN–13: 978-0-89957-826-2

First Published: May 2008

Cover Design by ImageWright, Inc.
Editing and Text Design by Warren Baker
Editorial assistance provided by Patrick Belvill and Weller Editorial Services, Chippewa Lake, MI

Printed in Canada
13 12 11 10 09 08 –T– 7 6 5 4 3 2 1

Twenty-First Century Biblical Commentary Series®

Mal Couch, Th.D., and Ed Hindson, D.Phil.

The New Testament has guided the Christian church for over two thousand years. This one testament is made up of twenty-seven books, penned by godly men through the inspiration of the Holy Spirit. It tells us of the life of Jesus Christ, His atoning death for our sins, His miraculous resurrection, His ascension back to heaven, and the promise of His second coming. It also tells the story of the birth and growth of the church and the people and principles that shaped it in its earliest days. The New Testament concludes with the book of Revelation pointing ahead to the glorious return of Jesus Christ.

Without the New Testament, the message of the Bible would be incomplete. The Old Testament emphasizes the promise of a coming Messiah. It constantly points us ahead to the One who is coming to be the King of Israel and the Savior of the world. But the Old Testament ends with this event still unfulfilled. All of its ceremonies, pictures, types, and prophecies are left awaiting the arrival of the "Lamb of God who takes away the sin of the world" (John 1:29).

The message of the New Testament represents the timeless truth of God. As each generation seeks to apply that truth to its specific context, an up-to-date commentary needs to be created just for them. The editors and authors of the Twenty-First Century Biblical Commentary Series have endeavored to do just that. This team of scholars represents conservative, evangelical, and dispensational scholarship at its best. The individual authors may differ on minor points of interpretation, but all are convinced that the Old and New

Testaments teach a dispensational framework for biblical history. They also hold to a pretribulational and premillennial understanding of biblical prophecy.

The French scholar René Pache reminded each succeeding generation, "If the power of the Holy Spirit is to be made manifest anew among us, it is of primary importance that His message should regain its due place. Then we shall be able to put the enemy to flight by the sword of the Spirit which is the Word of God."

The Pastoral Epistles provide the most thorough statement of church government found anywhere in the New Testament. British scholar Donald Guthrie has observed, "Their appeal lies in their blend of sound practical advice and theological statement, which has proved invaluable to Christians both personally and collectively." Paul's combination of personal advice and apostolic injunction has set the pattern for church government for the past twenty-one centuries.

While these epistles have always been viewed collectively because of their nature and content, it was not until 1703 that D. N. Berdot popularized the term pastoral to describe them. Although these epistles are written to specific individuals (Timothy and Titus), Canadian scholar Ronald Word, has remarked, "They are both personal and official, for they have wider interests than those of a purely private letter."

American scholar Homer Kent Jr. made a career out of studying these important letters in detail. He summed up his opinion of them, saying, "Not only is the content rich in doctrinal and practical discussion, so pertinent to the Christian life, but the historical, geographical, and personal notices make the letters colorful and intensely human."

Contents

Background of the Pastoral Epistles

These three letters from the apostle Paul to his coworkers Timothy and Titus are collectively called the Pastoral Epistles. The term was first applied as far back as 1703.[1] This designation is appropriate because the recipients were two young pastors who needed Paul's encouragement and instruction. Virtually all scholars agree that these three books of the New Testament were penned by the same person within a few years of each other. As such, they can be considered as a unit. An attack on one is an attack on all.

The question, then, often comes up, "Why should I study these three books? I'm not a pastor." Preachers would certainly do well to heed the admonitions the great apostle issues, but all believers can glean vital truths from this portion of the Bible. Indeed, right there in 2 Timothy 3:16 is the statement, "All Scripture is . . . profitable. . . ."

William Hendriksen provides several other reasons.[2] These three New Testament books furnish information on church government, on qualifications for church leaders, and on women's roles, both in the home and in the church. First Timothy is the most pastoral of the three. Little is known about Paul and his travels after the close of the book of Acts, but some of the passages in these letters help to fill in the gaps. Hence, they likewise supplement our historical knowledge of the church in the first century. Perhaps the most vital reason for examining them is that they teach sound doctrine. It seems that many church bodies today are disinterested in solid theology and unaware of the danger of neglecting it. On the other hand, Paul has not composed a dry, doctrinal lecture. Hendriksen reminds us that purity of doctrine leads to purity of life.[3] Finally, the Pastoral Epistles are worth our time and effort "[b]ecause in these epistles as well as in the others God speaks to us."[4]

Authorship

Until the early 1800s, there was no serious challenge to the notion that Paul was the penman behind these works. Both external evidence (confirmations from outside the Bible) and internal evidence (confirmations within the text itself) support Pauline authorship. Modern scholars who reject that conclusion base their beliefs on a faulty interpretation of the data. More will be said about those specific issues later on in this section. For now, the evidence favoring Pauline authorship will be presented, beginning with the external.

An array of documents from the early church fathers suggests that they not only knew of 1 Timothy, 2 Timothy, and Titus, but also recognized them as part of Holy Writ.[5] About AD 95, Clement of Rome wrote his *Epistle to the Corinthians*. In his letter he alludes to 1 Timothy 1:18 (sec. 37), 2 Timothy 1:3 (sec. 45), and Titus 2:10 (sec. 26). Another ancient saint, Polycarp (ca. AD 110), wrote, "But the beginning of all troublesome things is the love of money. Knowing therefore that we brought nothing into the world, but neither have we anything to carry out, let us arm ourselves with the arms of righteousness."[6] His words bear a strong resemblance to 1 Timothy 6:7, 10: "For we have brought nothing into the world, so we cannot take anything out of it either. . . . For the love of money is a root of all sorts of evil, and some by longing for it have wandered away from the faith. . . ." Polycarp's allusions to the Pastoral Epistles are frequent in his works. That he was a disciple of the apostle John makes it all the more certain that he considered these three letters to have genuinely come from the hand of Paul.

Clement of Alexandria (ca. AD 155–215) quotes 1 Timothy 6:20–21 and describes this passage as being from "the apostle."[7] A man contemporaneous with Clement of Alexandria, Tertullian, directly declared that 1 Timothy 1:18; 6:13, 20, and 2 Timothy 1:14 are statements of Paul.[8] Others who cite or allude to the Pastoral Epistles include Ignatius, Justin Martyr, Hegesippus, and Irenaeus.

Those who rejected the three letters were generally Gnostic heretics. They did so, however, because they disagreed with the books' teachings, not because they denied Paul composed them. The fact that some church fathers countered the claims of the heretics indicates that the orthodox opinion of the day was that these were authentic Pauline epistles. Finally, note that every one of the manuscripts, versions, and ancient lists of Paul's writings include the Pastoral Epistles (and in the same order as in our Bibles today).

Although the internal evidence is not as strong as the external, there is certainly nothing within the text that would cause one to doubt the Pauline authorship of 1 Timothy, 2 Timothy, and Titus. Just the fact that the author identifies himself as Paul in the first verse of all three letters should be sufficient proof. Nevertheless, we will examine the internal evidence by contrasting it with the five main arguments against Pauline authorship. These arguments are as follows:

1. *The Pastorals do not fit within the historical structure of the book of Acts.* Scholars on all sides of the issue agree that the travels described in the Pastoral Epistles cannot be harmonized with Luke's accounts in Acts. The critics, based on the assumption that Paul died at the end of Acts, conclude that the apostle could not possibly have written them. However, that assumption rests on shifting sand. Acts does not state whether or not the apostle went to be with the Lord at that point, so other factors must be utilized to determine which scenario is more probable. One of those factors is the likelihood of a conviction. The Romans were somewhat perplexed as to what to do with Paul. The charges against him were not specific (Acts 25:27). Agrippa, one of the higher ranking Roman officials who heard Paul's case, believed that Paul "might have been set free if he had not appealed to Caesar" (Acts 26:32). To the Romans, Paul had done nothing deserving of death.

Furthermore, it would be odd for Luke not to report the execution of the one who dominates the second half of Acts. By contrast, the beloved physician gives the impression throughout those chapters that the apostle *will* be released. Some scholars assert that Acts 20:25 thwarts that inference because Paul tells the Ephesian elders, ". . . all of you . . . will see my face no more." Other reasonable interpretations can be applied to that verse, though. He may have meant that exact group of men ("all of you") would not see him again. Some of them might die before the great missionary could make it back to Ephesus. As well, his words are not necessarily a prophecy, but simply reflect Paul's "gut feeling" at the time (cf. Acts 20:23). Finally, no verse of Scripture that demands Paul's presence in Ephesus after this farewell address. First Timothy 3:14 expresses his desire to visit Ephesus, but it is possible he never did.

Some of the apostle's own words exhibit an assurance that he will be set free from this first incarceration. He took advantage of this "furlough" from his missionary journeys to write Ephesians, Philippians, Colossians, and Philemon (sometimes called the Prison Epistles). He confidently told the Philippians "I trust in the Lord that I myself also shall be coming [to Philippi] shortly" (Phil. 2:24). Philippians 1:23–25 and Philemon 1:22 likewise suggest that Paul expected to do some more traveling. Spain was one country he wished to see (Rom. 15:24, 28). That he accomplished that goal is known with some certainty from documents outside the New Testament. Clement of Rome declared that Paul went "to the extreme limit of the west."[9] The Iberian Peninsula would be those limits for someone writing from Rome.

The Muratorian Canon (AD 175) commented on the works of Luke and criticized the otherwise careful historian for not reporting on "the journey of St. Paul to Spain." In his last inspired correspondence, Paul remarked to his coworker, "I have finished the course" (2 Tim. 4:7). Finally, two other items are noteworthy. First, no tradition states that Paul did not go to Spain, and second, some historians believe Roman law required the release of any citizen who had not been convicted within two years after arrest.[10]

The Life and Ministry of Paul

Reference	Event	Date
Acts 9:1–19	Paul's conversion	AD 32
Gal. 1:18	Three years in Damascus and Arabia	AD 32–35
Acts 9:23–29	First trip to Jerusalem	AD 35
Gal. 2:1	In Tarsus approximately nine/ten years	AD 35–44
Acts 12	In Antioch	AD 44–46
Acts 12:25	Trip to Jerusalem for famine relief	AD 46
Acts 13–14	First missionary journey	AD 47–48
Acts 15	Jerusalem Council	AD 49
Acts 15:36–18:22	Second missionary journey	AD 49–52
Acts 18:23–21:30	Third missionary journey	AD 52–56
Acts 21:31–40	Arrested in Jerusalem	AD 56
Acts 24:23	Caesarean imprisonment	AD 56–58
Acts 27	Voyage to Rome	AD 58
Acts 28	First Roman imprisonment	AD 59–61
	Possible release and final travels	AD 61–64
	Martyrdom with Peter	AD 64 or 67

Therefore, it is most probable that Paul's activities after Acts unfolded as follows: he was released from the house arrest mentioned in Acts 28:30–31, went on some more expeditions for the Lord,[11] and inscribed the Pastoral Epistles. Some time later he was again arrested, taken to the imperial capital, and martyred.

2. *The form of church government proffered in the Pastorals is too advanced for the first century.* Scholars (almost always liberal) who hold this position insist that Paul could not have composed these verses because in his day there were no paid ecclesiastical offices (1 Tim. 5:17) or standardized qualifications for church leaders (1 Tim. 3; Titus 1). Additionally, a hierarchy of bishops, elders, and deacons did not develop until long after the apostle's ministry. As a general response, we may ask, "Why is it so difficult to believe the early church was organized?" In specifics, 1 Timothy 5:17 will be dealt with first. That verse says, "Let the elders who rule well be considered worthy of double honor." There is a measure of disagreement as to whether double honor refers to a salary or simply to respect. The very next verse does discuss wages, so it is probable Paul had remuneration in mind. At that time there were no church buildings, and thus the Christians had to meet in homes (or in some other structure; Acts 19:9). Likewise, with no "senior pastor," the group of elders would often be responsible for whole communities (Titus 1:5). That situation obviously required much time: caring for widows, comforting the bereaved, studying the Word, and so on. It is not surprising then that the men had to be paid.

Concerning the qualifications, it is common sense to desire (and require) competent men to guide and lead the body of Christ. Even in its earliest days, it was being invaded by false teachers. The church would rapidly depart from its nature and purpose if its leaders were not men of spiritual maturity and insight. The "problem" of an ecclesiastical hierarchy is really no problem. Some time before Paul began his ministry, deacons (and perhaps elders) were already in place. Acts 6 makes it clear that deacons were appointed within a very brief period after the coming of the Holy Spirit.[12] The same can be said for elders, who were in the church before the first missionary journey (Acts 11:30). It must be remembered as well that bishop and elder are the same office. In Titus 1:5–7, Paul tells Titus to appoint elders (*presbuteros*), and then in listing the qualifications for these men he calls them "overseers" (*episkopos*; "bishop," NKJV). The fact that these two words are interchangeable implies that there is no difference between the terms *bishop, elder, overseer,* and *pastor-teacher.*

Were deacons of a lower rank than elders in the early church? 1 Timothy 3:13 gives that impression, but there is no hint in the New Testament that the

elders "lorded it over" the deacons. The elders were and are the spiritual super-
visors and teachers, whereas the deacons perform most of the other acts of
service necessary for the church.[13] Functionally, then, elders were "over" deacons (just as they were to supervise every aspect of the church), but those who
qualified for the office of deacon were not just people who were willing to do
manual labor. Deacons, too, had to be "men of good reputation, full of the
Spirit and of wisdom" (Acts 6:3) and be "beyond reproach." (1 Tim. 3:10).
Consequently, it is baseless to claim that Paul was not aware of church government to this extent.

3. *The Pastoral Epistles do not reflect Paul's theology.* Critics specifically point
to the Fatherhood of God, the union of the believer with Christ, and the
power of the Holy Spirit in one's life as doctrines that are lacking in the three
letters. These alleged deficiencies are easily explained. First, the Fatherhood of
God was not emphasized by Paul during his ministry. As a result, one would
not necessarily expect to encounter it in these epistles. Second, the type of literature must be considered. The apostle is writing a letter presenting practical
advice, not a theological treatise. Third, these are arguments from silence,
which usually are of less significance. Finally, what doctrine *is* found is in harmony with Paul's known beliefs.

Liberal commentators often apply the term *pious fraud* to New Testament
books they believe were not inscribed by the person named in the first verse. The
usual factor compelling them to reach such a conclusion is that they see the
internal evidence as pointing to a second-century environment. They explain
the Pauline features of a book by saying that someone well versed in Paul's literature wrote it and placed the apostle's name on it to give it authority.

It does not require much reflection to realize that the term *pious fraud* is a
contradiction. A person cannot be considered pious if he purposely deceives
others by placing someone else's name on the letter. God is the author of the
Bible, and therefore no portion of it can be deceptive. Too, this way of thinking contradicts their other argument that the vocabulary in these letters does
not mesh with Paul's known writings (see argument 5 below). A final note:
Second Timothy especially has many remarks of a personal nature. "Demas
. . . has deserted me" (2 Tim. 4:10), "Only Luke is with me" (4:11), and ". . .
bring the cloak which I left at Troas" (4:13) are just a few instances. A pious
fraud would not concern himself with such matters but would emphasize the
teaching he was trying to propagate.[14] This argument is absolutely devoid of
substance.

4. *The false teaching being refuted in the Pastoral Epistles is a second-century
heresy.* Liberals assert that some of the terms found in the Pastoral Epistles,
especially 1 Timothy, are ones that appear frequently in writings about

Gnosticism. This heresy, which derives its name from the Greek word *gnōsis* ("knowledge"), denied the physical resurrection of Christ, delved into speculation and mysticism, and claimed to have superior knowledge. Since this false teaching did not arise until the second century, Paul could not have spoken against it. This line of thinking, like the previous three, has no solid evidence undergirding it. Three passages in particular are put forth as proof that the writer of 1 Timothy was repudiating Gnosticism. One is 1 Timothy 1:4— "nor to pay attention to myths and endless genealogies." These myths are the speculations of the Gnostics, or so the argument goes. This supposition is in error because the Gnostics were firmly anti-Semitic, and the people espousing the myths were Jews. They are described as "teachers of the Law" (1 Tim. 1:7). Titus 1:14 also mentions "Jewish myths."

A second passage is 1 Timothy 4:1–3. It contends that asceticism, another teaching promoted among Gnostics, is the result of "paying attention to deceitful spirits and doctrines of demons." To assume 1 Timothy 4:1–3 is directed toward this peculiar sect is unfounded. Many such orders encouraged their members to avoid pleasure. Besides, verse 1 predicts that this heresy will be a mark of "later times."

The most significant verse in this matter is 1 Timothy 6:20, where Paul urges Timothy to stay away from "the opposing arguments of what is falsely called 'knowledge.'" This phrase is a favorite weapon of the critics because it strikes a blow at the heart of Gnosticism, namely, superior knowledge. In fact, Paul uses the word *antithesis* (in the Greek), the exact title of a document penned by Marcion, one of the most influential Gnostics of the second century. The concept, however, was not new with the great apostle. Aristotle spoke of it as well.

Lastly, it must be kept in mind also that although this false teaching was in full bloom in the second century, there is no reason its roots could not have begun to grow in Paul's day.

5. *The linguistic peculiarities of the Pastoral Epistles are not Pauline.* A final argument devised by the critics proposes that the vocabulary and style of the Pastoral Epistles do not match the known writings of Paul, yet this hypothesis falls apart when the details are scrutinized. The critics zeroed in on 1 Timothy and came up with some 175 words that are not found elsewhere in Paul's epistles. Since there are only 538 different words used in 1 Timothy, that figure works out to a very high percentage. Again, though, ponder the details: 3 of the words in question are proper names, 11 were spoken by Paul in Acts, and cognates (forms or derivations) of 55 of them were utilized by the apostle somewhere else in the New Testament.

Two final factors must be reckoned with. First, the "vocabulary" argument is generally not as persuasive as other factors can be. The body of literature from which the study is conducted is simply not large enough (in this situation) to deduce whether or not a particular word is a favorite one of the author's. If it were impossible for the writer to have known the term (such as an anachronism), then a charge could be substantiated.

Second, the subject matter of the Pastoral Epistles is distinct from that of Paul's other writings. In these he is communicating with individuals, whereas in his other epistles (with the exception of Philemon) the recipients are the members of a church. If I write a love letter to my wife, I am going to use a different set of words than if I were writing to a company to complain about a product.

Furthermore, the "full discussion of widows, qualifications of bishop and deacon, and directions for worship are recognized by all students as new subjects in the Pastorals."[15] Thus, one would expect a new set of words to surface. As mentioned before, the early church was nearly unanimous in upholding Pauline authorship.

A handful of secondary arguments also lends support to the conclusion that the apostle Paul authored the Pastoral Epistles. Scholars have noted a rather large number of words and expressions found in Paul's other letters not encountered in these. But that assertion does not mean that the *style* of the Pastoral Epistles is markedly different, for it is also true that several phrases and stylistic mannerisms (wordplays, understatements, etc.) emerge here and in his other correspondence.[16] That perhaps Luke served as Paul's amanuensis (secretary/stenographer) may likewise explain some peculiarities. Finally, Paul was now in his sixties so it is expected that his vocabulary would have changed in some form since he was a young man.

Date

Bits of information taken from the Pastoral Epistles themselves and from writings of the early church fathers supply enough data to ascertain a rather accurate date for the composition of these epistles. Of course this date assumes (safely by all indications; see above) that Paul did not die during his first Roman imprisonment as recounted in Acts 28. Conservatives further argue that this two-year sentence took place between AD 59 and 63. Fathers such as Clement of Rome, Eusebius, Gaius, Dionysius, and Origen all concur that Paul died in Rome during Nero's reign as Caesar.[17] Eusebius wrote, "It is related that in his [Nero's] time Paul was beheaded in Rome itself, and that Peter likewise was crucified."[18] Nero himself passed from the scene in AD 68. Armed with this knowledge, conservative scholars teach that Paul authored 1 Timothy, Titus, and 2 Timothy (in that order)[19] between AD 63 and 67. Second Timothy is believed to be the apostle's last inspired letter because 1 Timothy and Titus show him at liberty, whereas in 2 Timothy he writes of his chains (1:16–17) and impending death (4:6).

Purpose

It is impossible to discern Paul's exact itinerary with 100 percent certainty after he was let go from his first Roman incarceration. He names places that he has visited, but about a dozen routes fit the facts. "It is not a problem of conflicting data, but of insufficient data."[20] Some of the locations listed include Ephesus (1 Tim. 1:3), the island of Crete (Titus 1:5), Nicopolis (3:12), Troas (2 Tim. 4:13), Miletus (4:20), Corinth (possibly; 4:20), and of course Rome (1:16, 17). He also set foot in Spain somewhere along his travels, as discussed above.

Even though there is some overlap in Paul's purposes for writing each letter, it is helpful to examine them one book at a time. The factors that motivated the apostle to pen 1 Timothy fall into two classes. His first concern was Timothy's personal well-being. Functioning as Paul's representative, Timothy was left in Ephesus to oversee the churches there (1:3). The presence of aggressive false teachers made his ministry all that more treacherous. Paul had confronted these would-be "teachers of the Law" (1:7), but he was expecting more trouble from them (6:3–5).[21] He was not able to return from Macedonia as quickly as he thought (3:14–15) and therefore sent this letter to his associate to encourage him in the faith. He exhorted Timothy to rebuke them despite his youth (4:12). The letter itself would help Timothy because it would be tangible proof that Paul had bestowed his apostolic authority on him.[22] The great missionary even dispensed medical advice (5:23)!

A second set of motivating factors has to do with church leadership and pastoral duties. Paul imparted much instruction on public worship (2:1–12), and qualifications for church leaders (3:1–13), as well as on how Timothy was to relate to various age groups in the body (5:1—6:5). This young pastor had his work cut out for him, but he also had Paul's loving and wise hand to guide him.

The impetus behind 2 Timothy is likewise twofold. In it Paul seeks to meet Timothy's needs while using the occasion to express his own longings as well. The situation at Ephesus had not changed much. If anything it had grown worse. Paul reminds his young colleague that he knows of the adversity in which Timothy finds himself. At least three times the subject of suffering comes up (1:8, 2:3, 4:5). Thus, the apostle once again has to embolden Timothy with words of perseverance (1:7). He must not give in to his foes but keep preaching the Word (4:2), and thus maintain sound doctrine.

Purpose of Paul's Epistles

Date	Book	Purpose
AD 48	GALATIANS	Salvation is not by law-keeping. The Christian lives by grace not by law!
AD 51	FIRST THESSALONIANS	Consolation during persecution. Comfort concerning those who are asleep in Jesus. Instruction about the resurrection and Rapture.
AD 51	SECOND THESSALONIANS	Further instruction about the Rapture, the Day of the Lord, and the Man of Sin.
AD 55	FIRST CORINTHIANS	Issues concerning carnality, food offered to idols, marriage, Paul's apostleship, the resurrection.
AD 55	SECOND CORINTHIANS	Continuing discussion about church problems, giving, Paul's apostleship.
AD 56	ROMANS	The great doctrines concerning salvation, God's plans for Israel, guidelines for Christian living.
AD 59	EPHESIANS	The calling of the believer, the nature of the "body" of Christ, Christian living issues.
AD 60	COLOSSIANS	The danger of worldly philosophies, incipient Gnosticism, the exalted Son of God.
AD 60	PHILIPPIANS	The humiliation and exaltation of Jesus Christ, the outworking of the Christian experience.
AD 60	PHILEMON	Practical instruction about Christian slaves, brotherhood, courteous and gracious treatment of others, the law of love.
AD 62	1 TIMOTHY	Qualification of church officers, instruction about prayer, women, heresy.
AD 62	TITUS	Qualification of church elders, pastoral work, exhortation for Godly living.
AD 64	2 TIMOTHY	Paul's departure, the abandonment of his friends, final instructions.

This epistle reveals Paul's desperate situation too. The conditions depicted make it clear that this is not the same incarceration spoken of in Acts 28. At that time Paul was treated well and his friends could visit him. Now he was chained up like "a criminal" (2:9), and his friends wouldn't associate with him anymore (4:16). Why the change? Nero blamed the Christians for the great fire of AD 64, and now they were being hunted down. Apparently Paul was in Spain when this took place. Upon his return, he found himself in the midst of a very different societal attitude toward believers.

Paul had now been incarcerated a second time in Rome (1:8, 17) and was lonely and in need of exhortation himself (4:11). He believed he was near the end of his earthly life (4:6). Timothy was thus urged to make "every effort" (4:9; cf. 4:21) to get to Rome as quickly as possible, bringing with him a cloak for the approaching winter (4:13), some treasured reading materials (4:13), and John Mark (4:11). No doubt the great preacher of the gospel sought solace in these things. Though the situation was desperate, it was not depressing and certainly not hopeless. Paul could look back with satisfaction on a life of dedicated service. He could honestly say, "I have fought the good fight" (4:7). This godly man was now ready to go to be with his Lord and Savior.

Second Timothy is as personal as 1 Timothy is pastoral. Very little in 2 Timothy has to do with church policies and politics. In all likelihood Timothy knew Paul was dead, or close to death, by the time he received this letter. It must have stirred his heart deeply, as it has many other Christian workers.[23]

Titus's circumstances were nearly identical to those of Timothy. It seems Paul and Titus had traveled to Crete, a Mediterranean island south of Greece, some time before the letter was written. When Paul departed to other fields of ministry, Titus stayed to "set in order what remains, and appoint elders in every city, as [Paul] directed [him]" (1:5). It was Titus's task to finish the work of organizing the Cretan churches. There is no record as to how and when the church was begun there. Perhaps some present in Jerusalem on the Day of Pentecost went back and witnessed to their friends and family (Acts 2:11).

A handful of clues within the text gives the reader an idea as to the conditions on the island. The people (at least the false teachers) didn't take kindly to the apostle's "substitute," or at least to his teaching, as 2:15 suggests: "Let no one disregard you." The imposters expended much of their energy on minor matters rather than focusing on the more significant aspects of the Law (3:9). The body of Christ was not being edified but was confused and upset (1:11). Titus was not to tolerate them but to muzzle them (1:10–11). He was therefore instructed to name godly elders, set an example of moral living (3:1–3), and make sure only sound doctrine was taught (2:1). It is the opinion of many that this is some of the most beautifully written theology to come from Paul's hand.

This letter bestowed more authority on Titus and imparted some information to him, such as Paul's desire to meet him in Nicopolis (3:12), in addition to the matters already noted. The apostle's compassionate encouragement assisted Titus in carrying out his heavy responsibilities.

Biographies of Timothy and Titus

That Timothy and Titus were the recipients of these letters is put beyond doubt by the direct statement of Scripture (1 Tim. 1:2, 2 Tim. 1:2, Titus 1:4). Both of these men were faithful and diligent servants of the Lord Jesus Christ, and two of Paul's ablest coworkers. Since the Pastoral Epistles are addressed to individuals and not to congregations, their personal tone is no surprise. Second Timothy especially has numerous verses pertaining to the apostle's relationship with his son in the faith. However, these words were not to stop with Timothy and Titus. All three epistles conclude with a plural "you" ("Grace be with you"). Paul even threw in an "all" at the end of Titus.[24] The Pastoral Epistles were expedient for believers in the first century, and continue to be so on down to us in the twenty-first century. Biblical truths are not bound by culture or time.

The New Testament offers no meager amount of information concerning Timothy's background. Acts 16 says that Timothy was from Lystra and that his mother was Jewish but his father was a Gentile. In 2 Timothy 1:5 we learn that his mother's name was Eunice and his grandmother was Lois. These devout women must have had a vital hand in his religious upbringing. Even as a young man Timothy was known as a godly person, the result of being instructed in the Scriptures from childhood (2 Tim. 3:15). Not only in his hometown of Lystra, but also in the neighboring community of Iconium, "he was well spoken of" (Acts 16:2). Paul likewise noticed him and decided to bring him along for the rest of the second missionary journey (Acts 16:3–4).

Bible students are often curious as to why Paul circumcised Timothy (Acts 16:3). The first church council had already determined that ritual was not necessary for salvation (Acts 15), and therefore Paul must have insisted on it for practical reasons. People knew (or would find out) that Timothy's father was a Gentile, and instead of having to explain the situation in every village and town about circumcision not being a requirement for conversion, the apostle just went ahead and did it.

Timothy must have enjoyed many hours of conversation and travel with his mentor, for he is mentioned as being with Paul in a score of New

Testament verses.[25] He is with him in Berea (Acts 17:14), Corinth (18:5; 1 Cor. 4:17), and Ephesus and Asia (Acts 19:22). Timothy, among others, rejoined Paul at Troas at the end of the third missionary journey (20:4). Paul sent him to Thessalonica to encourage the believers there (1 Thess. 3). This young man from Lystra was also known in Philippi (Phil. 1:1), Colossae (Col. 1:1), and Rome (Rom. 16:21). If he is the Timothy of Hebrews 13:23 (which is plausible), then it implies he spent some time in jail too. Surprisingly, his name is found in all of Paul's letters except Galatians, Ephesians, and Titus. Because both 1 and 2 Timothy locate him in Ephesus, it is evident that he conducted almost his entire latter ministry in that city.

Timothy was one of Paul's most faithful and trustworthy associates. Paul had enough confidence in Timothy to assign him to the most arduous situations, those of Thessalonica, Corinth, and Ephesus. On the other hand, the apostle often had to deal with Timothy's timidity. Phrases such as "Let no one look down on your youthfulness" (1 Tim. 4:12), "Do not neglect the spiritual gift within you" (4:14), "God has not given us a spirit of timidity" (2 Tim. 1:7), and "Be strong" (2:1) were indispensable if he was to have an effective ministry.

Titus similarly surfaces numerous times in the New Testament. He is named in 2 Corinthians (2:13; 7:6, 13–14; 8:6, 16, 23; 12:18), Galatians (2:1, 3), and 2 Timothy (4:10). Paul identified him as "my partner and fellow worker" (2 Cor. 8:23). He sent Titus to Corinth to help defuse the troublesome predicament there (7:6–7; 12:18). The epistle to Titus intimates that the two of them went to the island of Crete, but Titus was left there to organize and teach the body of Christ (Titus 1:5). From Titus 3:12 we learn that Paul later sent a replacement to Crete so Titus could meet up with Paul in Nicopolis (3:12). Indeed, Titus was near that area at the end of the apostle's time on earth (2 Tim. 4:10; Dalmatia was the region north of Nicopolis). The ancient historian Eusebius advances the tradition that Titus returned to Crete where he served the Lord the rest of his life.[26]

Section I

First Timothy

CHAPTER 1

The Goal Is Love
1 Timothy 1:1–20

Preview:

Timothy is a young pastor in the city of Ephesus. Some false teachers have entered the church, and Timothy must confront them. However, he is timid, and so Paul writes this letter to encourage his young colleague. He does so by reminding Timothy of the power of God. The apostle uses his own life as an illustration to teach about that power.

Salutation (1:1–2)

The addition of the word "mercy" makes this salutation by Paul distinct from his others (cf. Phil. 1:1; Col. 1:1; 1 Thess. 1:1).[1] "Grace" and "peace" are much more frequent. Timothy would certainly need mercy in carrying out his duties. To Westerners this letter-writing style is quite unusual because the writer's name is given first. We normally sign our name at the end of a letter, but in Paul's day it was customary to place it at the very start.

Paul identifies himself as "an apostle." In its most basic sense, "apostle" means sending someone out for a special purpose. In the New Testament it becomes a technical term for a person commissioned by Christ for the purpose of proclaiming the gospel.

In light of the fact that Paul is writing to a friend (as opposed to a church), it appears as if he is bragging by calling himself an apostle. However, that is not really the case, because this document is more than a personal correspondence. As noted in the introduction, one of the purposes for 1 Timothy was to invest more authority in Timothy's ministry. This young pastor was having a rough go of it, and Paul could help by making it clear that Timothy did have apostolic approval. So including the word "apostle" in his greeting was not a show of pride, but a reminder to the people of whom (better, Whom) they were dealing with. Any disrespect shown to Timothy was a sign of rebellion toward the Lord.

Indeed, Paul refers to the Source of his authority in the next phrase ("of Christ Jesus"). He didn't receive his assignment from mere men. He has delegated authority from the Lord Himself. Galatians 1:1 expresses the matter explicitly: "Paul, an apostle (not sent from men, nor through the agency of man, but through Jesus Christ, and God the Father . . .)." In addition, the use of "Christ Jesus" and not "Jesus Christ" may be more than just literary variance. In his earliest letters (Galatians, 1 and 2 Thessalonians, etc.) he tended to use "Jesus Christ" more than "Christ Jesus." Gradually, however, "Christ Jesus" became more common. In the Pastoral Epistles, "Christ Jesus" appears twenty-five times while "Jesus Christ" is encountered only five times.[2] "Christ" puts an emphasis on His roles as Messiah and Savior, whereas "Jesus" draws attention to His humanity. Whenever Paul is talking about a believer's relationship to the Lord, he writes, "in Christ," not "in Jesus." Obviously "Christ" was more meaningful for Paul than "Jesus" was.

Just so this point isn't missed, Paul adds, "according to the commandment of God." This may be the same command noted in Titus 1:3. The same word is translated "authority" in Titus 2:15.

"[Commandment] refers to a mandate or an injunction that must be obeyed. The Greek term is used of commands from kings and from gods."[3] The verb form of "command" is used in the Septuagint[4] five times, and in each case it has to do with a royal decree (Esther 1:8, 3:12, 8:8, 11; Dan. 3:16).[5]

The point is that it is definitely the Lord's will for him to be in this position. Now there is no doubt that this man from Tarsus is following divine orders in carrying out his ministry.

Paul was commissioned by Jesus just a few days after he was converted, a rather unusual situation. Normally a person has to grow and mature in Christ before he goes out to serve the Lord. Paul was on his way to Damascus when the Lord appeared to him. Jesus said that Paul "is a chosen instrument of Mine, to bear My name before the Gentiles and kings and the sons of Israel" (Acts 9:15; cf. 22:14–15; 26:16–18; Gal. 1:14–15).

Other rather rare phrases are introduced in the second half of verse 1, namely, "God our Savior" and "Christ Jesus, who is our hope." Although uncommon in the Bible, God the Father being described as the Savior should be no shock. Isaiah 43:11 declares, "I, even I, am the LORD;/And there is no savior besides Me" (cf. Ps. 106:21; Isa. 43:3; 45:15, 21; 49:26; 60:16; Hos.

13:4). It is to God the works of salvation are ascribed in the New Testament as well. "God was well-pleased . . . to save those who believe" (1 Cor. 1:21). "God . . . made us alive" (Eph. 2:4–5). Too, this notion has theological importance because it affirms the deity of Jesus. Skeptics may acknowledge Him as a historical figure but generally deny that He was God. Since God is the Savior and Jesus is the Savior, then Jesus is God.

The concept of hope in the Scriptures is not wishful thinking, contrary to its usage in modern English ("I hope it doesn't rain Saturday"). The Bible teaches that hope is a sure thing. A person with hope has confident expectation. The Scriptures can be trusted to say what they mean and mean what they say. "It is never a fearful dreading of what lies ahead; rather it is an eager and confident anticipation of what God has in store for believers"[6] (cf. 1 Tim. 5:5, 6:17; Titus 1:2, 2:13, 3:7).

For Christ Jesus to be our hope is a very comforting thought. It means we have every reason to believe He will take care of us. It is impossible for those who are in Christ to be in a hopeless situation. That is certainly something Timothy needed to hear. One would think he turned that phrase over and over in his mind as he went through the rigors of ministry—*Christ Jesus our hope.*

The recipient of this letter is revealed in verse 2. Timothy was a young pastor and a dear friend to Paul. His godly heritage prepared him well for the life of service to which he was committed. He embodied the meaning of his name, "honoring or worshiping God." More on Timothy can be found in the introduction.

Paul reveals his fatherly concern for him by referring to Timothy as "my true child in the faith" (cf. 2 Tim. 1:2; Titus 1:4). The apostle did not view him as just another worker, but as a son. "Of course, Timothy was not Paul's physical child, for he had a Greek father (Acts 16:3). But in the realm of Christian faith, Timothy owed his spiritual birth to the agency of Paul."[7] It is assumed that Paul lead Timothy to the Lord on his first missionary journey even though there is no record of Timothy's conversion in the Bible. First Corinthians 4:14–17 may fortify this supposition.[8]

Why does Paul make use of the word "true" (or "genuine") here? Probably to indicate the certainty of Timothy's confession. In the realm of the family, it was used for a legitimate offspring, as opposed to a bastard. Timothy did not just *claim* to be a Christian, but lived his life in such a way so as to prove he had trusted Christ as his Savior.

The phrase "in the faith" (*en pistei*) has generated some debate. Does Paul mean Timothy is a son "by faith"—that is, because he has faith in Jesus? Or does he mean by Timothy's faithfulness he has shown himself to be a genuine child of God? Or does he mean *the* faith, that body of truth revealed in the Bible?

Some discount this last suggestion because the Greek does not have the word "the," but it seems to be the best choice. All the major English translations have "the faith," and Paul calls Titus "my true child in a common faith" (Titus 1:4).

An extra-long benediction is then pronounced upon Timothy (another slightly different feature of the salutation). Outside of 1 and 2 Timothy, "mercy" is not found in any of Paul's introductions.[9] His usual greeting is "grace and peace to you" (or the like). Knowing timid Tim was facing very aggressive and obnoxious people, Paul felt inclined to throw in some "mercy" for his friend.

Grace, the flip side of mercy, is both simple and profound. The simple feature of grace is its definition: unmerited favor. Within a Christian context, it concerns the distribution of blessings from the Lord to us, His people, despite our sin and disobedience. When He gives us some good thing we don't deserve, that is grace. When He withholds something we do deserve (such as punishment), that is mercy. Why He would treat us so is what makes grace profound.

Why does God love us? Because we are valuable to Him? Absolutely not. He loves us because of who He is, not because of who we are. He graciously and sovereignly chooses to bless His children.

The third item listed is peace. This kind of peace is not merely the absence of war, but "is the daily, continual experience of the soul in harmony with God."[10] Jesus said, "Peace I leave with you; My peace I give to you; not as the world gives, do I give to you" (John 14:27). Believers can and should trust Christ to the degree that they will not be overly concerned about any circumstance. Worry is a sin (Phil. 4:6). The term "peace" had its origins in Hebrew. From ancient times to today, *shalom* has been a popular Jewish greeting. The concept has to do with the bestowal of health and well-being on another.[11]

Paul then reiterates the only true Source of grace, mercy, and peace (cf. James 1:17). That God is the Father is unequivocally stated here. It is a powerful and precious truth that a mere human beings can have such intimate, "parental" relationships with their Creator and Redeemer. In verse 1 God was our Savior, and now He is identified as our Father. The description of Christ's person and work is likewise expanded. Gratefully, He is our hope, but He is also our Lord. As His slaves, believers are to submit to Him without hesitation.

The observant student will notice that the word "our" appears three times in the first two verses. Having a close walk with the Lord is not reserved for a few elite. The invitation is open for all to draw near to Him (James 4:8). The false teachers may have been declaring the opposite, that only a select group of "super-Christians" can be close to Him. Our *relationship* with God can never be broken, but our *fellowship* with Him can be hampered.[12] A close fellowship is brought about as we keep ourselves pure and exercise the spiritual disciplines (Bible study, worship, prayer, fellowship, etc.)

Charge Concerning Sound Doctrine (1:3–20)

In this section Paul talks about doctrine, the Law, and the gospel from both a negative and positive point of view. He takes this approach as a charge and warning to Timothy. The false teachers who had infiltrated the church in Ephesus were not teaching the Law accurately or applying it appropriately, and thus the people were learning false doctrine. Doctrine (or theology) and duty cannot be divorced. How a person thinks will influence his or her behavior. Good theology becomes a recurring theme in the Pastoral Epistles (1 Tim. 1:3, 10; 3:15; 4:1, 3, 6; 6:1, 3, 20; 2 Tim. 1:13; 2:15, 25; 4:2–4; Titus 1:9, 13; 2:1–3, 7, 10). The misuse of the Law and the resulting immoral conduct are what concerned the apostle.

These problems stimulated Paul to discuss the power and nature of the gospel in verses 12–20. Paul presents himself as an example of how the Law can be used correctly. Even he, a persecutor of the church,[13] was wonderfully saved by the gospel. On the other end of the scale, the gospel can be abused with horrible and eternal consequences.

Throughout this book, the great missionary is imparting his wisdom and encouragement to Timothy to help him combat the serious problems within the Ephesian church.

Heresy	Falsehood
(Heteros, that which is CONTRARY)	*(Psudē, that which is a LIE)*
Certain men teach **strange** *doctrines (1 Tim. 1:3)*	**False** *brothers (Gal. 2:4)*
If anyone advocates a **different** *doctrine (1 Tim. 6:3)*	**False** *witnesses (Acts 6:13)*
Do not receive a **different** *spirit (2 Cor. 11:4)*	**False** *apostles (2 Cor. 11:13)*
Beware of **another** *gospel (Gal. 1:6)*	*Speaking* **lies** *in hypocrisy (1 Tim. 4:2)*
	False *prophets (2 Pet. 2:1)*
	False *Christs (Matt. 24:24)*
	To **lie** *against the truth (James 3:14)*

The Effects of Heresy (1:3–11)

With 1:3 Paul begins to delve into the first topic of his letter: the apostates[14] in the church and the necessity of rebuking them. The church in Ephesus cannot be healthy and whole as long as these deceivers have influence. We tend to think of false teaching as something that started within the last two hundred years, but, as can be seen in the New Testament, it was a problem from the very start.

Some knowledge is gleaned from this verse regarding Paul's travels after his first Roman imprisonment (see under "Authorship" in the introduction). Paul and Timothy had gone to Ephesus, but Paul later decided to move on to Macedonia, leaving Timothy in Ephesus to continue the work. It may be that Timothy also wanted to move on but Paul was confident his young associate could handle the situation.

Notice that Timothy was not just to ask them to stop spreading heresy, he was to command them to cease. The word "instruct" (NASB, NRSV) can also be translated "give orders," "direct," or "command" (NIV). Apostasy must be dealt with sternly. If even a "small amount" of unbiblical instruction is taking place, it needs to be squelched. Once the door of compromise is opened, there is no stopping the flood of deviance that will surely follow. Paul does not tell Timothy to tolerate the false teaching; he told him to get rid of it.

Paul's words imply that not all of the teachers in the church were bad, just "certain men." Whether they were believers or outsiders is ambiguous. What these "certain men" were promoting were "strange doctrines." Whatever was being espoused was heterodoxy—that is, something incompatible with the Bible (cf. 1 Tim. 6:3).[15]

Paul gives some details about these "strange doctrines" when he speaks of them as "myths and endless genealogies." In the New Testament, a myth is always an untrue tale or legend.

The expression "pay attention to" (NASB) means not just an occasional allusion to these fables and lists, but a devotion to them.[16] This gibberish was the focal point of their instruction! What these myths were is not entirely clear. More than likely they were of Jewish or Gnostic origin.[17] The former is the better choice for two reasons. First, these teachers were would-be Law teachers and thus were probably Jewish (1:7). Second, Paul specifically mentions "Jewish myths" in Titus 1:14.

It may be that these myths are references to the books written between the testaments, such as the Jewish Apocrypha scrolls, some of which may go back to 300 BC. Though the fourteen most well-known apocryphal works certainly have historical, cultural, and religious value because of their antiquity, for the most part they were not to be considered part of inspired Scripture. Some of them, such as *Bel and the Dragon* and *The History of Susanna*, were simply fiction, or at the least contained historical inaccuracies and fictional portions. The writings of Tobit and Judith are tales of pure fiction filled with historical errors and questionable morality.

For many Jews who did not know better, these books were admired, read, quoted, and considered of religious value to the genre of the literature of the Jewish faith. Many Jews probably quoted them more than they did the Old Testament. The stories in these scrolls may have formed the basis for much tradition. And the belief in salvation by works, which some of them seem to have set forth, influenced the average Jew to strive for eternal bliss by Law keeping.

And then there was the Talmud, that great body of commentary literature that went back to Babylon. With the Mishnah and Midrash, it was an encyclopedia of Jewish knowledge that sometimes granted ancient exegesis to understanding the Old Testament. But in time, it became by some to be more honored than the inspired Scripture. It would be more quoted than Isaiah or Moses. It formed the backbone of rabbinical Judaism that could be terribly harsh and legalistic. The letter of the Law would in time overshadow true biblical knowledge and smother both godly righteousness and faith.

Paul was raised on all of this material. After his conversion he realized how the Apocrypha and possibly the Talmud had distorted God's original message in the Old Testament. He was determined to cut through this body of literature and return to the pure message of the Old Testament, but as well, proclaim the new revelation that centered on the Lord Jesus Christ.

Hendriksen believes the phrase "myths and endless genealogies" should be taken as a unit. That is, the myths and genealogies are woven into one story. If the two terms were to be considered separate concepts, then the myths could be as Hendriksen described them, and the genealogies could be the false teacher's personal family history. That he is related to some esteemed rabbi of past generations "qualifies" him to properly interpret the Law. By coupling that endorsement with his extensive "knowledge" (the myths), he could overwhelm the congregation.

The apostle explains that this sort of subject matter only leads to guesswork ("mere speculation").[18] It is totally inept in being able to direct people to the Lord and help them grow, and it only results in envy, fighting, and strife (1 Tim. 6:4).

Bible students debate what Paul had in mind when he wrote, "the administration of God" (v. 4). The most basic meaning of "administration" is "a stewardship." A steward in ancient times was one who was entrusted with the responsibility of managing the (financial) affairs of a household.[19] It has also been defined as "a plan," and in this context would therefore refer to *God's plan of salvation,* a plan that is accomplished "by faith," not by the Law. The Lord has entrusted believers with the sacred duty of furthering His cause.

Verse 5 marks a shift in the letter's tone. Paul began with the negative ("Stop the unorthodox teachers") but has now moved to the positive ("the goal . . . is love"). The NIV translates the first part of the verse: "The goal of this command is love." Is the apostle claiming that an instructor's goal is to stimulate love in and for others (which the heretics were not doing), or is he saying he gave this command (v. 3; same Greek word) out of love and not just to throw his weight around? Both considerations are true, but the former is more in line with the context. Paul did issue this order out of love,[20] but the purpose (or goal) of all Bible teaching is to foster a love for God and for others.

Jesus said that the two greatest commandments are to love God with all your heart, soul, and mind, and your neighbor as yourself (Matt. 22:36–40). By contrast, the infidels were seeking prestige.

The apostle here utilizes the strongest Greek term for love, *agapē*. It is virtually impossible to define love, but it can be described in terms of how it is to be seen in our actions and attitudes (1 Cor. 13). One display of love is found in Ephesians 5:25. There, Christ's self-giving love for the church is the standard by which husbands are to love their wives. *Agapē* is an act of the will to deny oneself for the good of others. The fact that Paul highlights love in his solution to the problems in Ephesus strongly implies it is that characteristic that is lacking in the false teachers. In that same vein, it may be that Timothy had become somewhat embittered toward the troublemakers and he needed to hear about love as well.[21]

It is almost shocking to read the sources suggested by Paul for this love. He lists the heart, the conscience, and faith. "This trilogy is not exhaustive, nor does it claim to be. . . . It is . . . three concepts particularly appropriate to the Ephesian situation since the opponents were depraved in mind (1 Tim. 6:5) with seared consciences (1 Tim. 4:2) and corrupt faith (2 Tim. 3:8)."[22]

How can love emanate from a heart that "is more deceitful than all else and is desperately sick" (Jer. 17:9)? Jesus made it clear that "out of the heart of men, proceed the evil thoughts, fornications, thefts, murders, adulteries" (Mark 7:21). Of course the answer is that the apostle wasn't signifying the natural heart. He was thinking of the supernatural heart. One that is clean and pure, having been (positionally) purged of corruption and evil by the Holy Spirit at conversion (Acts 15:8–9; cf. John 13:5–11).[23] The "heart" is considered the innermost being, the real you inside, and "the person as he or she really is within himself or herself and before God."[24]

The conscience is an indicator of right and wrong, an inner judge to assist us in making moral decisions.[25] It is inherent in all people as part of being made in the image of God (Rom. 1). To have a "good conscience" is to live one's life knowing he or she is obeying the Lord. This person's conscience is clear and is not bothering him or her. A caution must be given here, because the conscience is not a perfect barometer. Since it can be seared, it is not 100 percent reliable (1 Cor. 4:4; cf. Jer. 17:9 and James 1:25; 2:12).[26]

The last concept presented is "a sincere faith." Some synonyms for "sincere" are "without hypocrisy," "unfeigned," and "genuine." Faith is trust in the Lord.[27] We should not be deceived that because this idea is last it is least important. On the contrary, it is the most vital one. A person lacking faith in God will not have a pure heart, a good conscience, or be able to love. Hypocrisy is one of the most frequently heard charges leveled at the church by non-Christians. Let us not be double-minded (James 1:5), but be wholly committed to Christ.

As mentioned above, this is not an exhaustive list for the sources of love. The Lord is the original and ultimate Source. "All love comes from God and it comes to us only as we are united to him by faith."[28]

The apostle now draws attention back to the heterodox teachers. Again he doesn't name them but refers to them as "some men" (v. 6). "Straying" means "miss the mark, deviate, depart." "These things" are the pure heart, good conscience, and sincere faith of the previous verse. The heretics' decision to move away from those values means they chose to forsake love. They weren't so much attracted to the deviant doctrine intellectually as they were morally. They didn't just suddenly realize they had drifted away, but made a deliberate choice to do so.[29] Consequently, they had steered themselves into nonsense. They were now engaged in "fruitless discussion" (NASB; "meaningless talk," NIV). They weren't merely wasting time, they were leading people down the wrong path.

Going into verse 7, Paul does not let up on his criticism of the false teachers. Their all-consuming passion is to be teachers of the Law, yet they don't even know what they are talking about! Additionally, they are not motivated by a love for Christ but by a love for themselves. However, before those issues are pursued, it is necessary to ask, "How is Paul using the word 'Law' here?" The term is understood in various ways in the New Testament. It can be viewed as encompassing the entire Old Testament (Rom. 3:19), or everything in the Old Testament except the Prophets (Matt. 5:17), or simply the Pentateuch (the first five books of the Old Testament authored by Moses; Luke 24:44).[30] In all probability the whole of the Mosaic Law is in view since the apostle broaches that subject in the next passage (vv. 8–11).

The troublemakers must have been smooth talkers, because they had a following despite the fact that they didn't comprehend the things they were teaching. To make matters worse, they gave their instruction shamelessly and boldly. They probably sounded logical and spiritual, but they were actually complete charlatans—all the more reason for Christians to pray for discernment.

Up to this point Paul has been exposing the heretics' misuse of the Law, so in verses 8–11 he discloses the proper approach to the Law. He begins by assuring Timothy (and us) the Law is not inherently bad (cf. Rom. 7:16). As a matter of fact, it's good! By "good" the apostle means "beautiful, useful, free from defects."[31] It is a sure guide for morally and ethically acceptable behavior.[32] It is not the Law's fault that this unfortunate situation in Ephesus has arisen. Furthermore, this view of the Law is a commonly held opinion in the Christian community ("we know"). With a play on words, he says the Law is good when it is used lawfully. Under what conditions can it be employed lawfully? The answer is given in verses 9 and 10.

Paul's Teaching on the Law

The believer has died to the Law through Christ (Rom. 7:4).

The Law arouses passions and sins (Rom. 7:5).

The believer has been released from the Law (Rom. 7:6).

The Law is not sin (Rom. 7:7).

The Law gives knowledge of sin (Rom. 7:7).

The Law is holy, righteous, and good (Rom. 7:12).

The Law amplifies sin (Rom. 7:13).

The Law is spiritual (Rom. 7:14).

The Law is weak because of human flesh (Rom. 8:3).

Salvation does not come by works of the Law (Gal. 2:16).

Justification is not by the Law but by grace (Gal. 2:16).

Christ redeemed us from the curse of the Law (Gal. 3:13).

The Law leads believers to Christ (Gal. 3:24).

Believers are justified by faith and live by faith—not by the Law (Gal. 5:4).

The new covenant replaces the covenant of the Law (2 Cor. 3:6–9).

In short the answer is: when it is directed at sinners. The Law of Moses[33] was not created for upright people but for those who rebel against the things of the Lord. The apostle is teaching that God's rules and commandments are there to correct moral behavior and are not to be the object of speculation ("myths and genealogies").[34] "Paul is stressing that the opponents' application of the law to all people is wrong; it does not apply to the Christian who is made righteous through faith and who lives righteously."[35] A gruesome list of vices that are specific manifestations of this rebellion is found in the rest of verse 9 and all of verse 10.[36]

The list commences with three pairs of general terms that serve as an introduction to the more particular iniquities named later down the list.[37] All six terms are nearly synonymous, but some elaboration on their differences will be helpful to experience the full weight of their horror. The first is "lawless." A literal translation would be "no law" or "without law." This describes someone who either recognizes no law or fights against the law. The latter is more applicable to this passage because the false teachers did not deny the Law but were terribly misusing it. They were fighting it in that they were pummeling its true intention. Joined with "lawless" is "rebellious." A rebellious person is one who is undisciplined. He knows the Law but has no desire to obey it. If there is any distinction between these two words, it is that "lawless" is more of a disregard for law, whereas "rebellious" indicates an active violation of it.

The next pair is "ungodly and sinners." "Ungodly" can also be rendered "impious, irreligious, irreverent." It speaks of someone who has no respect for or fear of the Lord. It might be said that the "ungodly" have an unruly attitude and "sinners" (cf. Matt. 11:19, Luke 5:30) exhibit unruly behavior.

The last expression is equally evil: "unholy and profane."[38] If the essence of God could be captured in a single word, that word would be *holy*. In extolling His virtues, the seraphim in Isaiah 6 did not shout, "Wise, wise, wise." The only attribute they repeated was "Holy, holy, holy." Holiness and purity are not synonyms but are closely related. Holiness means "set apart, distinct." A person (or thing) is set apart for sacred use. Purity can be defined as "without defect or corruption." What sets the Lord apart is His purity.[39] Accordingly, "unholy" is an attitude or action that is out of harmony with God's nature. "Profane" is the opposite of holy as well. It is something that is common or ordinary,[40] and the word is related to the word *desecrate*. Persons who are unholy and profane have, at best, no use for the sacred in their lives, and, at worst, speak evil of the Lord.[41]

Before this list is further scrutinized, it should be pointed out that some scholars see parallels between it and the Ten Commandments (Exod. 20;

Deut. 5). The three expressions just examined have to do with offending the Lord. The first part of the Decalogue concerns a person's relationship with Jehovah (no images, no taking the Lord's name in vain, keeping the Sabbath holy, etc.). The correspondence is even more pronounced in the rest of the list. The table below lays out the details.

The author now talks about some specific sins. The first two naturally go together and have to do with the parent-child relationship. The Greek terms meaning "father killer" and "mother killer" are not found anyplace else in the New Testament, nor are they used in the Septuagint.[42] That would certainly be the most horrendous way to dishonor one's parents.

Perhaps Paul wanted to make this a separate point because slaying one's mother and father is not like an "ordinary" murder.

1 Timothy 1:9–10	Ten Commandments
Father- and mother-killers	Honor your father and mother
Murderers	You shall not kill
Sexually immoral	You shall not commit adultery
Kidnappers	You shall not steal
Liars and perjurers	You shall not bear false witness

"Murderers" (*androphonos*, literally "man-killer") needs little explanation. Intentionally taking the life of another human being has been viewed with horror in virtually every society that has ever existed. Even if done in self-defense, it is not an easy event with which to deal. Murder is a serious sin to the Lord because the victim was created in His image (Gen. 9:6). Only He has the right and authority to establish the timing of a person's demise. "How it must have hurt Paul to write this. It brought back to his mind memories of the past, *Paul's own* past (Acts 9:1, 4, 5; 22:4, 7; 26:10)."[43]

Verse 10 contains the balance of Paul's list. Here the apostle uses two Greek words dealing with sexual immorality (*pornos*[44] and *arsenokoitēs*). An array of English equivalents has been suggested for these words: "immoral men and homosexuals" (NASB), "adulterers and perverts" (NIV), "fornicators and sodomites" (NRSV, NKJV). The former term (*pornos*) is an "umbrella word" because it encompasses any and all forms of sexual immorality (homosexuality, incest, etc.). It covers all possible ways the seventh commandment could be broken. The other one (*arsenokoitēs*) is literally "male-bed."

"Kidnappers" (NASB) is another rare word found in this passage. It doesn't appear in any Greek literature before Paul's day. It was often used for "slave trader" (so NIV) but later came to mean "kidnapper," since slaves were people who were captured in war for use by another person. Like "homosexual," the first portion of the word means "male," and thus a literal translation would be "men stealers."

The apostle then thoroughly covers the ninth commandment with two final terms: "liars" and "perjurers." By writing both, he includes all bearers of false witness, whether it is in a courtroom or not. It could be that the tenth commandment is inherent in these terms as well because all lying involves coveting of some kind.[45]

To make sure nothing is missed, Paul ends verse 10 with: "and whatever else is contrary to sound teaching." The text is actually "the" sound teaching (NIV, NRSV)—that is, the doctrine attained from the Old Testament and from the apostles. Note again that Paul doesn't write, "and whatever else is contrary to good behavior." What we *believe* directly affects how we *behave*.

This is the first explicit statement among many in the Pastoral Epistles that stresses the significance and importance of good theology. By "good" is meant theology that is the result of a proper (i.e., literal or plain) interpretation of Scripture. It is not conjured up by the mind of man, nor is it based on difficult passages.

Our English word *hygiene* comes from the word here translated "sound" (*hugiainō*), which literally means "healthful, healthy." Wickedness and sin are diseases of the soul. The apostate teachers were spiritually sick, and their teaching "spread like gangrene" (2 Tim. 2:17). The body of Christ is infected and weakened by such men.[46]

One of the connotations of the word "teaching" involves authority, an underlying issue in 1 Timothy.[47] A teaching is only as valid as the authority behind it. Paul speaks for God. The errorists of Ephesus have nothing to back them up. They claim to be using the Hebrew Scriptures, but in reality they are misusing them. The clear conclusion is that the church in Ephesus should silence these troublemakers and listen to Timothy, Paul's official representative.

The apostle brings this section to a close by amplifying what he means by "sound teaching." Paul is saying that sound teaching is that which is in harmony with the gospel. For the NASB's "according to," other versions have "that conforms to" (NIV, NRSV). Any belief that conflicts with the gospel as presented by the apostle Paul is flawed. The false teachers were wrong because their teachings were inconsistent with the gospel.

Two words in verse 11 need further explanation: "glory" and "blessed." Although both are frequently spoken by Christians, most believers would have a hard time nailing down a precise definition of them. We might say "glory" is the sum total of all God is. Furthermore, it "is more than a visible manifestation; it is an indication of the essence of God; he is glory."[48] Someday all Christians will get to share in that glory (2 Thess. 2:14; cf. 2 Cor. 3:7–11).[49] The Greek word for "blessed" (*makarios*) is rarely used to describe the Lord (the more common word is *eulogeō*). This is an odd use of "blessed," because we normally associate it with humans, using it to describe a favor bestowed on someone by the Lord. As good a definition as any is set forth by Wayne Grudem: "God's blessedness means that God delights fully in himself and in all that reflects his character."[50]

Paul realizes what a precious treasure he has ("I have been entrusted").[51] His is a heavy responsibility. Not only must he guard the gospel from theological corruption, but he is also obliged to share it with others wherever he ventures (cf. Gal. 1:15–16; Titus 1:3). He later instructs Timothy to make sure this duty is perpetuated (2 Tim. 2:2).

Note that the last verb in this verse is in the passive voice ("was entrusted"). God gave the message of good news to Paul. He did not manufacture a message and then exploit it for his own fame and fortune. On the contrary, he was willing to give his life for the truth of the gospel and its dispersion.

The Effects of Sound Doctrine (1:12–17)

In this paragraph, Paul makes use of his own life and ministry to demonstrate the effective work of God in someone's life. No one is beyond hope, neither himself (even as a persecutor of the church) nor the false teachers in Ephesus. In addition, this display of the Almighty's power would encourage Timothy to press on through the hardship he was experiencing as the apostle's designated spiritual supervisor of Ephesus (notice "our" Lord in v. 12). Paul is so grateful that he finally has to break out in praise (v. 17).

After standing up for the gospel (vv. 3–11), the very next thing from the missionary's pen is gratitude (v. 12).[52] It is sad this trait is so lacking in Christians. A believer who truly meditates on God's grace, especially as it relates to salvation, will be overcome with humility—and thankfulness. Let us not take His blessings for granted. Paul didn't, and the result was a deep commitment to Christ (cf. Luke 7:47). For emphasis, the full title of the One who is the recipient of the gratitude is written out: Christ Jesus our Lord.

Paul spells out those things for which he is thankful. First, Christ empowering him. Second, judging him trustworthy. Third, saving him. Fourth, being allowed to serve Christ. God is looking for faithful men and women.

The apostle launches into a lengthy review of his past, focusing on his conversion and call. He acknowledges that it was the power of Christ that delivered him from his sinful and violent state. When he speaks of Jesus strengthening him (cf. Phil. 4:13), he is not referring to daily empowerment but to the initial infusion of spiritual energy it took to save him and equip him for service.[53]

This man from Tarsus is absolutely shocked the Lord would choose him for such a crucial spiritual assignment. In His omniscience and sovereignty, God knew Paul would be a trustworthy person and so appointed him the apostle to the Gentiles.[54] This is not to say he deserved it. Nobody deserves to be in God's family. Another lesson we can learn from Paul is that people don't have to "get their act together" or "clean up their life" before Jesus will save them.

"Putting me into service" ("appointing," NIV) harks back to verse 1. There Paul makes it clear that he is an apostle because it is God's will. He is no self-declared "guru" of Christianity. Perhaps the unorthodox teachers were questioning his credentials, and so he had to lay some stress on the matter in this letter. The humility evidenced here fits in well with the tone of the paragraph. Paul doesn't trumpet, "I'm an apostle!" He meekly contends, "I'm a servant." Even those who are called "senior pastor" or "bishop" should remember they are merely slaves of Christ and servants to the Christian community.[55]

Our amazement that Paul would be shown such favor is compounded by the fact that (v. 13) he used to murder Christians (Acts 9:1) and speak insultingly toward the Lord (Acts 22:19; 26:11).[56] His zealousness for the Law drove him to the point of hunting down believers in Christ (Phil. 3:4–6). The third shameful term he gives about himself is "a violent aggressor," someone who completely disregards the rights of others. "It is a word of intenser significa-tion than either the word 'blasphemer,' or 'persecutor,' and means that what he did was done with a proud, haughty, insolent spirit."[57]

By these statements Paul is implying that he has personal experience with some of the iniquities singled out in verses 8–10. "His description of himself must not be attributed to false humility or exaggeration, but was undoubted-ly the way he felt about his past life. Those who live closest to God are usual-ly the most keenly aware of their own faults."[58]

He goes on to say that he was "shown mercy." God didn't treat Paul the way he deserved to be treated. John MacArthur remarks, "Mercy differs from grace in that grace removes guilt, while mercy takes away the misery caused by sin."[59]

The end of verse 13 is somewhat misleading in many English translations. It is better to translate *hoti* as "since" instead of "because," because the apostle was not telling the reason why he was shown mercy. What he was saying is that he was a more likely candidate for mercy than someone who knowingly and willfully worked against God and His will (Ex. 33:19). He accepted the truth when it was revealed to him (Acts 9).

Before Paul's conversion he felt it was right to oppress believers. He saw Christianity as a threat to Judaism. He now admits that the things he did were wrong, albeit done in ignorance (Rom. 10:2). Hence, *unbelief* is distinguished from *disbelief*; he just didn't know the truth at that point (Luke 23:34).[60] "Paul never wants to leave the impression that he is condoning sin, even when grace and mercy prevail (cf. Rom. 6:1ff.)."[61]

The great missionary sizes up the true nature of salvation in mentioning "grace" (v. 14). Salvation has always been, and always will be, by grace through faith (Eph. 2:8–9). In fact, this grace Paul received wasn't just adequate, it was superabundant.

Along with grace (or it may be better to say, "as a result of being given grace") came faith and love. Exactly what is meant by "with the faith and love which are found in Christ Jesus" though? Are these the Lord's faithfulness and love, or Paul's? The best solution is to understand Paul to mean that these are gifts bestowed on him by the Lord. They were issued to Paul to counteract the iniquities and flaws of his life (2 Tim. 1:13). He was given "faith" as an antidote to his "unbelief" (v. 13). He would need love (*agape*) to minister to those whom he previously hated with a passion. Finally, the author doesn't want us to miss the point that these characteristics originate only "in Christ Jesus." This is one of dozens of places where Paul inserts "in Christ" in an epistle (nine times in the Pastoral Epistles). This saying speaks to the profound union and identification believers have with their Savior.[62]

Beginning in verse 15, Paul reveals some general principles of which his personal testimony is an illustration. Without doubt, one of the basic yet vital teachings of the New Testament is spelled out here: Christ left heaven and came to earth to provide salvation for sinners (Luke 19:10). This event was not just a change in location but an indescribable act of humility on the part of Jesus.[63] He not only rescued us from hell, but also placed us in a right relationship with God. To say that the apostle highlights this point is an understatement. He makes use of *two* expressions to indicate that he has absolutely no hesitation in making this declaration.[64] First he says that it is "a trustworthy statement,"[65] and then he adds that it deserves "full acceptance."

"Trustworthy" is the same word translated "faithful" in verse 12. The Christian can totally believe this truth without reservation or qualification.

The author then makes a startling statement: he professes to be the "foremost" (literally, "first") sinner (v. 15).[66] Paul is not exaggerating here, because he is contrasting his outrageous transgressions with God's amazing grace. His former associates in the party of the Pharisees would definitely be stunned by such a statement, because on the outside he looked like a very religious man (except for killing Christians!). In Philippians 3:5–6 he writes that he was blameless as reckoned by the Mosaic Law.

No fewer than three interpretations have been suggested concerning what Paul meant when he said he was the "foremost" of sinners.[67] The first possibility teaches that he is inferring that he is the most evil person who has ever lived, since he did such terribly wicked things to the church (1 Cor. 15:9; Eph. 3:8). In other words, he is judging himself by God's standards, not by the world's. The weakness with this understanding is that Paul wrote, "I am," not "I was." A second possible interpretation takes "foremost" in the sense of most prominent. His escapades were known far and wide (Acts 9:13, 21). This view has some merit, since in verse 16 Paul's conversion is held up as a radical example to show that the Lord is willing and able to save someone as vile as this man from Tarsus. The third suggestion has much going for it, too. A third suggestion is as follows. He was the chief of sinners in that every time he recalled his murderous actions, he would again be humbled and amazed at God's mercy. Those memories may have haunted him with regularity.[68] That may also explain why he penned, "I am" and not "I was" (cf. 1 Cor. 15:9–10; Eph. 3:8). All factors considered, the second view seems to make the most sense.

Verse 16 elaborates on the sentiments found in verses 13–15. In fact, this verse repeats two critical words seen in verses 13–15: "mercy" (v. 13) and "foremost" (v. 15).[69] In verse 13 Paul discloses that the Lord was willing to be extra patient with him because he was acting in ignorance and not in defiance. Here it is reported that the primary impetus ("for this reason") for saving this murderous Pharisee is so he could be an example, a supreme object lesson to illustrate the extent of the Lord's grace and mercy. If Saul of Tarsus can be brought into the kingdom, then no one is beyond the reach of God's saving hand.

These last few verses may be an indication that this epistle was intended for the congregation's ears and not just for Timothy's eyes, because he already knew Paul's testimony.[70]

The apostle's conversion not only exhibited Christ's grace and mercy, but also His "utmost patience" (NRSV). The Greek has "all longsuffering." The

Savior endured Paul's iniquities until the time of his conversion came. Patience is a quality desperately lacking in our rat-race society. The idea is not just a willingness to wait, but also has the idea of not giving up despite the obstacles and determining to carry on to the desired goal.[71] Christians can and should lead the way in this area. Just as God is patient with us (Rom. 2:4), we are not to be quickly irritated by others (Gal. 5:22; Eph. 4:2).

Paul's testimony is to be an example "for those who would believe in Him for eternal life." This wide-open invitation anticipates 1 Timothy 2:4. People can wholly trust Jesus as Savior and thereby be with Him forever.

By verse 17 Paul is so full of praise that a grand doxology gushes from his quill. The heart picks up where the intellect has had to stop.[72] This section (vv. 12–17) began on a note of blessing and is now ending similarly, with honor and glory to the Lord.[73] No fewer than five accolades are presented here to describe the high position and nature of Jehovah. The first of these is King.[74] This noun speaks of His position as the Sovereign of the universe. As His subjects, we should submit to Him with all our being. Each of the remaining expressions highlights one of the Lord's attributes. "Eternal" is literally "of the ages." He has always existed in eternity past and will always exist in eternity future. The next accolade proclaimed by Paul is "immortal." This word is sometimes translated "incorruptible."[75] The idea is that since God cannot become decayed, death can never overtake Him.

Extolling the Lord as well is the word "invisible." It is too simplistic to think the apostle was just stating that the Father cannot be seen. He was insinuating much more. In His full majesty, very God of very God, He is dazzlingly holy; so much so that humankind cannot and should not cast their eyes upon Him (cf. 1 Tim. 6:16; Ex. 33:17–23). No one has ever seen God (John 1:18), but Jesus has revealed Him (John 12:45; 14:9). This concept is in no way implying He is unknowable. On the contrary, Jesus told His disciples they could have a personal relationship with the Father (14:7, 23). Our God is not aloof as are the gods of other religions. His attributes are seen in nature (Rom. 1:20). He cannot be seen with our physical eyes but He can be with the eyes of faith (Heb. 11:27).[76]

That thought leads into the final feature listed in verse 17.[77] Our great God is the only true and living God. Other gods exist solely in the imaginations of people. The one exception would be Satan, for he is called "the god of this world" (2 Cor. 4:4). The Lord is very clear about His uniqueness:

> "You are My witnesses," declares the LORD,
> "And My servant whom I have chosen,
> In order that you may know and believe Me

And understand that I am He.
Before Me there was no God formed,
And there will be none after Me.
I, even I, am the LORD,
And there is no savior besides Me." (Isa. 43:10–11)

Paul rounds out this paragraph by ascribing to God "honor and glory forever and ever." Honor and glory have nearly identical meanings and are often paired with each other in the New Testament (Rom. 2:7, 10; Rev. 4:9, 11; 5:12, 13; 7:12). The Almighty alone deserves our complete respect, praise, and adoration. The last word, "amen," is a transliteration of an Aramaic word, and it roughly means "so be it" (cf. Deut. 27:15–26, 1 Tim. 6:16, 2 Tim. 4:18). It is a shout of joy affirming the attributes of God just spelled out.

Handling Sound Doctrine Responsibly (1:18–20)

Verses 18–20 are actually more closely associated with verses 3–11 than they are with verses 12–17. Paul stresses "faith and a good conscience" in verse 5 as he does here. In verses 3 and 4 he pointed out that the false teachers were leading people astray, and in verse 20 he specifically mentions two by name (cf. also "entrusted," v. 11, "entrust," v. 18).

Confronting false teaching is not easy or fun (but it is necessary), and so Paul does all he can to comfort and encourage Timothy. Here he uses a term of endearment to do so—"my son." Too, just saying (or writing out in this case) the person's name ("Timothy") helps the recipient to realize that Paul cares about him and is not just barking out orders.

To which command (v. 18) is the apostle referring? The most sensible answer is the command to stop the infidels. Paul left Timothy in Ephesus for that purpose (v. 3). In fact, the word "command" here is the same exact word used in verse 3 (rendered "instruct" in the NASB). He has been "entrusted" with this command and is thus obligated to carry it out. God's truth is precious, and it must be preserved.

Perhaps a more difficult question is, what are these prophecies (v. 18) and why does Paul mention them? That these prophecies were "previously made" may indicate that they were uttered when the elders laid hands on the young evangelist (1 Tim. 4:14; cf. 2 Tim. 1:6 and possibly 1 Tim. 6:12), perhaps at some sort of ordination or commissioning service.

The wrench in the works is that the word "concerning" can mean "to lead" (of place), or "to come before" (in time).[78] Thus, the verse could be suggesting that the prophecies lead Paul to Timothy (as a replacement for Barnabas, Acts 15:39), or these utterances could have had something to do with what a fantastic, though hardship-filled, ministry Timothy would have.[79] If the former is correct, then Paul would be saying that he is confident Timothy can achieve his goal since the Holy Spirit would not have directed Paul to him if he were unqualified. The weakness of that conclusion is that it involves a great deal of speculation.[80]

In harmony with the theme of this chapter (Paul's encouragement of Timothy), it is better to understand the apostle to be referring to the success of Timothy's ministry. He is being reminded that the prophecies spoke of his success in ministry, as well as that they gave him authority to preach and teach. William Hendriksen's paraphrase is noteworthy: "The charge was not new, arbitrary or unfair, but entirely in agreement with the previous prophetic utterances concerning you."[81] Therefore he can now be more resolute about approaching the troublemakers. From that time down to today, many young pastors have found encouragement in recounting their call to ministry.

Paul was no stranger to spiritual warfare, so it is no shock here that he throws in a military (or possibly athletic) term (v. 18). "Fight" is actually "fight as a soldier" (cf. 2 Tim. 2:3–4). What are his weapons? Surprisingly, the prophecies. Paul writes that "by them"[82] Timothy may wage spiritual war. He hopes that bringing them to mind will inspire Timothy and convince him that he will come out on top. In our life of ease, we often forget that a battle is raging.

Last, the apostle describes the fight as "good." He is not saying that war is enjoyable, but that what Timothy is fighting for is noble and right. There could be no greater cause than to defend the truth.

Paul's Use of Athletic Imagery	
1 Timothy 1:18; 6:12	"fight the good fight"
1 Timothy 4:7, 8	"discipline"
1 Timothy 4:10	"labor and strive"
2 Timothy 2:5	"competes as an athlete"
2 Timothy 4:7	"fought the good fight"
2 Timothy 4:7	"finished the course"
2 Timothy 4:8	"the crown (wreath)"

Use of the word "rejected" (v. 19) throws into relief the fact that the false teachers did not subtly float away from the faith but deliberately turned their back on it. The first step, however, was to jettison their "good conscience"[83] so they wouldn't feel bad about what they had done. They repudiated their internal moral compass and decided to live any way they pleased. Consequently they destroyed themselves spiritually ("shipwrecked"), and would probably become defensive when confronted. Ergo, it is vital for Timothy to keep trusting God and not do anything that would violate *his* conscience. Any slipup would cost Timothy his personal integrity, and his ministry would be all but ruined (cf. 1 Tim. 4:16).

The apostle is not afraid to "name names." He points out two apostates in particular, Hymenaeus and Alexander (v. 20). This may be the same Hymenaeus mentioned in 2 Timothy 2:17. If true, then we know that his heresy was teaching that the resurrection had "already taken place" (2 Tim. 2:18; see v. 17 for more explanation). Alexander was a rather common name (Acts 4:6; 19:33; Mark 15:21; 2 Tim. 4:14). The Alexander of 2 Timothy 4:14 may be the same man Paul identifies here, since in both passages the man lives in or near Ephesus, and both opposed Paul's teaching. Otherwise we know nothing of the men here in 1:20.[84] That these two men were not the only heretics is evidenced by Paul's use of the word "among." Perhaps Hymenaeus and Alexander were the worst offenders.

Paul's accusations would not go over well today. Tolerance is the order of the day, and we certainly wouldn't want to hurt people's feelings by mentioning their names. Such reasoning is hogwash. It is absolutely necessary for believers to "earnestly contend for the faith" (Jude 1:3), never being afraid to do what is right.

Scripture does not specify the nature of the blasphemy mentioned in verse 20. It is not likely that the offenders were making direct statements attacking the Lord and His character, for in that case no one in the church would have latched onto their teaching. The irreverent remarks came in the form of claiming to speak for God when in reality they were espousing falsehoods.[85]

The words "delivered over to Satan" have generated much debate. The explanation could be as simple as that these two were kicked out of the church. They would no longer have the warmth and protection of Christian fellowship but would be out in the world, which is Satan's realm (2 Cor. 4:4). Jesus taught that a transgressor who refuses to repent is to be put out of the local assembly (Matt. 18).[86] On the other hand, it could mean that the devil was allowed to menace them much as he did Job. The only passage in the New Testament that parallels this one is 1 Corinthians 5:5. There it is revealed in plain language that pain was inflicted on the offender's flesh for the sake of his spirit.[87] That this sentence was carried out with the knowledge and backing of the congregation (1 Cor. 5:2, 7) is probably the case here too.[88]

Whatever "delivered over to Satan" means, it is certainly the worst possible thing that could happen to someone.[89] It is not enough to silence the troublemakers; they must be taught a lesson. Students of the Scriptures who think the penalty is too severe must keep six things in mind: (1) Blasphemy is a very serious transgression (Matt. 26:65; Mark 14:64; John 10:33; and especially Matt. 12:31), one with which Paul was familiar (1 Tim. 1:13). It would do Christians a world of good if we would meditate on the greatness and holiness of God. (2) The immediate purpose of church discipline is punitive, but the goal is repentance. The punishment is designed to get the Christian to straighten up (Gal. 6:1) and become a faithful and productive member of the congregation. Second Timothy 2:25–26 more directly states this truth (cf. Titus 1:13). "[Paul] is hoping and praying that by means of this dire affliction these false teachers may come to see themselves as grievous sinners and may be brought to genuine repentance, so that they will no longer rail at the truth and thereby revile its Author."[90] (3) Consider 1 Corinthians 11:27–30. Some Corinthian Christians had died because they participated in the Lord's Table "in an unworthy manner." (4) God sometimes makes use of the devil to bring about His purposes. In the Old Testament, Israel was attacked by its foes as a form of discipline (1 Kings 11:14). Paul's thorn in the flesh was "a messenger of Satan."[91] (5) When people turn their backs on God or malign His truth, that is the evil they have chosen for themselves (Rom. 1:24–28).[92] (6) Paul was not inflicting the punishment, God was[93] (cf. 2 Kings 2:23–24), and His judgments are always right (Ps. 19:9). Part of our faith is trusting Him even when we don't understand what He is doing (Isa. 55:8–9).

Hymenaeus and Alexander wanted "to be teachers of the Law" (v. 7) but they had a lesson to learn themselves ("be taught not to blaspheme").

All this means Hymenaeus and Alexander were indeed Christians. The church has no business castigating those who are not believers (cf. Acts 5:1–11).[94] Someone who is not a Christian is already under Satan's influence (1 John 5:19).[95]

Conclusion

This chapter reveals how to deal with false teachers in the church. They must not be allowed to continue to spread their heresy, but they must be confronted. They must be shown how their teaching is unscriptural. This duty is difficult, especially for someone shy, as Timothy was. But Paul reminded him that our God is all-powerful. He is more than capable of handling any situation, and He would be with Timothy during this ordeal. If the Lord could change Paul from a vicious killer to a devout and outspoken Christian, He can do anything.

Study Questions

1. In light of verse 3, what do you think of pastors who preach "feel good" sermons? Who rebuke backsliders?

2. Paul talks about love in verse 5. Does love mean always being kind and sweet to other people?

3. A concept found throughout the Pastoral Epistles is "sound doctrine" (v. 10), but many Christians think theology is boring. Why is it important to have a general understanding of basic doctrine?

4. Paul was grateful to be serving the Lord (v. 12). What is your attitude about ministering to others? Do you see it as a blessing or a burden?

5. Almost everyone was probably of the opinion that Saul of Tarsus would never be saved. Do you think there is someone beyond saving? Why or why not?

6. Verse 15 raises two vital questions about the person and work of Christ. (1) Do the words "Christ came into the world" show that He existed before He was born on earth? (2) The verse goes on to say that He came to save sinners. Did Christ die only for the elect or for all sinners?

7. Only God is to receive our praise, adoration, and worship. What is an idol? Do you have any in your life?

8. The apostle reminds us in verse 18 that we are in a spiritual battle. Discuss good and bad methods of spiritual warfare—things such as binding Satan, prayer walks, and territorial spirits. What advice does James 4:7 give? Ephesians 6:12?

9. Also in light of verse 18, do you believe the hardships of the Christian life are virtually ignored in our churches by overemphasizing joy and peace? What about in our evangelism?

10. Paul cautioned Timothy that in dealing with the false teachers, he should be careful not to lose his faith and good conscience (v. 19). Do you believe a Christian should stay in a liberal church in order to be "light"? Consider 1 Corinthians 15:33 and 2 Corinthians 6:17.

11. Church discipline is no pleasant matter, but it must be done or the spiritual vitality of the church will be drained. In verse 20 Paul publicly names two unrepentant men. What do you think about announcing an offender's name in public? What are some dos and don'ts? See also Matthew 18:17.

CHAPTER 2

The Goal Is Worshipfulness
1 Timothy 2:1-15

Preview:

*False teachers were not the only problem afflicting the church in Ephesus. Paul
also found it necessary to write at some length about the conduct of public worship. It seems the proper function of prayer, and roles of men and women in the
services were not being observed. These concerns spill over into chapter 3 as
well. The present chapter can be divided into two components. The first discusses prayer (vv. 1–7), and the second establishes the ecclesiastical roles of
men and woman (vv. 8–15).*

The Purpose and Content of Prayer (2:1–7)

Prayer for All (vv. 1–2)

Prayer is without a doubt on the writer's mind as he pens these words. That is
the subject matter of verse 1 and then again immediately after this section in
verse 8. However, a closer look reveals that salvation is a key feature of this
paragraph too. It could even be said to be the dominant feature. Therefore, a
proper overview of verses 1–7 must include an understanding of the relationship between prayer and salvation. The most natural conclusion is Paul wants
believers to pray for those who don't know Christ as personal Savior. Robert
Mounce concisely and correctly summarizes the first part of chapter 2: "Prayer
is the context, salvation the content."[1]

This passage is tied into chapter 1 by the word "then" (or "therefore").
The apostle has been expounding upon the greatness of God and the wickedness of the heretics, and his words have ignited the compassion in his heart,

turning his thoughts to the gospel. The great apostle is also the great missionary.

Another way to connect this passage with chapter 1 is to say that in chapter 1 the heretics showed how church is *not* to be done, and in chapters 2 and 3 Paul shows how it *is* to be done.

He does not beat around the bush but immediately starts into the most pressing need. "First of all" not only suggests a list of issues he wants to comment on, but, more important, is also a clear indication that prayer should receive a high priority in our private devotions and in our group worship. It was an indispensable element in the early church (Acts 2:42, 3:1, 6:4, 12:5).

Timothy is not commanded, but encouraged, to follow through on the advice offered here. "Urge" (cf. 1:3) is a gentle word. It means "to call alongside," and is the verbal root of the word Jesus utilized to describe the Holy Spirit (*paraklētos;* John 14:26).

The reader quickly notices that Paul doesn't just use the general term "prayer" here, but he amplifies the idea with the words "entreaties and prayers, petitions and thanksgivings" (so NASB; the NIV has "requests, prayers, intercession and thanksgiving"). These four words have nearly identical definitions, but it is helpful to elaborate on their distinctions. Whether these are types of prayers or different characteristics of prayer is not terribly significant to the interpretation of the passage.[2]

"Entreaties" (cf. 1 Tim. 5:5) are pleas, requests, or petitions for oneself.[3] They are a crying out to God for help. A sense of urgency is inherent in this word; in fact, the root meaning is "to lack, be deprived." The next term, "prayers," is the usual word for conversing with deity. It can also be used as a place of prayer (Acts 16:13, 16). Hendriksen makes a distinction between these first two terms, saying that "entreaties" involve keenly felt needs, whereas "prayers" have more to do with ongoing needs (food, spiritual growth, etc.).[4] In noun form they are directed only to God in the New Testament, never to a human.[5]

"Petitions" means to speak to someone on behalf of someone else, to intercede. (It can be distinguished from "entreaties" in that "entreaties" are requests for oneself.[6]) The Greek word (as a noun) is rare, occurring only here and in 1 Timothy 4:5. Romans 8:27, 34; and 11:2 are just a few of its occurrences in the New Testament as a verb. Both the Holy Spirit (Rom. 8:26) and Jesus (Heb. 7:25) intercede for the benefit of believers (cf. Luke 22:31–32). Subsequently, those two members of the Godhead not only are familiar with our problems and heartaches, but they express compassion for us, too. In the secular literature "petitions" was occasionally used of an official petition to a king (cf. 1:17). Thus it connotes a confidence or boldness to approach a superior.

The fourth and final word Paul has in his list is "thanksgivings" (the Greek word is plural, *eucharistias*, from which we get the word *eucharist*). It is defined as expressing gratitude for benefits or blessings, the giving of thanks. It is found frequently in the apostle's greetings to churches (Phil. 1:3; Col. 1:3) and is part of the Jewish practice of giving thanks before a meal (Mark 8:6, Acts 27:35). Christians would be more content and complain less if they spent more prayer time thanking the Lord and less time making requests.

Underlying verse 1 is the notion that we are completely dependent on the Lord in all matters. No one is to be excluded when we go before the Lord. We are to pray for "all men."[7] Neither bigotry nor bitterness is an excuse for erasing people from our prayer list. Regardless of whether we like them, we need to thank the Lord for them and intercede for them. The phrase "on behalf of" reinforces this intercessory aspect of prayer. "That Paul begins his teachings on church order with this topic sheds light on the primary focus for the church. If the primary aim of the church were fellowship, knowledge of the Word, or the holiness of the saints, all those goals could perfectly be accomplished by taking us to heaven. The central function of the church on earth is to reach the lost."[8]

The exhortations to pray become a little more specific at this point. Believers are now urged to lift up in prayer all those who are in a position of authority (cf. Rom. 13:1-7). Why these particular people? A handful of reasons can be suggested. First, in our prayer circles we tend to concentrate on people with whom we are personally acquainted. Our leaders are often not in our forethoughts. Second, generally speaking, politicians and dictators are not well liked among the citizens. Third, Paul may have noticed this problem was especially acute in Ephesus and wanted to correct their attitude toward their rulers. Fourth, an explicit answer is discovered in the remainder of the verse. Christians will more readily be able to go about their business (making disciples) if the interference from wars and the government is minimal (cf. 1 Thess. 4:11-12). Part of being a good Christian is being a good citizen.[9] In no way is Paul suggesting a believer is to have a life of ease.

This admonition to pray "for kings and all who are in authority" is extra incredulous when one remembers the "king" at the time was the notorious Nero.

Some Bible students endorse the interpretation that the "tranquil and quiet life" is the result of prayers for "all men" (v. 1), not just for those in positions of power. Indeed, Paul directed in Romans 12:18 that we are to "be at peace with all men." This decision is not either/or, however, since "all who are in authority" is a subset of "all men." Too, it is not just the Christian community that benefits from good government, but all citizens do (cf. Jer. 29:7).[10] There is no question the *pax Romana* (the peace provided throughout the empire by the powerful Romans) facilitated the spread of the gospel.

The words "tranquil" and "quiet" have nearly the same definition. "Tranquil" has more to do with outward disturbance, and "quiet" relates more to inner peace.[11] Paul is certainly not suggesting that the Christian life should be one of ease or that it will be free of conflicts. His own life testifies otherwise.[12]

Believers Are to Be Good Citizens

Render to Caesar (the government) the things that belong to Caesar (Mark 12:17).

Be subject to government authorities (Rom. 13:1).

Believers are to obey the laws of the land (Rom. 13:2).

Believers are to pay their taxes (Rom. 13:6).

Believers are to respect and honor government authorities (Rom. 13:6).

Believers are to pray for kings and all in authority (1 Tim. 2:2).

What the apostle is declaring is that Christians themselves should not be the source of uprisings. Their conduct should reflect "all godliness and dignity." Believers should be known for their respectability, piety, and trustworthiness. Our words and deeds need to conform to the Lord's moral standards. These characteristics are found in chapter 3 in the list of qualifications for church leaders.

Mounce elaborates on the term "godliness": "It also has an observable behavioral element so that it becomes a description of proper conduct (1 Tim 5:4), so much so that someone can appear to be [godly] but deny its true power (2 Tim 3:5)."[13]

Paul may have been motivated to pen these admonitions because the unorthodox teachers were causing trouble among the brethren. Unruly behavior and harsh words bring unnecessary reproach upon the Lord and upon the church.[14]

Salvation for All (vv. 3–4).

To pray as Paul has urged is pleasing to the Lord.[15] Why? Because these kinds of sincere prayers result in many benefits: civil authorities are blessed, people are drawn to the Savior (v. 4), and Christians are more likely to be able to live godly lives.[16]

The adjective "good" (*kalos*[17]) has the idea of being beautiful and admirable. "Acceptable" means something that is welcome and well received. "In the sight of," when used in reference to God, has the connotation of "in the opinion or judgment of."[18]

This verse is a sobering reminder for those who are not inclined to lift their superiors before the throne of grace. God expects His children to pray for all people, even (or perhaps especially for) those in authority.

The reader should not miss the significance of the expression "God our Savior" (cf. 1:1). Since Jesus is our Savior, it stands to reason that He is also divine. Any who deny His deity have no proper interpretation for this phrase.

As one can imagine, verse 4 has triggered much debate and discussion. If God wants everyone to be in heaven, then why won't they be there?[19] Isn't the Lord able to carry out what He wants?

If there is one thing that is certain about this verse, it is that it does not teach universalism. Jesus Himself said that some people will go to hell. "Do not marvel at this; for an hour is coming, in which all who are in the tombs shall hear His voice, and shall come forth; those who did the good deeds to a resurrection of life, those who committed the evil deeds to a resurrection of judgment" (John 5:28–29). Ergo, there must be some other explanation.

The key to this verse is the word "desires." Notice that Paul (under the inspiration of the Holy Spirit) did not write, "forces." The Lord woos people to Himself, but He does not make them come against their will. Love is not love if it is the result of pressure and coercion. We love God because we want to. Jesus predicted that He would draw all people to Himself (John 12:32), yet not all will believe (John 5:28–29). Nevertheless, Paul exhorted his readers to pray for all people (1 Tim. 2:1).

It is beyond the purpose of this volume to further scrutinize God's sovereignty versus humankind's free will, or even to do a word study on the word "desires," which would be helpful.[20]

The Greek word here for "knowledge" (*epignōsis*) is a more intense one than just simple knowledge. It could be translated "full knowledge" or "recognition." To be saved, a person must recognize and trust the truth of the gospel and not have merely an intellectual understanding of it.

Here is another place in the Pastoral Epistles where the apostle emphasizes the importance of the truth. A score of passages can be found that state or imply how vital sound doctrine is, in this case the salvation message (cf. 2 Tim. 2:25). Theology is the business of all Christians, not just of seminary professors.

The errorists were teaching that only a select few could possess this "full knowledge," which in turn caused the believers to question whether or not they were even saved in the first place. Paul combats that heresy by reiterating that the gospel is to be offered to all. In fact, the word "all" appears six times in the first six verses of this chapter.

One Mediator for All (vv. 5–6)

No fewer than three crucial doctrines are packed into this rather short passage. The first is monotheism (cf. 1:17). In every synagogue service, the Jews would recite a doxology that, among other things, stressed this belief in one true God. It is called the Shema (Deut. 6:4–9). It begins, "Hear, O Israel! The LORD is our God, the LORD is one!" This served as a reminder that all other gods are false. There is only one God, and He reigns over the entire universe.

A second doctrine has to do with Christ's unique function. Jesus is the one and only Savior, or as He is called here, the one Mediator (cf. John 14:6). What is a mediator? It is someone who is invested with authority to come in and settle a dispute between two parties.

Iniquity separates humanity from the Lord. It is like a huge, impenetrable wall blocking a person's access to the Almighty. A Mediator is therefore necessary because sinful people cannot draw near to a holy God. Christ stepped in and brought the two together by taking that iniquity upon Himself (Isa. 53:6). Furthermore, by implication the apostle is refuting the false teacher's exclusivism (as he seems to be doing throughout vv. 1–7). They teach that only those "in the know" are the true believers. In stark relief Paul is insinuating that Jesus, as the only Deliverer, must be the Deliverer of all people, not just of the Jews.[21] There is nowhere else to turn for salvation.

The third teaching inherent in this passage concerns Jesus' unique personality.[22] He is both fully God and fully man. Verse 3 highlighted His deity, whereas here His humanity is pointed out. Paul wrote "the *man* Christ Jesus," not "the *Jew* Christ Jesus" (cf. Rom. 5:15; Phil. 2:7–8).[23] By the way, Jesus did not shed His human nature when He ascended back to heaven. He will forever be the God-man.

One of the best techniques a speaker or writer can employ to make sure particular points get across is to repeat them. That the power of the cross can reach every single person was no doubt Paul's reason for writing "all" six times in six verses, as noted above. Otherwise, it would not make much sense to pray for "all men" (v. 1)—and doing so pleases "God our Savior" (v. 3).

Verse 6 makes a clear statement in that regard. The passage had spoken of Jesus as Mediator (v. 5), and now it is said that He "gave Himself as a ransom for all."[24] It could be argued that this means "for all time," but that doesn't harmonize as well with the context of "all men" above. How could the Scriptures be plainer in teaching that Christ died for every single person (cf. 1 John 2:2)?

Christ the Only Mediator
Christ is the only mediator between God and humanity (1 Tim. 2:5).
Christ as an intercessor sits at God's right hand to care for His own (Ps. 110:1; Rom. 8:34).
There is no other means of salvation (Acts 4:12).
He presently lives to intercede for the believer (Heb. 7:25).
He is a mediator of the new and better covenant (Heb. 8:6; 9:15; 12:24).

A ransom is a payment made for the life of another. That is what our Lord did. He died in our place so that we could have eternal life (cf. 1 Peter 1:18–19).[25] No one forced Him to the cross (cf. John 10:18). He "gave Himself" because of His gracious love for us.

Determining the proper interpretation of the last part of verse 6 is no easy assignment. What is this "testimony," and who is to proclaim it?[26] Because the first half of the verse is about the crucifixion, some Bible students believe the testimony was the actual act of Jesus' death. Others look to the next verse, which says, "For this I was appointed a preacher," and conclude that Paul is the one who is to bear the testimony. The best resolution is not to see this as either/or but as both/and.[27]

Jesus' work on the cross definitely had an impact on people (Mark 15:39), yet Paul (along with all Christians) is to make the gospel known in as many places as possible.

The last few words are an idiomatic expression literally meaning "in its own seasons" ("at the proper time"). Christ came in accordance with God's timing (Gal. 4:4), and this era has been designated the one in which to proclaim the Good News. See also Titus 1:3.

Last, it should be mentioned that verses 5 and 6 could be part of an early creed. The words do flow off the tongue well, and in fact the NRSV writes them out in poetic form.

Paul's Qualifications (v. 7)

After reminding Timothy of the nature and extent of the gospel, Paul lists three offices he holds in his service to the Lord[28] (cf. 2 Tim. 1:11). What is the "this" he is to proclaim? It is the good news of the gospel. His ministry is to explain and share the gospel with all who will listen, and of course that should be the goal of every disciple of Christ.

The great apostle's humility is subtly evident here. He does not announce, "I proclaim myself an apostle," or "The Jerusalem church voted me into office." He utilizes the passive voice ("was appointed") to imply that it was God Himself who designated Saul of Tarsus to be His spokesman (cf. Gal. 1:1). This statement of fact bolsters his authority. The heterodox teachers should listen to him (through Timothy) because he is conducting his ministry under the direct authority of the Lord.

Why does Paul find it necessary to add, "I am telling the truth, I am not lying"? Doesn't Timothy trust him? As in other cities, Paul's status as a true apostle was called into question. He likely inserted those words to further counteract the lies of the troublemakers. They had not only been spreading heresy, but also brainwashing the people to think it was Paul who was in error. It was they who had superior knowledge they claimed. In addition, it is significant that he places those words right after "apostle" and not at the end of the verse. The errorists may have made much of the fact that he was not one of the original twelve disciples.[29]

Since the false teachers were probably Jews and thereby taught that Gentiles should be excluded from the knowledge of salvation, the apostle is adamant that Gentiles are the very people he is targeting in his evangelistic efforts.[30] They too are part of the "all" of verse 4.

As noted above, Paul names three offices or positions that he is privileged to occupy. The first is preacher ("herald," NRSV, NIV). A preacher is someone who proclaims a message, and within a Christian context that message consists of the truths of Holy Writ, especially the gospel. Another hat he wears is that of apostle. An apostle is one who has been sent out on a sacred mission. Paul and Barnabas were commissioned by the church at Antioch by order of the Holy Spirit (Acts 13:1–3).

A third office listed in this verse is teacher, and more specifically a teacher to the Gentiles. Paul does witness and minister to Jews, but his primary audience is made up of Gentiles (Acts 9:15, 13:46). This office is needed to do follow-up work. Once a person is converted, in order to grow in Christ, he or she must be taught the Word of God. An ignorant believer is of little use to the Lord (2 Peter 1:8).

The last portion of the verse reads, "in faith and truth." Not a few interpretations have been suggested for this expression. (1) These terms may hark back to verse 4. One must have faith to be saved, and one must be saved to know the truth.[31] (2) The words are an hendiadys[32] and should be rendered, "the true faith." (3) Paul is being faithful to God in teaching the truth, in contrast to the troublemakers who are teaching with selfish motives and are spreading falsehoods. (4) Paul is teaching what is of the faith (the body of knowledge revealed by God; cf. Jude 1:3) and is true. There is not a great deal of difference between 2, 3, and 4,[33] but 3 states the meaning best.

Men and Women in Public Worship (2:8–15)

This chapter commenced with Paul encouraging the Ephesian believers to pray for "all men," and then briefly discussed the goal and purpose of prayer. Logically, the next step would be to write about the "how" of prayer, and that's exactly what he does. It can be deduced from this section (vv. 8–15) that the congregation was acting unbecomingly during public worship services. He first addresses the men, but the balance of the chapter is directed at the women.

Men in Prayer (v. 8)

The writer indicates that he is drawing matters to a close with his "therefore." Paul has been expounding upon the philosophy of prayer, and now it is time to take action.

The emphasis in this verse is not on the lifting of the hands. What Paul is concerned about is holiness. Of the various postures for prayer encountered in the Old and New Testaments, not one is established as the "correct" one. The lifting or spreading of the hands is just one of the methods used by the faithful (Ps. 141:2; Isa. 1:15). What is important is that the posture reflect the heart attitude of the one who prays.[34]

By the phrase "in every place," Paul means that whenever public prayer is offered, it should be done by godly people. He doesn't mean that they should constantly have their hands lifted.[35] That Paul has to include the words "in every place" implies that some house churches were allowing inappropriate worship practices.

What was it about them that was inappropriate? Based on the statements made in the rest of this passage, it seems first that the men were being hypocritical in their public prayers, and second the women were taking over the worship services. Our comments on the subsequent verses will expand on these suggestions. Whatever problems the apostle was addressing, it is not far-fetched to think the false teachers were exasperating them.

Paul deems it wrong for a man to take the people before the throne of grace when he is harboring sin in his own life. He is not praying with "holy hands"—that is, he is not spiritually pure. No believer is perfect, but to knowingly cling to iniquity and then think God will listen to one's prayer is ill-founded. For an unrepentant man to stand before the congregation and utter words of piety is hypocrisy.

Paul offers some elaboration on the form of this unholy attitude when he writes, "without wrath and dissension" ("anger or argument," NRSV). The term "wrath" has reference to anger and bitterness toward another. The Greek word for "dissension" (*dialogismos*) in and of itself is not evil. From it, we get the English word *dialogue*. However, because it is closely associated here with wrath (as also in Phil. 2:14), the writer does put a negative connotation on it. Some are of the opinion that this is not an audible dialogue but one that takes place inside a person's head. He is debating within himself how he is going to vent his anger at the one who offended him.[36]

Others contend that there is feuding among the members, maybe over the teachings of the errorists. This idea of "disputing" (so NIV) is probably what Paul was trying to get across. Whatever the case, such wicked thoughts disqualify that person from leading the public prayers (cf. Matt. 5:22–24).

Since Paul was inspired to employ the Greek word for males here (*anēr*), as opposed to humankind in general, a question arises as to whether he is asserting that women are not to lead the worshipers in prayer. Those who believe that assertion is true look to evidence just two verses away (vv. 11–12). Verse 12 in particular declares that women are to "remain quiet" during the service. First Corinthians 14:34–35 expresses the same sentiment: "Let the women keep silent in the churches; for they are not permitted to speak, but let them subject themselves, just as the Law also says. And if they desire to learn anything, let them ask their own husbands at home; for it is improper for a woman to speak in church."

Those who disagree point to 1 Corinthians 11:5. There it is assumed that women are to pray. The first group counters by saying 1 Corinthians 11:5 may not be a church setting but possibly a women's Bible study. At the very least, anyone reading Paul's epistles gets the idea that it is the men who are to have the leadership roles in the church.

Finally, it is again noticed (just as in v. 1) that Paul does not command these things but "wants" the men to do them. On the other hand, his apostolic authority negates the notion that his words are to be taken lightly, or that that is just his opinion. Remember that he is writing under the inspiration of the Holy Spirit.

Women in Worship (vv. 9–12)

Beginning in verse 9, Paul addresses women directly. Just as men are to strive for holiness, so women ("likewise") are to be careful how they beautify themselves.

Does God really care what clothes we wear? Verse 9 answers that question with a "yes." He is *more* concerned with what's on the inside (our character), but keep in mind that how a person looks on the outside reflects what that person is like on the inside (cf. 1 Peter 3:3–5). Inappropriate dress ultimately reflects on the Lord.

Verse 9 does not mean that Paul doesn't care how the men dress. He is focusing on the women here because men and women are "wired" differently. A man can be invoked into having immoral thoughts by merely looking at a woman who is clothed immodestly, but generally the opposite is not true. There is a difference between looking nice and being seductive.

New Testament Women and Godliness

Righteous Elizabeth (Luke 1:6)

Mary favored of God (Luke 1:30)

Pious Anna the prophetess (Luke 2:36)

The forgiven woman, Mary (Luke 7:36–50)

The women contributing to the disciples' needs (Luke 8:1–3)

The ministering servants: Mary and Martha (John 11)

The devoted women (Acts 1:14)

Praying Mary, mother of John Mark (Acts 12:12)

The pious worshiper of God, Lydia (Acts 16:14)

Believing Damaris (Acts 17:34)

Philip's prophetess daughters (Acts 21:9)

Godly and brave Priscilla (Acts 18; Rom. 16:3)

The servant Phoebe from Cenchrea (Rom. 16:1)

Timothy's Godly grandmother Lois (2 Tim. 1:5)

Timothy's Godly mother Eunice (2 Tim. 1:5)

The word "modestly" connotes a sense of honor and self-respect, as well as a concern for the feelings of others. "Discreetly" means having good judgment, moderation, and control of one's passions.

Some details on improper adornment are listed in the second half of the verse. "Braided hair" indicates that the woman took the time to give herself a nice hair style. "Gold" is gold jewelry of some kind, perhaps woven into the hair. "Pearls" were sought after just as much as, if not more so, than gold was (Matt. 7:6; 13:45–46). "Costly garments" would be raiment made from the finest linen and probably dyed purple (cf. Acts 16:14). Purple dye was expensive because it was very time consuming to concoct. Perhaps that is why it became the symbol of royalty.

Why did the apostle pick these particular adornments? Do they have something to do with only his culture, or does this verse apply today? For whatever reason, these accessories were considered improper by Paul. It may be that that is how the prostitutes of the day looked (cf. Isa. 3:16–24). The principle certainly applies today in that Christians (men and women) should attire themselves in such a way as not to draw undue attention to themselves.

The text is not saying that it is inherently wrong to shop at an expensive clothing store or wear jewelry, because a woman can have on bland clothing yet still look seductive. Nevertheless, Christians should make sure they are making these purchases with the right motives.

Last, although the context is a church service (vv. 11–12), these admonitions are not to be limited to those times. Believers always need to maintain an appearance that brings honor to the Lord.

Women are not to adorn themselves so much with gold as they are with good works (v. 10). It is better to be known for exhibitions of Christian character than for displays of the latest fashion. Years from now people will not remember the clothes worn, but they will remember the acts of grace and kindness.[37]

As one would imagine, verses 11 and 12 have produced much controversy. At first reading, Paul appears to be a chauvinist. Four points can be made to show that this is not the case. First, Paul involved women in his ministry (Acts 16:13, 18:18; Rom. 16:1). Second, he is writing these instructions under the inspiration of the Holy Spirit. Third, he explains his reasoning in the following verses. Fourth, that he would want women to learn anything at all was against the mind-set of the day.

The reader must also remember that these remarks have nothing to do with intellect, ability, or character. All believers have equal worth in the sight of God (Gal. 3:28). The matter is one of bringing order out of the chaos caused by the curse.

After humankind fell (vv. 13–14), God's wonderful creation was thrown into confusion. Someone had to be put in charge or the situation would have remained chaotic. The Bible teaches that in the home and in the church, the man is to assume the leadership role.

Much agitation could be eliminated if Christians focused on what women *can* do instead of on what they *can't* do in their service to the Lord. Here the apostle is stating that a woman is not to have an official teaching position over men. Women are to teach other women (Titus 2), and they can have a tremendous impact in the lives of children, among many other possibilities.

Women Are of Equal Value (vv. 13–15)

The passage presents two reasons as to why women are in the subordinate role to men.[38] First, Adam was created before Eve was (v. 13). At first this may seems like a trivial reason, but the firstborn had special privileges. A passage dealing with what a father should will to his children says, "But he shall acknowledge the first-born, the son of the unloved, by giving him a double portion of all that he has, for he is the beginning of his strength; to him belongs the right of the first-born" (Deut. 21:17). Such honor was not limited to the Jewish culture. In the tenth plague on Egypt, it was the firstborn who was killed (Exod. 11:5, 12:12, 29, 13:15).[39]

Second, it was the woman who was deceived (v. 14), which implies that Adam ate the forbidden fruit knowing full well that he was sinning! Reading between the lines, one gets the idea that because Eve tried to take over the leadership role in the family (consciously or unconsciously), God made a firm statement that the man is to be the head (cf. Gen. 3:16; 1 Cor. 11:3).

First Timothy 2:15 is one of the most challenging verses in the New Testament. Part of the difficulty is that "shall be preserved (or saved)" is singular, whereas later in the verse Paul writes in the plural, "if they continue." Space does not permit an examination of all interpretations derived from this verse, but two will be given.[40]

One view teaches that Paul is referring to the birth (and subsequent death, burial, and resurrection) of Christ. The Greek has the definite article, "the childbirth," an indirect allusion to Genesis 3:15. One obtains salvation by having faith in that "seed." There is no subject specified in the Greek, and thus this suggestion has the advantage of harmonizing with the immediate context. The closest subject is "the woman" (v. 14), Eve. Verse 14 also reports her fall into transgression (vv. 13–14; cf. 2 Cor. 11:3), and so it would seem logical for Paul to next talk about her salvation. The apostle then moves from speaking of her (singular) to women in general (plural). That they are genuinely saved will be evident by their "love and holiness with propriety" (NIV).

The problem with this viewpoint is that it teaches a works salvation. To be saved, a woman must "continue in faith and love and sanctity with self-restraint." Salvation is always by grace through faith (Eph. 2:5–9). Good deeds have nothing to do with it (Rom. 11:6).

Another view espouses the idea that women are "saved" from a perception of inferiority. They cannot be in authority in the church, but they will find satisfaction in their station as wife and mother if they are loving and faithful and show self-restraint by not usurping the leadership role of their husbands. A flaw in this theory is that Paul rarely, if ever, uses "preserved" (or "saved") in this fashion. In his writings, that verb means spiritual salvation.[41] This understanding doesn't clear up all the difficulties, but it does seem to be the one with the fewest problems.

If a person stopped reading at the end of verse 14, he or she would get the impression that because women are not to be teachers of men in the church, and because it was Eve who was deceived, women are beyond all hope. The apostle corrects that misperception in verse 15.[42]

Because this passage is not easily understood, it should not be used to support a particular doctrine.

Corporate worship is one of the most crucial elements in a Christian's spiritual diet. Any kind of disruption will prevent the service from having its maximum effect. Prayers need to come from a pure heart. Men should fulfill their duties as leaders. Women would do well to submit to the teaching authority of the church and dress in a way that is pleasing to the Lord. These and other characteristics allow the body to thrive and grow.

Study Questions

1. Are you faithful in praying for your leaders?

2. Should Christians be involved in politics? Does 2 Timothy 2:4 throw light on this question?

3. What does 1 Timothy 2:3–4 say about the nature of Jesus?

4. How does 2:5 relate to John 14:6 and Acts 4:12?

5. Is it really all that important that Christ is fully man and fully God?

6. In 2:7 Paul confirms that he was appointed an apostle. Does the office of apostleship still exist today?

7. Do you believe there is a wrong way to dress for church? If so, how? Similarly, what does Scripture have to say about Christians who dress like the world (green hair, multiple body piercings, etc.)?

CHAPTER 3

The Goal Is Character
1 Timothy 3:1–16

Preview:

In chapter 2 Paul spoke of proper worship in the church. Now he draws our attention to proper leadership in the church. A local body of believers is only as good as its leaders. Ministering as an elder or deacon is a high calling, and consequently the requirements are high. The Lord deserves no less. A reading of chapter 3 reveals, however, that the emphasis is on character, not on skill.

Qualifications for Elder (3:1–7)

In the very first verse, the apostle stresses the dignity associated with the office of elder. He does this by prefacing his words with a solemn declaration: "It is a trustworthy statement" ("Here is a trustworthy saying," NIV). He then goes on to call it "a fine work" ("a noble task," NIV). Service to God should not be entered into lightly.

To say that it is good for a man to aspire to this office requires some clarification. Just desiring to be a leader does not make a man fit to serve in that capacity. By implication Paul is also stating that this desire is not to be motivated by selfishness, but it is something the Lord has put on the candidate's heart. Nowhere in the New Testament are church officers elected. They are appointed (Titus 1:5). The other members recognize the candidate's qualities and affirm that he meets the stringent standards. Otherwise, they would not be comfortable with him being a leader, and his ministry would be ineffective. "Campaigning" for this position is a sign of pride.[1]

The titles "bishop," "overseer," and "elder" are used interchangeably in the New Testament. Titus 1 (a parallel passage to 1 Tim. 3) is an example. There, in verse 5, Paul writes "elders" (*presbuteros*), yet just two verses later he uses a different Geek word, *episkopos*, translated "overseer" in the New American Standard Bible and New International Version[2] (cf. Acts 20:17 with 20:28). There is no evidence that one office is superior to another.

Here in 1 Timothy 3:2 the apostle begins the list of qualifications using an all-encompassing phrase, "above reproach." By it he does not mean that the man has to be perfect. What is intended is that the candidate is to have no major blemishes in his character whereby he would be disqualified as a godly example to the congregation.

The expression "above reproach" is one word in the Greek (*anegklētos*) and is a compound of *ana* ("up, above") and the noun *klētos* ("to call"). This means the elder-overseer does indeed have a high calling and is to be "irreproachable, blameless." Nothing can be laid to his charge.

The candidate is to be the "husband of one wife" ("married only once," NRSV). The main idea behind this expression is that he must be a one-woman kind of man. In Paul's day, polygamy (whether by an actual marriage contract or by concubinage) was not very common in the general population, but it was among the wealthy. At the very least, then, Paul was making it clear that men who were not faithful to their one wife did not qualify.

That is the most natural reading of the expression, but since polygamy was not that much of a problem, the apostle must have been thinking of some other social ills as well. Divorce comes readily to mind. A recently divorced man should not serve as an elder since he would no longer be a godly example.

Of course, even this does not answer all possible situations and questions. What if he was divorced before he got saved but has now remarried? Or what if his wife left him (perhaps because he had become a Christian) to marry another man, and now he too has remarried? These and other questions can be answered only by much prayer on a case-by-case basis.

Nevertheless, some other definite conclusions can be drawn from this phrase. (1) Although it is ideal that the candidate be married, he is not *required* to be married to be a church officer. Paul was single and encouraged other Christians to remain single if at all possible (1 Cor. 7). (2) Only men are to be placed in positions of authority (cf. 1 Tim. 2:12).[3]

This matter was obviously a grave one for Paul, because he brings it up here, later in 3:12 concerning deacons, and in Titus 1:6.[4]

Other features that should mark the candidate will now be analyzed one at a time.

1. *Temperate*. Some synonyms for this word are *sober-minded, watchful,* and *circumspect*. Albert Barnes views it this way: "A minister [or elder] should have a watchful care over his own conduct."[5]

2. *Prudent*. This quality springs from a life of temperance. A prudent man is serious about spiritual matters. He has his priorities straight and possesses good self-discipline. Many conclude that this kind of man must always be cold and stoic, but that is not what Paul is trying to get across here.[6] A church leader will not do well if he cannot develop a warm, personal relationship with the others in the congregation.

3. *Respectable*. The root word here is translated "proper" ("modestly," NIV) in 1 Timothy 2:9. The candidate needs to be a man who is virtuous and worthy of honor.

4. *Hospitable*. The Greek word literally means "lover of strangers." This characteristic involves more than just having people over. To those of Paul's day, it would mean a willingness to take in travelers, especially Christians. There were inns in those days (cf. Luke 2:7; 10:34), but they sometimes had a reputation for immorality.

5. *Able to teach*. This is the only skill in the entire list. The elder should be able to communicate God's Word in such a way that the congregation is edified. To do so, he must know the Scriptures well. A parallel passage, Titus 1:9, states that he must "be able both to exhort in sound doctrine and to refute those who contradict." It is the sacred duty of all believers to conduct personal Bible study, and this is especially true for the leaders in the church.

6. *Not addicted to wine or pugnacious*. It is appropriate that these two criteria are positioned side by side (v. 3). It would not do to have as a leader someone who is known to be a drinker. Alcohol not only impairs judgment, but more significantly it is also a poor testimony. "Pugnacious," a word not heard much anymore, means "brawler" or "striker." A man who drinks too much often winds up in a fight. Of course, even an elder who is a teetotaler should not have a quarrelsome spirit.

7. *Gentle*. A contrast to pugnacious. The concepts of patience and forbearance are encompassed by this word. People respond better to a gentle leader than they do to a domineering personality.[7]

8. *Uncontentious* is likewise the opposite of pugnacious. An uncontentious person is one who is reluctant to fight. He is peaceable.[8]

9. *Free from the love of money.* An inordinate affection for riches is forbidden too (cf. 1 Tim. 6:10; Luke 16:14). No follower of Christ can serve both "God and mammon" (Matt. 6:24).

10. *Manages his own family well.* His home life is to be taken into consideration as well, a subject verses 4 and 5 address. This is a logical requirement, because those are the people who know him best. It is in the home where a man's true colors (and leadership skills) come out. The idea here is that managing one's family well isn't just a matter of having things under control, it is doing it with "all dignity." The philosophical reasoning behind all this is expressed in the form of a rhetorical question (v. 5). Mismanagement in the home is a sign that he will not be an effective servant-leader in the church either.[9]

11. *Not a new convert.* Verse 6 is based on good common sense. Someone who has been a Christian only a short time more readily gives into worldly and fleshly enticements. He has not had time to build up his resistance. In fact, any immature believer, regardless of how long he has been saved, will likely end up embarrassing the church and Christ. Paul asserts here that the most probable trap for a quickly promoted novice is pride. He thinks he is really something because the church has recognized his leadership skills. When the devil got puffed up, God kicked him out of heaven ("the condemnation incurred by the devil").

12. *A good reputation.* Verse 7 continues this admonition, requiring the candidate to have a good name. Not only must his spiritual maturity and home life be evaluated, but his reputation among his neighbors and coworkers needs to be factored in as well. A person with a bad reputation is not "above reproach."

In verse 6 it was the devil who *received* the judgment. Here, it is the evil one *laying out* the snares to entrap the careless Christian.

Qualifications for Deacon (3:8–13)

Elder is not the only church office discussed in the New Testament. Paul's thoughts now turn to the position of deacon. "Deacon" can simply mean "servant," but the fact that qualifications are spelled out shows that it is used in this passage as a technical term for the office of deacon.[10]

Church Offices

Apostles—*helped found the church; building up the body (Eph. 4:11–12)*

Prophets—*helped found the church; building up the body (1 Cor. 14:29–32, 37–40; Eph. 4:11–12)*

Evangelists—*helped spread the gospel; building up the body (Eph. 4:11–12)*

Pastors—*building up the body of Christ (Eph. 4:11–12)*
> *As an overseer (1 Tim. 3:1)*
> *As a teacher (Eph. 4:11)*
> *As an elder (Titus 1:5)*

Elders—*governing the body of Christ*

QUALIFICATIONS	PURPOSE
Above reproach	*Teach the truth*
Husband of one wife	*Be an example*
Temperate	*Reprove*
Prudent	*Correct*
Respectable	*Train in righteousness*
Hospitable	*Speak sound doctrine*
Able to teach	*Instruct to deny ungodliness*
Not addicted to wine	*Instruct to live sensibly*
Not pugnacious	*Instruct to look for the blessed hope*
Gentle	*Give attention to the Scriptures*
Uncontentious	*Teach others to teach*
Not driven by money	
Manages his own house well	
Not a new convert	

Deacons—*serving the body of Christ (Acts 6:1–6 ; 1 Tim. 3:8–13)*

QUALIFICATIONS	PURPOSE
Almost identical to elders	*Serve the local body of Christ*
	Supplement the work of the elders
	Give aid to the needy and the widows

The word "likewise" in verse 8 is a strong hint that the qualifications for deacon are right up there with those for elder (cf. Acts 6:1–7). Deacons, too, are to be men known for their "propriety of manner and conduct,"[11] sincerity ("not double-tongued"), and sobriety, and for not having riches as their primary goal in life. All of these except "not double-tongued" are enumerated above in verses 3 and 4.

"Not double-tongued" means that the candidate must be a man whose word can be trusted. There is some distinction between "free from the love of money" (v. 3) and not "fond of sordid gain" (v. 8). This distinction is found in the word "sordid." The former is a more sweeping statement and means that the person is not obsessed with making money, whether legally or illegally. The latter means that he holds to the conviction that stealing is wrong.

By "mystery of the faith" (v. 9), Paul means the doctrinal truths of Holy Writ. A "mystery" in the New Testament does not refer to something unknowable, but to something that was unknown yet has now been revealed. This verse is disclosing, then, that although a deacon is not required to teach,[12] he must still be convinced that what he believes is absolutely true. He has no hesitation in affirming the apostles' teaching. A "clear conscience" implies he is living in accordance with those truths.[13]

Like elders, deacons must be "beyond reproach" (v. 10). To determine if this is so, the candidate has to be "proven" or "tested." Has he been faithful in the ministries in which he has already been involved? What is he like at home (v. 12)?

More will be said about verse 12 below, but for now we need to look at verse 11. The first thing that must be determined is the meaning of the word *gunaikas*, which can be rendered in English as "wives" or "women." In other words, is Paul talking about the wives of the deacons, or about female deacons?

Those who are of the opinion that women can officially function as deacons contend that "women" is the better selection. However, it is context that determines the meaning of a word. A consideration of the adjacent verses leads to the conclusion that "wives" is what Paul had in mind. Ponder the following observations.

If "women" was the intended translation, then the author was abruptly switching the topic from male deacons to female deacons and then back to male deacons (v. 12) in the midst of this list. Why would female deacons have to be singled out? Wouldn't the same qualifications apply to them as to men?[14]

In the very next verse (v. 12), Paul is obviously using *gunaikas* in the sense of wife ("husbands of one wife"). The reasonable deduction is that he is utilizing it in the same manner in verse 11.[15] Another argument related to the context is that the word "deacons" found in verses 8 and 12 is a masculine noun in the Greek in both cases.[16]

Finally, inserting "wives" in verse 11 places it in the same category in which verse 12 is found—namely, the family. For a man to meet the standards established for deacon, his wife needs to be characterized by the traits listed in verse 11. Paul then completes his discussion of the man's home life in verse 12. There is no substantial evidence in the New Testament that women held the office of deacon.[17]

Therefore, it seems best to understand this verse as alluding to the wives of the deacons. This interpretation makes sense, because a wife who commits a moral or ethical blunder reflects upon her husband and limits his capacity to minister (cf. 1 Cor. 11:7).

Verse 11 goes on to say that these wives must be women who are "dignified, not malicious gossips, but temperate, faithful in all things."[18] Two of those traits ("dignified" and "temperate") were named before in verses 2 and 8. As noted above, "dignified" contains the notion that this person is of such a high caliber that she is worthy of respect, and "temperate" is defined as being level-headed, not excessive in any way.

The phrase "malicious gossips" could also be translated "slanderers" (so KJV). The Greek word behind it is rendered "devil" in Matthew 4:1. Because their husbands are deacons, these women might be privy to confidential tidbits of information and hence would need to be very careful not to talk with others about what they know. Last, they can enhance their testimony by being "faithful in all things," including to Christ, to their husbands, and to the duties God has assigned to them.

More parallel themes between the qualifications for elder and deacon are found in verse 12. A good deacon is one who is a godly man, a godly husband, and a godly father.

Verse 13 may be a follow-up thought to verse 10. It is implied that a deacon's ministry should be monitored and evaluated. Those who have served faithfully acquire a "high standing."[19] The thought here is that the faithful deacon will grow "in favor with God and men" (Luke 2:52). This promise does not mean that he will automatically be "promoted" to the office of elder, and it certainly doesn't mean that he is superior to other Christians.

Another promised reward for outstanding service is an increase in boldness. "Confidence" here denotes courage to speak out. But this confidence is not in themselves; it is in God and His truth ("the faith"). Verse 9 also spoke of being sure of one's belief in "the faith." As a result of this assurance, the pious deacon will have less fear to share the gospel.

Verse 13 is an encouragement to all who minister in the name of the Lord.[20]

The Great Duty of the Church (3:14–16)

Paul, in a world where danger and delay plagued travelers, was not sure when he could come to Ephesus to see Timothy. But the crucial nature of his message could not wait. In hopes of getting it there sooner, the apostle sent it by courier.

The verb "conduct" (v. 15) denotes lifestyle, not just individual behaviors. At several points in the Pastoral Epistles, Paul talks about how mature Christian living is expressed. When he writes "household of God," he is not thinking of a building, but a family (cf. Gal. 6:10; Eph. 2:19; 1 Pet. 4:17),[21] which is how a local body of believers should think of themselves. We are all brothers and sisters in Christ, and thus we should act as such. In other words, he is not so much talking about how Christians are to act "in church" (although that is part of it) as he is how we are to act "in Christ."

He defines "household of God" as "the church of the living God" (cf. "church of God," v. 5). The church is not a man-made institution.[22] It was established by the Lord and for His glory (Matt. 16:18). The deity we worship is "the living God." He is not a dead idol. He is a personal and active God. He is the only true God (Isa. 45:6, 21).

A final descriptive clause concerning the church is discovered at the end of verse 15: "the pillar and support of the truth." "Support" is better rendered "foundation" (so NIV). It is the great duty of the church to know, proclaim, and protect God's truth as it is revealed in the Holy Bible. Like a precious vase, it must be guarded from all attacks (cf. 1 Tim. 6:20). There will be an accounting for those disciples (individually and collectively) who do not study and defend "the faith" (Jude 1:3). A structure collapses sooner or later when a pillar cracks or the foundation is weakened.

Duties of the Church

To be working for Christ and waiting for His return (1 Thess. 1:9–10)

To be a pillar and support of the truth (1 Tim. 3:15)

To be a source of instruction (1 Tim. 6:17–18)

To be a place from which the love of the brothers is seen (1 Thess. 4:9–10)

To be a source of admonition for the fainthearted (1 Thess. 5:14)

To contend for the faith (Jude 1:3)

To be used of God to snatch some out of the fire of judgment (Jude 1:23)

The last verse of chapter 3 is packed with wonderful truths. It starts out by declaring that these are the beliefs to which all Christians adhere ("common confession"). But what is this "mystery of godliness"? Whatever (or whoever) it is, it is worth the effort to find out, because Paul uses "great" to describe it (or Him). Based on what follows, Jesus Christ is the most probable answer to our question. He alone fits all six lines of what is with little doubt an early hymn or creed. He was the "mystery" Messiah in that He was not "revealed in the flesh" until He was born to the virgin Mary.

In what sense did this perfect God-man need to be justified ("vindicated in the Spirit")? The answer is that His life and ministry would have been all for naught if He had not risen from the dead. All three members of the Trinity participated in the resurrection (Gal. 1:1; John 10:17–18), including the Holy Spirit (Rom. 8:11), and it was the resurrection that affirmed Jesus' person, teaching, and work (Rom. 1:4).

The next line says, "beheld by angels." Angels are associated with Jesus at several significant points of His earthly life: His birth (Luke 1:35), after His temptation (Matt. 4:11), during His passion at Gethsemane (Luke 22:43), at His resurrection (Luke 24:4), and at His ascension (Acts 1:10).

Later He was indeed "proclaimed among the nations." His followers obeyed His command to go and preach the gospel among the Gentiles ("nations;" Acts 9:15; 10), and thousands took hold of this good news (Acts 2; "believed on in the world"). As already noted, His earthly ministry ended with the ascension ("taken up in glory").

More than a few Bible students have pointed out the contrasting pairs in these lines: flesh/Spirit, angels/humans (nations), and world/heaven (glory).

Conclusion

The process for selecting men to serve as church officers is not one to be taken lightly. It will not be successful if done with much speed and little prayer. Don't pick leaders because they are willing to serve or just because they are good businessmen. Those qualities are good, but many other ones are quite necessary. Remember that these are the men who are not only going to be making decisions for the church, but will also be setting a Christian example. No one is going to live up to all the standards perfectly, but every one of the men must be above reproach. Too, these characteristics are not solely for the leaders. All believers should be cultivating them in their walk with the Lord.

From the evidence of the New Testament, one can discern the distinct roles of elder and deacon. An elder functions like an overseer or supervisor

(Acts 20:28), whereas a deacon is more in a supporting role (Acts 6). This is not to say there is not any overlap in their duties.

The apostle wraps up this chapter by reminding the church of its grand and noble obligation—to uphold the truth; an obligation made more difficult when immature or unfaithful men are at the helm.

Study Questions

1. What are some appropriate ways a church can find out the reputation of a candidate for elder or deacon?

2. How much can a man sin and still be "above reproach"?

3. Name some situations in which a man does not meet the requirement of being the "husband of one wife."

4. Does a man qualify for an office just because he is willing to be in that position? Explain your answer.

5. Explain more about the term "be tested" in verse 10.

6. In light of verse 11, how are we to distinguish between a prayer request and gossip?

7. Does your church do its part in upholding the truth? What does that look like? Do you as an individual Christian do your part?

CHAPTER 4

The Goal Is Discipline
1 Timothy 4:1–16

Preview:

The dominant purpose of chapter 3 was to lay out the qualifications a man must have to be considered for a church officer. Paul now writes to Timothy in a more personal way, reminding him to set an example for the flock. This virtue is becoming increasingly necessary because there will come a day when believers will lose interest in sound theology and be attracted to "doctrines of demons."

Warnings of Apostasy (4:1–5)

The word "but" ("now," KJV, NRSV) is a signal that Paul is continuing his thoughts of chapter 3. He wrote some glorious words about "the mystery of godliness" (3:16) but now warns Timothy that some Christians will sooner or later "fall away from the faith" ("depart from," KJV) and will follow after false teachers. How many is "some"? We don't know, but at least he didn't say all. God always has a remnant who are faithful to Him.

The apostle is not making up this prediction or trying to scare people unnecessarily; the Spirit of God is giving this admonition (v. 1). Paul is sure of what he is saying because he writes that the Holy Spirit declares it "explicitly" ("clearly," NIV). This apostasy will be quite evident at some point in the future.

This falling away (apostasy[1]) does not mean that Christians will lose their salvation (cf. John 10:28–29; Rom. 8:35–39). And Paul is definitely speaking to followers of Christ here, because they used to hold to "the faith," and because

65

non-Christians would have very little interest in a false preacher. It seems that these "some" will no longer want to listen to the exposition of the Word (2 Tim. 4:3). Instead, they will be drawn to legalistic teachers (1 Tim. 4:3).[2]

In the second half of verse 1, we have a contrast between the Holy Spirit and "deceitful spirits." Paul listens to the Holy Spirit (cf. Acts 13:2), while these misguided people listen to liars (1 Tim. 4:2). "Paying attention to" has the idea of heeding or even giving oneself over to. These false teachers are seducing Christians away from genuine Christianity and teaching them unbiblical notions. It is not surprising that these falsehoods originated with demons since their leader is "the father of lies" (John 8:44).

Satan is using ("by means of," v. 2) these hypocrites to spread his evil message. That these men are hypocrites (v. 2) implies that they are instructing the people to practice asceticism (no marriage, restricted diet, v. 3) while they participate in a variety of sensual pleasures. They have indulged so much that their consciences no longer bother them.

Concerning the hypocrites' directives, George Knight correctly observes, "Although Paul commended singleness as an estate in which one could give more time and energy directly to serving the Lord (1 Cor. 7:32, 35), he always insisted that marriage was not wrong (1 Cor. 7:28) and that God had indeed gifted many to marry (1 Cor. 7:7)."[3]

Paul notes the irony of the situation. The deceived believers were avoiding the very things the Lord has given people to use ("to be gratefully shared in"). "God . . . richly supplies us with all things to enjoy" (1 Tim. 6:17). The false teachers, claiming to represent the Lord, were actually making pronouncements that were directly counter to what God had intended,[4] which is exactly something one would expect Satan to promote. Finally, note with what attitude we are to enjoy them. It is to be done "gratefully" ("with thanksgiving," KJV, NIV).

At the end of verse 3, Paul asserts that these things are to be "shared in by those who believe and know the truth." It is one thing to *know* the truth, and it is another to *believe* it. Many people know *about* Christianity, but they don't believe it to be true. Believers alone can fully appreciate God and His provision for people.

We can partake of all the Lord created without guilt because He created it and because ("for," v. 4) whatever He creates is good (cf. Gen. 1:12; Mark 7:15, 19). This idea goes beyond just eating good food or having one's breath taken away at the sight of a beautiful mountain. It encompasses our circumstances as well.[5] Believers need to react to life's difficulties in a way that brings glory and honor to the Lord. Indeed, we should welcome everything "with gratitude" (cf. James 1:2–3).

Verse 5 teaches that common items can be set apart for a holy purpose ("sanctified"), even things like food (cf. 1 Cor. 10:31). The Word of God can do that because it informs us as to how we can use them for the glory of God, and prayer is a way to express our thankfulness. The heretics took God's good things (food, relations between husband and wife, etc.) and misused them.

Timothy's Spiritual Discipline (4:6–16)

In the remainder of this chapter, Paul tells his young friend Timothy how he can go about leading the congregation in the proper direction. One of Timothy's most important jobs was to protect them from heresy ("pointing out these things to the brethren"). He could do this best by setting an example, showing the people what it looks like to live out the truths of the Christian faith.

In addition to modeling a godly lifestyle, Timothy must also speak against the false teachers. Carrying out that responsibility is the main ingredient in the recipe for becoming a "good servant of Christ Jesus" (v. 6). Furthermore, Timothy must be careful not to let his tank run dry. To keep up his spiritual vitality, he needed to "nourish" his soul[6] "on the words of the faith and . . . sound doctrine." By "the words of the faith," Paul means the propositional truths revealed in Scripture. The phrase "sound doctrine" most probably "refers to Paul's own instructions to his young disciple."[7] Timothy has done well in maintaining this "diet," and Paul encourages him to remain resolute.

In verse 7 Paul commands Timothy to stay away from spiritual "junk food." These "worldly fables" ("godless myths," NIV) are mere superstitions, the type of misinformation elderly women sometimes try to pass down to the next generation ("old wives' fables," KJV). They may be the same as the myths mentioned in 1:4.

Beginning with the second half of verse 7 and continuing on down through verse 10, Paul emphasizes the value and importance of godliness by contrasting it with physical exercise. To be spiritually fit (develop a Christlike character), one must not only watch one's diet, but also exert oneself in the spiritual disciplines. The word "discipline" is perhaps better translated as "train," as it is in the NIV. The words "gymnasium" and "gymnastics" are derived from the Greek word used here (*gumnazō*).

Spiritual growth and maturity do not happen overnight, but require time and effort on the part of the individual Christian. Just as an athlete works hard to get his body in shape for the competition, so the believer must strive to be consistently involved in personal Bible study, prayer, worship (corporate and individual), and meditation to prepare for spiritual battle (cf. Eph. 6; 2 Tim. 2:15). The result, and goal, is godliness.

He notes in verse 8 that one type of exercise pays better dividends than does the other. Calisthenics are "of little profit" because they are limited to the here and now, whereas spiritual discipline (which leads to godliness) "is profitable for all things" ("in every way," NRSV) for now and the hereafter. It's good to keep yourself in shape, but spiritual growth should receive a higher priority.

To be more specific, Paul writes that godliness "holds promise for the present life and also for the life to come." This "life" is not just mere existence, because even wicked people have biological life.[8] The promise is the abundant life Jesus spoke of in John 10:10 (cf. 2 Tim. 1:1). Christ is not implying that every believer will be materially wealthy, but He is assuring His followers that He will give them a full life in that their lives will have meaning and purpose.

Spiritual training also pays off for "the life to come." When we stand before the judgment seat of Christ (Rom. 14:10; 2 Cor. 5:10), we will be glad we decided to pursue a lifestyle pleasing to Him. We will then have a "life that will be fully realized and enjoyed."[9] Luke 18:29–30 expresses a similar idea: "[Jesus] said to them, 'Truly I say to you, there is no one who has left house or wife or brothers or parents or children, for the sake of the kingdom of God, who shall not receive many times as much at this time and in the age to come, eternal life.'"

Since verse 10 picks up the theme of verse 8, verse 9 is somewhat of a parenthetical statement. For the third time in this epistle (see also 1:15 and 3:1), Paul writes: "It is a trustworthy statement deserving full acceptance" (see comments at 1:15 for its significance). Bible students deliberate as to whether this "trustworthy statement" refers to verse 8 or to verse 10, but there is no reason to think it doesn't apply to both. Paul simply inserted an affirming remark in the middle of his discussion on the value of spiritual discipline and godliness.

When Paul writes, "for this we labor and strive" (v. 10), the "this" is looking back to the godliness (and its accompanying promise of life) in verses 7 and 8. The word "labor" denotes working hard (and is translated so in 5:17) until one is weary or exhausted. "Strive" means straining and struggling. It is from this Greek word (*agonizomai*) that we get the English words *agony* and *agonize*. These terms reinforce Paul's ongoing admonition that great effort is required for spiritual growth.

Christians should be willing to endure this anguish "because we have fixed our hope on the living God" (v. 10). The concept of "hope" in the New Testament is not wishful thinking, but a certainty that is yet to come to full fruition. We can have complete assurance that the Lord will come through on all of His promises. That assurance would not be rational if God were not real, but He is in fact "the living God" (cf. 3:15). The god of the false teachers is a stark contrast because he is neither living nor can he give life.

Steps to Spiritual Maturity

Be filled (controlled) with the Word of God (Col. 3:16).

Be filled with the knowledge of His will (Col. 1:9).

Be filled by the Holy Spirit (Eph. 5:18–21).

Be filled with the fruit of righteousness (Phil. 1:11).

Do not grieve the Holy Spirit (Eph. 4:30–32).

Do not walk as the pagan Gentiles (Eph. 4:17).

Walk in love (Eph. 5:1–2).

Do not quench the Holy Spirit (1 Thess. 5:19).

In what sense is God "the Savior of all men, especially of believers"? What this verse does not mean is that all people will eventually be saved. Jesus Himself declared, "Do not marvel at this; for an hour is coming, in which all who are in the tombs shall hear His voice, and shall come forth; those who did the good deeds to a resurrection of life, those who committed the evil deeds to a resurrection of judgment" (John 5:28–29).

Jesus is the Savior of all men in the sense that He is the one and only Savior. "And there is salvation in no one else; for there is no other name under heaven that has been given among men, by which we must be saved" (Acts 4:12). He is the One who died for the sins of the world.[10] He is the Savior "especially of believers" in that they have recognized and trusted Him as Savior. He is their personal Savior. In other words, Jesus is *the* Savior, but believers alone can truthfully say, "He is *my* Savior." As with 2:4 and 2:6, Paul is also emphasizing the universal *availability* of the atonement, not its universal *application*.

From verse 11 to the end of the chapter, Paul firmly exhorts his young colleague by firing off a barrage of admonitions. Timothy is told to "prescribe and teach these things" ("Command and teach these things," NIV). "These things" would include all the matters that were brought up in this chapter and maybe even farther back in the letter. Timothy must admonish his congrega-

a

tion to shun false teaching and work hard at the discipline of godliness. The NRSV renders 4:11 as: "These are the things you must insist on and teach."

Carrying out these orders is a difficult enough task, but to proclaim them to people older than yourself adds that much more difficulty to the endeavor. Apparently Timothy was one of the youngest men within the Christian community in Ephesus, and so some of the elderly members may not have taken too kindly to this young guy "bossing them around." Paul was confident that Timothy could clear this hurdle by practicing what he preached (v. 12). Setting an example of godliness in the way he spoke, acted, loved, and exhibited faith in Christ would cause the people to show more respect for their pastor.

The apostle was planning a return trip to Ephesus ("Until I come," v. 13), yet in the meantime Timothy was to make sure the believers heard and understood the Word of God. Very few of them had a copy of the Scriptures, and so the only time they could hear the sacred text was when they met for worship. It was Timothy's responsibility to see that this was done. After that, he needed to follow through by teaching them doctrine and encouraging them to live it out.

Verse 14 is another word from Paul to lift Timothy's spirits. When Timothy felt like quitting, he should remember that he had been equipped by God to serve in this capacity. To give up would be to disregard ("neglect") this gift. Actually, this was not one gift but a combination of gifts. Timothy was a preacher (2 Tim. 4:2), pastor (2 Tim. 4:2), teacher (1 Tim. 4:11), and evangelist (2 Tim. 4:5).[11] Paul underscores the seriousness of the matter by writing "do not neglect" in the imperative (command) mood. The word "bestowed" ("given," NIV) is in the passive voice, indicating that Timothy did not actively obtain the gift; rather, it was graciously granted to him by the Lord.

To confirm and affirm that Timothy indeed had these gifts, it appears some sort of "commissioning service" took place (see also 1 Tim. 1:18; 2 Tim. 1:6). At this event, his fitness for ministry was affirmed by both God ("prophetic utterance") and man ("laying on of hands by the presbytery"). A "prophetic utterance" is not necessarily a revelation about the future, although some of what was said could have been regarding the difficult yet successful ministry Timothy was to have. It is more logical to think that most of the utterance had to do with God's official "stamp of approval" on Timothy. By laying their hands on this young man, the presbytery (or "board of elders")[12] publicly demonstrated that they, too, believed Timothy was fit for the pastorate and gave him their blessing.

John MacArthur sums up verse 14: "Timothy's call to the ministry was thus confirmed subjectively, by means of his spiritual gift, objectively, through his prophetic call, and collectively, through the affirmation of the church. For

Timothy to bail out of the ministry would be to fly in the face of that clear consensus. Paul urges him to remain faithful to his calling."[13]

The last two verses of chapter 4 (vv. 15, 16) contain a string of commands designed to highlight the gravity of Timothy's responsibility. As with verse 11, "these things" harks back to virtually everything Paul has brought up in this letter, including praying for those in authority, worshiping properly, choosing leaders who have character, and, most important, protecting the flock from doctrinal error.

Timothy must work hard ("take pains") to grow in Christ ("progress") because (among other reasons) it will show up the errorists. "But they [the false teachers] will not make further progress; for their folly will be obvious to all" (2 Tim. 3:9).[14] The people will soon get the idea that the teachings of the opponents are a dead-end street, whereas a true understanding of the Scriptures will result in genuine maturity. That all four imperatives in verses 15–16 ("take pains," "be absorbed," "pay close attention," and "persevere") are in the present tense enhances the idea that these disciplines are to be observed continually.

Paul is adamant in his tone because he knows his young friend is not above the enticements of these charlatans.[15] The apostle commands Timothy to "pay close attention to yourself" (v. 16). Like spiritual growth, spiritual decline is a slow drift, not a sudden fall. One day the wayward Christian wakes up and realizes (hopefully) how far he is from the truth of the Bible. If Timothy personally starts believing false doctrine, it is certain that his teaching will become infused with heresy as well.

The last part of verse 16 is peculiar. What does Paul mean when he writes that Timothy has to do these things to "insure salvation both for yourself and for those who hear you"? He is not saying that believers can lose their salvation, because they can't (John 10:28–29). There must be some other explanation.

The answers given by commentators generally fall into two classes. Some assert that this verse relates to Philippians 2:12, the end of which says, "work out your salvation with fear and trembling." Colossians 1:22–23 could also be considered a parallel passage: "yet He has now reconciled you in His fleshly body through death, in order to present you before Him holy and blameless and beyond reproach—if indeed you continue in the faith firmly established and steadfast, and not moved away from the hope of the gospel that you have heard" (cf. Rom. 11:22).[16] In other words, they are working out their salvation, not to keep it, but to improve it (sanctification). Proponents of this view also point out that almost all occurrences of "save" in the Pastoral

Epistles are in a context of eternal life (1 Tim. 1:15, 2:4; 2 Tim. 1:9, 4:18; Titus 3:5). First Timothy 2:15 is the one exception.

A second possible interpretation takes this clause to mean that Timothy will deliver himself and his hearers from doctrinal error by diligent study of the Word. The context seems to support this position. The immediate context concerns Timothy's personal life and ministry, using such phrases as "Let no one look down on your youthfulness" (v. 12), "Do not neglect the spiritual gift within you" (v. 14), and "Take pains with these things" (v. 15).[17] The general context of 1 Timothy focuses more on dealing with the false teachers than it does on eternal life. The decision is difficult, but I prefer this second suggestion.

Conclusion

This chapter can be summarized as follows: Paul warns Timothy that, sooner or later, followers of Christ will fall away from the truth and begin to favor false doctrines. However, he is not just to sit around and do nothing. He is to discipline himself to stay true to the Word, thus maintaining his godliness. Doing so is required to fulfill a second major duty—guarding the flock. They will succumb to the pious sounding charlatans unless Timothy intervenes. To be forewarned is to be forearmed.

Study Questions

1. What does "fall away from the faith" mean (v. 1)? Can Christians lose their salvation?

2. How do you understand the phrase "doctrines of demons"?

3. Some people believe an unmarried person is more spiritual and godly than a married person is. How does 4:3 shed light on this matter?

4. Paul writes that "everything created by God is good" (4:4). Does this include things like disease? What about plants used to manufacture illegal drugs?

5. Paul urged Timothy to be always nourishing his soul "on the words of the faith and of the sound doctrine which you have been following" (v. 6). Are you nourishing your soul?

6. What do you believe Paul meant by "the Savior of all men, especially of believers" (v. 10)?

7. Do you know what your spiritual gift is? Are you neglecting it?

CHAPTER 5

The Goal Is Respectfulness
1 Timothy 5:1-25

Preview:

Chapter 4 concerned itself mostly with personal instructions to Timothy. In this chapter, Paul continues to give directions to his young assistant, yet here the instructions are more relational than personal. Paul's purpose in writing chapter 5 is to make sure the elderly receive the honor and respect they deserve. Paul mostly speaks of widows, but also of the men serving as elders. That Paul spends many verses on this topic suggests that the older generation was not being properly treated within the Christian community of Ephesus.

Honoring Others (5:1-2)

Before Paul launched into a lecture on widows, he first taught Timothy about how he should approach the various age groups in the church, both men and women.[1] The basic idea is to act toward the members of God's family as you would toward your own family. Recall that the church is called "the household of God" in 3:15.

Whenever a confrontation was necessary, Timothy was to come with an attitude of wanting to help that person for the glory of God and not with an attitude of spiritual superiority (cf. Gal. 6:1). It is one thing to rebuke someone out of love, and it is another to do it harshly. "All vindictiveness and bitterness must be avoided, if the minister would manifest the spirit of Christ in his duties."[2]

That attitude comes about when we view other Christians as if they were in our own (blood) family. Since Timothy was a young man (1 Tim. 4:12), older men were the first group that came to Paul's mind. An elderly man is not about to listen to a younger one who comes to him with an air of disrespect. Likewise, Timothy was to treat an older woman as he would his mother, and a young man as he would his brother.

Extra caution must be exercised in approaching a young woman. Paul warns that it must be done "in all purity" (v. 2). The reasons for this are obvious. Any impropriety on Timothy's part would ruin his reputation and ministry, as well as bring shame upon the Lord Jesus. Christian men, especially pastors and others in leadership positions, should never be alone with a female (other than one's wife) in an enclosed room. This advice may seem legalistic, but lives and ministries have been destroyed merely by a false rumor (cf. 1 Thess. 5:22). To be godly, a believer has to be "above reproach" (3:2).

Sadly, some people have a hard time understanding how to apply verses 1 and 2. During their growing up years, they may not have had a loving father, or a sister with whom they were close. Such persons will need to learn how to apply these verses.

Honoring Widows (5:3-16)

In ancient times the elderly were highly esteemed. They were more experienced, wiser, and more mature, and thus were a valuable asset to the community. Just the fact that they had made it to that age was remarkable! Men generally outlived women in those days. Life expectancy for women was about thirty-six years, whereas for men it was between forty-two and forty-five.[3] That many women died in childbirth accounts for the shockingly low life expectancy for women.

For the next fourteen verses, the apostle elaborates on the responsibilities of the church toward widows. Based on what is written here, it is evident that this ministry was overtaxing the church (or was in some way being abused) and something had to be done.

Taking care of women who had lost their husbands was no small matter in ancient Israel. If a man died, his wife and children were virtually helpless. In fact, it was the neglect of certain widows that created the first widespread uproar in the early church (see Acts 6).

For a family line to end and have its name die out was one of the biggest disgraces in Jewish society. That was the main purpose of the Levirate marriage custom (Gen. 38:8; Deut. 25:5-10; Ruth 4:1-9; Matt. 22:24). If a brother died without leaving a male heir, the next available next of kin was to marry the widow and raise children in honor of his brother. In fact, the first child born in the Levirate marriage was considered the deceased's. This custom was also practiced among the Canaanites, Assyrians, and Hittites.[4]

Verse 3 is unambiguous: "Honor widows who are widows indeed." The word "honor" in the Greek is an imperative. Paul is ordering his fellow workman (and by implication all believers) not only to look after these bereaved women, but also, and more importantly, to hold them in high esteem. This would include taking an interest in their emotional, spiritual, and financial well-being.

Not all widows can be beneficiaries of this ministry; only those who are "widows indeed." Paul explains this expression over the next several verses. The general idea is that the church is to step in solely in those situations where the widow has absolutely no one to take care of her.

The apostle teaches the church how it can identify a "widow indeed" by providing some telltale signs (vv. 4–5, 9–10). One may even call these qualifications. If the widow has family in the area ("children or grandchildren"), they are the ones who are to take care of her if they are able. This is not just a good idea, it "is acceptable in the sight of God" since it is a way to honor one's mother according to the fifth commandment (Exod. 20:12). Her descendants have the responsibility of seeing to her needs.

If a widow's relatives don't know what to do, they need to learn (v. 4).[5] Paul is not talking about accumulating head knowledge; he wants the family to be disciplined in carrying out their duties.

Remembering the Widows
Widows should be cared for by the church deacons (Acts 6:1).
Widows should be honored (1 Tim. 5:3).
If possible, family should care for their own widows (1 Tim. 5:16).
Orphans and widows should be visited and not neglected (James 1:27).

All of this is simple common sense, isn't it? The widow's children know her best and should have a keen desire to help out. This is a way to recompense their mother for all she has done for them. How embarrassing it would be (and a poor testimony) to have someone outside the family ministering to this widow when a kin capable of doing it is right there! According to verse 8, that is being "worse than an unbeliever."

Verse 5 shifts the focus to the woman herself, and that is where Paul begins his "definition" of a widow indeed. He lays out three considerations.

First, she is a widow indeed if she "has been left alone"—that is, if no family is nearby to take care of her. Second, she has always been known to be a woman who trusts God, and continues to trust Him even though her husband died.[6] She looks to verses such as Psalm 146:9, "The LORD . . . supports the fatherless and the widow" (cf. Deut. 10:18; Ps. 68:5).[7]

The third consideration is the outworking of 1 Thessalonians 5:17 ("pray without ceasing"). A wonderful example of this is Anna. She was the widow who saw the baby Jesus. Luke says this about her: "She never left the temple, serving night and day with fastings and prayers" (Luke 2:37). The widows who meet these three criteria are the ones the church is obliged to take care of ("widows indeed").

By contrast, the church is not responsible for the type of widow depicted in verse 6. She has forsaken discretion and set her sights on pleasure alone (cf. v. 11). She probably thinks the pious widow has a boring life while she is living it up. In reality, she is dead.[8] The self-centered life leads to emptiness (Prov. 30:15). Furthermore, she cannot expect the church to help her. The members would not want to fund her sensual indulgences.

As in 4:11, Paul specifically tells Timothy to firmly instruct them about these matters (v. 7). But who are "them"? Is Paul referring to the widows, the widow's family, or the congregation? Of course all of these parties need to be "above reproach," but it seems that Paul is referring to the widow's family here. In this passage, he talks *about* widows but not *to* widows. The congregation is eliminated as a possibility for the same reason. They are not explicitly present in this passage.[9]

To say that Paul is referring to the widows' families is not out of harmony with the context. They were addressed in verse 4, and they are addressed again in the very next verse (v. 8).

In no uncertain terms, Paul declares how grievous it would be for a family to shirk its duties with regard to one of its own members (v. 8). Such neglect signals to the community that that family "has denied the faith." They have rejected the teachings of Jesus and the apostles, not in their minds, but in their actions. Titus 1:16 states, "They profess to know God, but by their deeds they deny Him, being detestable and disobedient, and worthless for any good deed" (cf. Matt. 5:16; James 2:17). We have a poor testimony when our walk doesn't match our talk.

The apostle takes it a step further and contends that this family dishonors the Lord more than an unbelieving family does. His point is that even pagan families know better than to forsake one of their members. For a Christian family to do so is a much more glaring wrong.

Verse 9 reveals there was some kind of list or register that contained the names of the truly needy widows. The church would become overburdened if it supported widows who really were to be taken care of by their families[10] (cf. v. 16). This list may have been made available to the entire Christian community so that no widow was overlooked. Remember there were no church buildings; worshipers gathered in private homes. A certain house church may not be aware of a needy widow across town, and thus the list would be helpful in that way.[11]

Paul then tells Timothy of two more contingencies for being on the list. The woman must be at least sixty years old and "the wife of one man" ("faithful to her husband," NIV). In verse 11 the apostle explains why the younger widows should not be included. The expression "the wife of one man" has produced as much debate as the words "the husband of one wife" have (3:2, see comments there). Paul cannot be asserting that the widow doesn't qualify if she had more than one husband, because in verse 14 he urges the younger widows to remarry. Therefore, he must be saying that she had to have been faithful during whatever time she was married.

A third requirement in order to be considered for the list is in verse 10. At first glance, it appears that a widow would have to be a "superwoman" to fulfill all the stipulations presented, but the main thrust of this prerequisite is found in the first few words and the last few words. Paul's main concern is that during her life she has busied herself by ministering to others, thus acquiring a good reputation.[12] Someone with an attitude of expecting handouts all the time is not worthy of the list. Similarly, selfish people are rarely grateful for what they have.

The body of verse 10 is taken up by specific good works. This is not an exhaustive list, but these good deeds are the more common ones of that culture, which are illustrative of a servant's heart and a humble attitude. Although raising children is mentioned, I don't think Paul would forbid a woman who *couldn't* bear children from receiving help from the church who otherwise was qualified. Two other items put forth are showing "hospitality to strangers" and washing "the saints' feet."

Contrary to popular belief, there were "hotels" in those days (Luke 10:34). The problem was, those establishments often had a reputation for immorality. Therefore, it would be better for any Christian passing through town to stay in someone's home. The woman who is willing to put someone up for the night is a woman with a selfless spirit.

Washing the feet of one's guests was a courtesy in ancient times (cf. John 13:5). Footwear was open-toed, and thus one's feet would become quite dirty, if not outright stinky. The wealthy would have a slave do it, but a poor widow would have to do this degrading task herself.[13]

The last two clauses in verse 10 are more general in nature. The apostle also wants to know "if she has assisted those in distress." This "distress" likely encompasses everything from aiding the sick to comforting the persecuted. Paul sums up his thoughts with "if she has devoted herself to every good work." Those are strong words! A widow is not just to give assistance occasionally, but is to be "devoted" to doing it at "every" opportunity.

Starting in verse 11, Paul explains why he doesn't want younger widows (less than sixty years old, v. 9) on the list. "Refuse" is the same Greek word translated "have nothing to do with" in 4:7. "Sensual desires" primarily have to do with the sexual aspects of marriage, but the term also includes all the attending blessings of a godly relationship between a husband and wife. The inclination to get married is natural and normal, and Paul is not against it. In fact, he encourages it in verse 14.

Some understand verses 11 and 12 to mean that some young widows had taken a pledge to remain unmarried in exchange for being supported by the church (put on the list), a pledge that also may have involved a vow to serve the Lord in the church, but they broke their pledge and remarried. Proponents of this view may look to 1 Corinthians 7 (especially vv. 8 and 32–34) to bolster their claim. There the apostle Paul asserts that a single person can dedicate more time and energy to serving the Lord than a married person can.

A problem with this interpretation is that the language seems unduly harsh ("disregard of Christ," v. 11; "incurring condemnation," v. 12; "follow Satan," v. 15) for a relatively minor offense.[14] As noted above, a young widow's desire to remarry is not inherently evil. There must be a better explanation.

That better explanation involves a different understanding of some of the phrases in verses 11 and 12. Paul is not rebuking younger widows for having sensual desires; he is rebuking them for having sensual desires *in disregard of Christ*. Second, the words "previous pledge" may also be rendered as "first faith."

Now let's put this all together. Apparently what was happening was that young widows were being put on the list but then later were marrying unsaved men. Such a boldly unbiblical action indicated their rejection of the Christian faith ("first faith"). I assume they were marrying unsaved men, because Paul equates their way of fulfilling their "sensual desires" as a "disregard of Christ" and as a way "to follow Satan" (v. 15). A potential flaw in this interpretation is this: wouldn't a sinning young widow come under church discipline just like any other member of the congregation? What difference does it make if she is on the list or not?

Two responses will be given. First, when a young widow is on the list, she is "officially" associated with the church, and therefore when she sins publicly, effectively rejecting the faith, it tarnishes the name of Christ. Second, verse 15 implies that this embarrassment has already happened a number of times, and Paul is trying to prevent further shame (and preserve precious church funds). Not all young widows will cause this trouble, but to place any young widow on the list is too great a risk.

Even if a young widow didn't cause this problem, Paul had another reason for not placing them on the list (v. 13). This reason can be summed up in the old adage "Idle hands are the devil's workshop." Since they don't have a job, those supported by the church will become bored and start going "around from house to house." Instead of using their time to minister to others, they will waste it being "gossips and busybodies."

What is Paul's solution to this dilemma? He advises young widows to get married and fulfill their duties as a homemaker (v. 14; cf. Titus 2:5). The verb "bear children" takes one's thoughts back to 2:15 ("women shall be preserved through the bearing of children"). This is not a popular notion today, but it is what the Bible teaches. Believers who ignore the will of God give the enemy an "occasion for reproach." You may remember that the false teachers were telling people not to get married (4:3).

This passage ends (v. 16) with a final admonition to family members to take care of their own so that the church will not be overwhelmed. Paul specifically mentions believing women because women are generally more caring people and because it is often not appropriate for a man to look after a woman. When families follow these guidelines, the church then has plenty of resources to aid widows.

Honoring Elders (5:17–25)

This portion of chapter 5 is quick to point out that elders are not to be approached and treated in the same manner as other people. The theme here is the same as in the previous paragraph, namely, honor. In fact, elders "are to be considered worthy of double honor" (v. 17).

This is not to say that an elder's sins are to be overlooked (v. 20), but, like any high-profile person, his reputation can be forever tarnished by a false accusation. A charge against anyone should be investigated, but one must be extra careful if an allegation is leveled against a man highly regarded in the community.

Verse 17 reveals the primary duties of an elder. He is to rule, preach, and teach (cf. "able to teach," 3:2). The verb "rule" means to "manage, lead, have charge over." Paul made use of it earlier in chapter 3 (vv. 4, 5, 12), and in each case it is translated "manage." The New International Version is noticeably different from the New American Standard Bible on the present verse: "direct the affairs of the church." The board of elders (cf. Prov. 11:14; 15:22; 24:6) is therefore responsible for overseeing the various aspects of the local church, but the spiritual aspects (teaching, spiritual growth of the members, etc.) are the ones accentuated.[15]

The "double honor" that is to be accorded elders could be taken as either salary or respect, or both. A number of times the Greek word for "honor" is rendered "value" or "price," including Acts 5:2 ("and kept back some of the price for himself"). It is likely that both compensation and respect are intended here (maybe that's why it's "double"), but it seems that the stress is on respect.

The context allows for this "both/and" interpretation. Wages are the subject matter of the very next verse, and verses 19 and 20 have to do with protecting an elder's integrity and reputation.

Verse 18, furthermore, is a very significant theologically. Note that Paul identifies both of the expressions as "Scripture." The first one is a quote from Deuteronomy 25:4, so there is no surprise that it is claimed as part of the Bible. On the other hand, the second quote is taken from Luke 10:7 (cf. Matt. 10:10). We now know that the Gospel of Luke belongs in the New Testament, but when 1 Timothy was written (about AD 65) the New Testament had not been completely compiled. Therefore, even at this early date, the apostle was already recognizing and declaring Luke's writings as part of the canon.[16]

Within the present context (especially vv. 17–20), Paul is admonishing churches not to neglect their elders. Since they "work hard at preaching and teaching," the church is under obligation to support and encourage these men.

Verse 19 is not unrelated to that responsibility. As the leaders in the church, the elders feel the wrath of disgruntled members. Those who are dissatisfied with the elders' resolution to a problem may seek revenge by positing a false charge against one of the elders. The apostle urges much caution here. The accusation must be solidly confirmed by "two or three witnesses" before judgment is rendered.

If the unfortunate occasion arises whereby an elder is found guilty of a transgression, the apostle demands that he be "rebuke[d] in the presence of all" (v. 20). A few notes of clarification are in order. Notice that Paul is talking about an ongoing sin ("Those who continue in sin"). One stumble by a spiritual leader may disqualify him from office, but it shouldn't necessarily be brought out in public. On the other hand, if making it known to the members is biblically warranted, we shouldn't be afraid to do it.

Paul *may* be skipping some church discipline steps here, or he may be assuming that his audience knows what they are. Matthew 18 sets forth a great deal of information on this unpleasant but necessary action. The Lord Himself declares that a believer accused of an iniquity should first be approached one-on-one. If that doesn't resolve the matter, then "two or three witnesses" (Matt. 18:16) should confront him.[17] If the Christian still will not repent, "tell it to the church" (18:17). The next step is excommunication (18:17; cf. 2 Thess. 3:6).

We said above that Paul *may* be skipping the first two steps. Perhaps he means in the case of a guilty elder, he should be publicly exposed right away because he has betrayed the congregation's trust. The remainder of verse 20 gives another reason to go public: "so that the rest also may be fearful of sinning." Whether "the rest" refers to the other leaders or to the congregation, this open rebuke should serve as a stern warning not to disobey the Word.

Two expressions in verse 21 throw into relief the gravity of these words. He begins, "I solemnly charge you. . . ." What the apostle has to say is no light matter; it is very important (much like Jesus' "truly, truly"). To "charge" someone is to strongly urge that person or tell him or her something.

He reinforces the seriousness of these items by adding, "in the presence of God and of Christ Jesus and of His chosen angels." Similar wording can be found in Revelation 14:10, "he will be tormented with fire and brimstone in the presence of the holy angels and in the presence of the Lamb."

Paul is admonishing Timothy to keep personal feelings out of the decision-making process. Judgment must be rendered as objectively as possible. All believers are in equal standing before the Lord, and playing favorites will only bring more trouble on the church.

Paul has been writing about carefully investigating an accusation against an elder, but in the remainder of chapter 5 (vv. 22–25), he discusses investigating a man *before* he is made a leader.[18] Verses 17–21 are the "cure"; verses 22–25 talk about the "prevention." However, verse 23 seems to be an "interrupting thought" the apostle inserts before he forgets it.[19]

The main ingredient in this "prevention" is patience (v. 22). Timothy must not rush the process and ordain (lay hands on)[20] a man only to find out later that he hasn't been living up to the qualifications of 1 Timothy 3. Taking one's time now may avert an unpleasant situation later.

I. Howard Marshall writes, "Here the thought is clearly that by showing some kind of positive attitude to a sinner one is approving of the person and thereby sharing in that person's sins in the sense of sharing in the responsibility and hence the guilt for them."[21] Paul later reinforces this advice by contending that some people's sins are not evident right away (v. 24; cf. 2 John 1:10–11).[22] In this, and in every other part of his ministry, it is important for the pastor to be "above reproach" (1 Tim. 3:2).

The final caution of verse 22 is for Timothy to abstain from immorality in any and all forms.

We will postpone our examination of verse 23 for now.

It is not much of a stretch to see the connection of verse 22 with verses 24 and 25. These last two verses of chapter 5 both speak about the same principle, but verse 24 deals with sin and verse 25 deals with good deeds.[23] In the former, Paul is telling Timothy not to ordain a man too hastily (because his sins will come out later; v. 22), yet in the latter he is saying not to reject a potential elder too hastily (because his good deeds may not be obvious yet).

The "flip side" of this counsel is also true. Some men are clearly not qualified because their sins are so conspicuous, whereas the good works of others are so prominent that they should be seriously considered for the office of elder. Men who are aspiring to the office of elder "may seem initially either better or worse than they really are, for both their good and their bad points may take a while to surface. Therefore time is needed to discover the truth."[24] The bottom line is that Timothy needed (as do all Christians) a discerning spirit.[25]

As noted above, verse 23 seems to be out of place in this passage. Perhaps the end of verse 22 triggered these thoughts on water and wine. The word "free" (NASB) is translated "pure" in other versions (NIV, KJV, NRSV, ESV). The impure drinking water was making Timothy sick. This young pastor was trying to maintain a good testimony in the community by staying away from alcohol altogether.[26]

Wine had two basic functions in the ancient world. It, along with oil, was used in the curative process on wounds (cf. Luke 10:34). Also, wine was a very common beverage because clean drinking water was difficult to obtain. Pouring a little wine into a cup of water helped to kill the germs, yet the mixture was weak enough whereby it was not intoxicating (cf. 1 Tim 3:8).

The words "a little" must not be overlooked. Paul is not here giving us permission to indulge in alcohol. God's warnings against drunkenness are well known (Gen. 9:21; 1 Sam. 1:13–14; Isa. 19:14; Hab. 2:15; Luke 12:45; Rom. 13:13; 1 Cor. 11:21; Gal. 5:21; Eph. 5:18).

Study Questions

1. Would verse 1 mean something different if the word "sharply" ("harshly" in NIV) were not in it?

2. How does your church treat its elderly members? Does your church have any "widows indeed"?

3. Do you think the widow described in 5:6 is saved?

4. What is the meaning of the phrase "wife of one man" (v. 9)?

5. In what ways could verse 10 be updated to the twenty-first century?

6. What is the "previous pledge" of verse 12?

7. What does "rule well" (v. 17) look like?

8. Why does Paul tell Timothy to be extra cautious in bringing an accusation against an elder (v. 19)?

9. What are some dos and don'ts when it comes to rebuking an unrepentant elder "in the presence of all"?

CHAPTER 6

The Goal Is Godliness
1 Timothy 6:1–21

Preview:

Paul concludes his first letter to Timothy with instructions for three groups of people: slaves, the false teachers, and the rich. Some Bible students are of the opinion that up to half the population of the Roman Empire was slaves, and therefore slavery was not a minor matter within the church. Timothy's biggest crisis was having to squelch the unorthodox teachers. As such, the apostle wanted to get in a few more instructions in that department. No fewer than seven verses are devoted to addressing the attitude of the rich. Having great wealth is not evil, but one's mind-set toward possessions can be if one is not careful.

Advice to Slaves (6:1–2)

For those of us who live in a country where slavery hasn't existed for a long time, the Bible's approach to the issue is puzzling. How could Paul and the other inspired writers not take a strong stand against such a horrible practice?

To give a full answer to this question is beyond the purpose of this commentary, but a few remarks are helpful. For one thing, the politics are different. Unlike many societies today, the Roman Empire did not give the vote to the populace. Caesar ruled that vast realm with tremendous power. A slave revolt probably would have done more harm than good. Thousands of slaves would have joined in just to be free, not to follow Christ.[1] Too, the efficient spread of the gospel depended to a large extent on the *Pax Romana*, the peace that was found throughout the empire. Paul, it seems, desired to change the situation with biblical love rather than political law.

Finally, we Westerners need to realize that slavery in the ancient East had nothing to do with race. People from all nationalities were part of the system. Many (most?) became servants to pay off a debt. Furthermore, the Old Testament made provisions for a slave to stay on even after the debt was paid (Exod. 21:5–6) if the owner agreed to it.

Another question to consider is why slave owners aren't given advice in this passage. That Paul dealt with them in his earlier epistle to the Ephesians seems to be the answer. "Masters, do the same things [act out of love to Christ, cf. Col. 4:1] to them, and give up threatening, knowing that both their Master and yours is in heaven, and there is no partiality with Him" (Eph. 6:9).

Those Christians masters must have given heed to Paul and treated their slaves well.

That said, let's move on to 1 Timothy 6:1–2. Based on the counsel Paul gives here, it can be inferred that the slaves who had become believers were the ones causing problems now. Perhaps their newfound freedom in Christ had caused them to question the institution of slavery.

There is some deliberation concerning verse 1 as to whether the apostle has Christian or non-Christian masters in mind. However, there is no reason not to see this as a both/and situation. All believing slaves should be respectful toward their owners, regardless of whether the owner is saved. Verse 2 is unquestionably directed to Christian masters.

Returning to verse 1, the word "yoke" is not necessarily to be taken literally in all situations. Some slaves must have had to endure it, but for the most part, slaves were not physically restrained as such. Indeed, some were entrusted with the everyday activities and business of the home, considered "part of the family" in effect.[2]

Paul is rather emphatic here, commanding his enslaved brothers "not [to] be disrespectful" but to show "all honor" toward their masters. He then puts forth two reasons for doing so. The first is "so that the name of God . . . may not be spoken against" ("not be slandered," NIV). In the Bible, a person's name is not just a label; it represents the whole of who he is.[3] You may have heard *name* used figuratively on TV: "Stop in the name of the law!" Thus "the name of God" means all of His attributes (authority, love, holiness, grace, etc.). Christians can tarnish "the name which is above every name" (Phil. 2:9) by having a bad attitude and exhibiting improper behavior.

The second reason slaves should respect their masters is "so that . . . our doctrine may not be spoken against." By "doctrine" Paul means those truths that he and the other apostles believe and proclaim. A slave's poor testimony might cause people to look on Christianity with disdain.

What could be thought of as a third motivating factor is found in verse 2—namely, a situation in which both the slave and the master are Christians. A number of possibilities could arise whereby the slave comes to resent his owner. The slave may be disappointed that his brother in the Lord hasn't released him and forgiven his debt. It is not outside the realm of possibility as well that in the local assembly the slave is an elder and the master is "just" a layperson. Subsequently, those positions of authority are reversed during the week, and the slave may come to believe this arrangement is no longer acceptable. He may reason in his mind, "Are we not all equal in Christ (Gal. 3:28)?"[4]

To avoid this problem, Paul says the slave must maintain a proper attitude. Instead of slacking off, he should labor that much more fervently for his master. Why this attitude? Because it is the owner who benefits from the slave's "good work,"[5] and because the owner is a beloved believer. A Christian slave could not have this kind of relationship with a pagan owner. "By the use of this word ["benefit"] Paul turns the service of a slave into an act of bestowing good on another, even his master. Paul has thereby made the difficult role of a slave the means by which the slave can benefit his master."[6]

People are always clamoring for their "rights," but the Bible stresses responsibilities.[7]

Verse 2 ends with "Teach and preach these principles." The NIV does a better job of capturing the essence of Paul's admonition here: "These are the things you are to teach and urge on them." "What Paul has been saying with reference to slaves (in verses 1 and 2) must be dinned into the ears of the people. Timothy must *teach* these things. However, not only upon *the minds* of the people and of their presbyters must he make an impression but also upon their *wills*. He must *urge* as well as *teach* these things."[8]

Advice about the False Teachers (6:3–5)

Verse 3 is "the beginning of the end" for this letter. Before he sends it to Ephesus though, Paul reviews some of the things he has said and brings up a few other matters.

We seem to have it in our head that if something is "different," it is automatically wrong or evil, but that is not always the case. However, a belief that contradicts the clear teaching of Scripture is absolutely wrong! In fact, the apostle declares that the person who knowingly teaches error "is conceited and understands nothing" (v. 4). Rightly does he use strong words here. The Bible is God's message to us. Woe to that person who tampers with it!

Paul begins by turning our attention back to the false teachers (described before primarily in 1 Tim. 1). Here he stresses that what these unorthodox teachers were espousing was a "different doctrine." Not different in the sense that they worded it differently, but in the sense that they deviated from God's Word. Similarly, they did "not agree with sound words" (v. 3). As in 1:10, the word "sound" means "healthy, free from error."[9] The things the errorists were declaring were not in harmony with the teachings of Jesus.

Furthermore, their message was not one that promoted holy living. Apparently these would-be religious instructors overemphasized the freedom we have in Christ. You can imagine them saying, "You can't lose your salvation, so live it up!" The word "godliness" is found once in 2 Timothy, once in Titus, but eight times here in 1 Timothy. Such prominence indicates that piety goes hand in hand with sound theology ("doctrine conforming to godliness," v. 3). You may have noticed that verses 3–5 are in the form of an "if-then" statement. If someone assents to false doctrine, then the result will be envy, strife, and the like.

One of those results, as previously noted, is that the man becomes "conceited and understands nothing" (v. 4; cf. 1 Tim. 1:6–7). He doesn't approach God's Word with honest motives. All he is interested in is drawing a crowd, yet he has the arrogance to claim he knows everything about the Scriptures. "In his conceit, he thinks he knows something, but he 'understands nothing.' He has zero spiritual understanding because in rejecting sound, Christocentric instruction, he necessarily embraces opposing views of Christ's sufficiency, his own sinfulness, and the way of salvation. As the *New English Bible* puts it, he is a 'pompous ignoramus.'"[10]

Paul goes on to reveal that this guy "has a morbid interest in controversial questions" (v. 4). "Morbid" in its noun form is translated "disease" in three verses of the New Testament.[11] This man has sick cravings, wanting to quibble about academic minutia with no desire to edify the body of Christ. That's a sharp contrast to the "healthy" truths Timothy is to preach (1:10).

Is comprehending and standing up for good theology really all that important? Yes! Look at what else results from unscriptural beliefs: "envy, strife, abusive language, evil suspicions, and constant friction" (vv. 4–5). The false teachers have utterly ruined the warm fellowship that believers are to have with each other. Those are not the things that should be said of the church. Christians are to be known for their faith, love, joy, and the other fruits of the Spirit (Gal. 5:22–23).

The principle here is this: what we believe directly influences our behavior. Whatever we allow our mind to dwell on (Phil. 4:8) will manifest itself in the way we act.

As they have continued to give in to their sick cravings, the troublemakers have not only negatively impacted the congregation, they have ruined themselves too. They have become "men of corrupt mind[s]" (NIV). Their minds are controlled by their selfish desires and not by the Holy Spirit. Such corruption has brought about two devastating results: (1) They are now "deprived of the truth." Impure minds have little regard for biblical matters. (2) They now believe "godliness . . . is a means of great gain." Not only are they spreading lies, but they are fleecing the sheep while doing it. We are not told exactly how they are profiting from godliness, but it is obvious Paul is speaking against it. "Paul was always careful not to use his calling and ministry as a means of making money. In fact, he even refused support from the Corinthian church so that no one could accuse him of greed (1 Cor. 9:15–19). What a tragedy it is today to see the religious racketeers who prey on gullible people, promising them help while taking away their money."[12]

Advice to the Rich (6:6–10)

The apostle seems to reverse himself when he writes, "Godliness actually is a means of great gain" (v. 6). However, he qualifies that observation by adding, "when accompanied by contentment." What he means by gain and what the false teachers mean by gain are two different things. They were trying to make a buck by (ab)using religion, a method that can never produce a "gain" because there will always be a craving for more. Paul contends that believers who have learned to be satisfied with what they have in Christ (which is much; Eph. 1:3) realize they have "great gain" (not just "gain"). The mature Christian is preoccupied with becoming more Christlike, not with building his bank account. The apostle had "learned to be content in whatever circumstances" he found himself (Phil. 4:11). We need to learn the same lesson.

Verse 7 takes our thoughts back to Job: "Naked I came from my mother's womb, and naked I shall return there (Job 1:21; cf. Eccl. 5:15). This thought is designed to put our way of thinking about physical things into proper perspective. It's okay to have nice things, but we must keep in mind their transitory nature (2 Pet. 3:10). Our mind should be directed to heavenly glory (Matt. 6:20), not to worldly goods (cf. Col. 3:1–2).

Of course some worldly goods are necessary, but how much is enough? Paul supplies the answer in verse 8: "food and covering." We should be happy (and grateful) even if we have "only" the basic necessities for physical survival. "Covering" includes both clothing and shelter. Recall that one of the qualifications for elder was that the candidate must be "free from the love of money" (1 Tim. 3:3). A passionate yearning for more "stuff" is destructive to one's soul and indicates a lack of trust in the Lord.

```
┌──────────────────────────────────────────────────────┐
│               The Christian and Riches                 │
├──────────────────────────────────────────────────────┤
│ Riches are deceitful (Matt. 13:22).                    │
│ Believers should not trust in uncertain riches (1 Tim. 6:17). │
│ Riches can be corrupted (James 5:2).                   │
│ Riches can choke out the Word of God (Luke 8:14).      │
│ Elders are not to pursue sordid gain (unlawful income) (1 Tim. 3:8). │
│ Elders are not to teach for sordid gain (Titus 1:11).  │
│ Elders are not to shepherd for sordid gain (1 Pet. 5:2). │
└──────────────────────────────────────────────────────┘
```

In verses 9 and 10 Paul elaborates on the destructive results of greed in no uncertain terms.

The consequences are unavoidable. Those whose primary goal in life is to accumulate wealth will "fall into" three things: temptation, a snare, and a multitude of lusts (v. 9). They will be a prisoner of their own sinful enticements, trapped by the very things they thought would make them happy.

Paul says an inappropriate hunger for riches is "foolish" ("senseless," NRSV, ESV) and "harmful" ("hurtful," ASV, KJV). The word "foolish" (*anoētos*) in a literal sense means "no understanding," and in this context it has more to do with morality than intellect. To put it another way, a craving for material things is morally unwise.

These fleshly longings will eventually cause the Christian to sink ("plunge") into "ruin and destruction." "It has been suggested that this combination of two nearly identical terms, which is not found elsewhere, may suggest an intensification: *'utter* destruction.'"[13] His testimony will be ruined, the people who love and trust him will be disappointed, and he will lose rewards at the judgment seat of Christ (cf. 1 Cor. 3:13–15).

The apostle explains why this is so ("for") in verse 10. The opening words are well-known to people who grew up in a society in which the Bible has had some influence. Despite its familiarity, its precise meaning demands a close examination. What it does not say is, "Money is the root of all evil." In fact, that is not even all that close to its proper interpretation.

First, Paul is talking about the *love* of money, not money itself. Everyone—from atheists to committed Christians—has to pay bills. Another piece of misinformation is that the verse teaches that the love of money is *the* root of evil (popularized by the KJV). The article ("the") is not in the Greek, and so it should be rendered "*a* root."[14] In other words, the love of money is just one of many routes wickedness can take to invade our lives. (It should also be noted that the last part of the phrase is "all sorts of evil," not "all evil.")

Two more consequences of this sin are then listed. The first is that it causes Christians to wander "away from the faith." By "the faith" he means the body of truth revealed by the Lord (cf. Jude 1:3). The verb "wandered" speaks volumes as to how this happens.

Inherent within the word "wandered" is the idea of going astray, or drifting (cf. Isa. 53:6). People don't suddenly bolt from the Lord; they move away inch by inch. It is something they have been pondering for some time, not some snap decision. That is why it is so vital for believers to let their minds dwell on things that are lovely, pure, and right (Phil. 4:8), and take their "spiritual temperature" often. That "wandered" is in the passive voice means something is happening *to* the Christian, and thus the Christian often doesn't even realize he or she is drifting.

A final consequence is the multiple injuries greedy Christians inflict upon themselves ("pierced themselves with many a pang").

Homer Kent comments, "They are the pains the sinners bring upon themselves . . . the present griefs which accompany the avaricious person. Pangs of conscience, disillusionment, spiritual unrest, and many other unhappy accompaniments, are the product of this course of life."[15]

Finally, note that Paul does not mention even one good thing that results from a craving for money.

Final Instructions to Timothy (6:11–21)

In this last portion of 1 Timothy, the apostle gives his final charge to his young colleague. The first topic concerns dealing with personal sin. It is not good enough to keep temptation at arm's length. The believer who desires to stay pure needs to quickly move away from evil ("flee"). The longer we allow wickedness to "hang around," the more alluring it becomes.

Paul is very personal here. The "you" is singular. He reminds Timothy that he is a "man of God" (v. 11), and a man of God handles personal sin by fleeing from it. When tempted by Mrs. Potiphar, Joseph ran from the house (Gen. 39:12).

Of course, whenever you run away *from* something, you are always running *to* something else. Disciples of Christ should "pursue righteousness, godliness, faith, love, perseverance and gentleness." If we are consciously and actively striving for these character traits, we won't have the time or energy to chase after ungodly things.

These terms are mostly self-explanatory, but some comments will be helpful. We cannot develop these traits if we don't know what they are. Paul picked these particular qualities probably not because they were lacking in Timothy, but because they were lacking in the heretics.

Righteousness is closely related to the notion of justice, doing what is right. It is conformity to God's moral and ethical standards. Godliness includes righteousness but is a broader term. In addition to the moral and ethical standards of righteousness, godliness encompasses values such as those listed as the fruit of the Spirit (Gal. 5:22–23). Anything—any aspect of life—that is not in compliance with God's principles, is ungodly.

By telling Timothy to pursue "faith," Paul is exhorting him to develop a deep trust in the Lord. Don't give up when life is at its worst, but keep believing that God will handle the situation in the best possible way. Interestingly, faith is listed as a spiritual gift (1 Cor. 12:9).

As is widely known, all occurrences of "love" in the Greek New Testament are derived from one of two Greek words, *phileō* or *agapē*. In verse 11, the apostle used *agapē* (cf. 1 Tim. 1:5). Christians should be known for their love of God and others (cf. John 13:35).

Within the word "perseverance" are the ideas of steadfastness, patience, and endurance. Job wasn't so much a patient man as he was a man of endurance. Bearing up under difficult circumstances builds character (Rom. 5:3–4). Most believers in industrialized nations have a wrong or poor attitude about suffering (cf. 1 Pet. 2:21). We are so self-centered in our thinking that we don't understand hardship from God's point of view.[16] He often uses it to chip off the rough edges and shape us into more Christlike people.

The last trait listed is gentleness. The Greek word found here is intriguing. It is actually a combination of two words,[17] a combination not found anywhere else in the New Testament. In a literal sense it means "to suffer gently." Hence, it carries the notion of exercising control while undergoing persecution. A good synonym is "meekness."

Christians are to earnestly seek after these character traits day by day.

Verse 12 begins with a stark contrast. Paul has just told Timothy to be gentle and earlier told him that a spiritual leader is not to be pugnacious (1 Tim. 3:3), but now he commands him to fight! What's more, he goes on to talk about a seeming contradiction: a "good fight" (cf. 1 Tim. 1:18). Of course, Paul is not speaking of fisticuffs, but of faith—"the" faith (so NIV, ASV, ESV, NRSV) to be more specific. It is a "good fight" because God's truth has eternal value and worth, and thus something for which we should fight. It is not enough to silence the errorists; Timothy must actively stand up for the sound teachings of the Bible too.

To spur him on in this arduous task, Paul instructs Timothy to look ahead and to look back. This young pastor should "take hold of the eternal life to which [he was] called." Looking forward to the day when there will be no more suffering, pain, or death helps soften the blow of our earthly trials. "For I consider that the sufferings of this present time are not worthy to be compared with the glory that is to be revealed to us" (Rom. 8:18; cf. 2 Cor. 4:17). Of course, some aspects of eternal life have already begun. Believers have forgiveness of sins, the peace of God, and the joy of serving Him.

The apostle also wants Timothy to think back to the time he "made the good confession in the presence of many witnesses." Exactly what event Paul has in mind here is not specified. It could have been a time when Timothy was undergoing persecution, or at his baptism, or at his ordination service (cf. 1:18; 4:14). At his baptism is probably the best choice. [18]

Whatever the case, this is an effective technique for bolstering discouraged Christians. Recalling one's public confession and expressed desire to serve the Lord fervently and faithfully will instill a renewed vigor into one's ministry.

Verses 13–16 is a whole paragraph given over to a charge to Timothy. This charge takes the form of a doxology, a glorious pronouncement as to who God is. This is one of four charges given to Timothy (5:21; here; 2 Tim. 2:14; 4:1). Paul enhances the solemnity of the occasion by stating that he is declaring it "in the presence of God . . . and of Christ Jesus." A descriptive element follows each divine name.

It is the Father who "gives life to all things" (v. 13). He is not only the Creator of all things, He is the Sustainer of all life as well. The point seems to be that the Father is not only willing but able to preserve Timothy through all of his trials and hardships.

Christ is identified as the One who "testified the good confession before Pontius Pilate." Jesus, even though facing torture and death, did not shrink back from proclaiming the truth. "Pilate therefore said to Him, 'So You are a king?' Jesus answered, 'You say correctly that I am a king. For this I have been born, and for this I have come into the world, to testify to the truth. Everyone who is of the truth hears My voice'" (John 18:37, but see all of John 18–19).

The contents of the charge to Timothy are detailed at the beginning of verse 14: "I charge . . . that you keep the commandment." "Keep" has the connotation of "guard" or "watch over" (cf. 1 Tim. 5:22, "keep yourself free from sin"). What is it he is to keep? Several possibilities have been suggested.

First, it could refer to the exhortations in verses 11–12, collectively understood. Second, it could be a baptismal charge to which allusion is made in verse 12. Third, it is an ordination charge. Fourth, it could refer to the whole Christian faith thought of as a kind of new law. Finally, it has been suggested that it is a commandment to Timothy to persevere in his own faith and ministry, as in 4:16, so as to save himself and others.[19] The fourth suggestion is probably the best one.

The false teachers had brought shame on Christ and Christianity. Timothy must now do all he can to restore the good reputation of Christianity within the Ephesian community and remove the "stain or reproach." "Stain" can be defined as "spotless, without defect." Peter used this word to describe Jesus, the Lamb of God, as "spotless" (1 Peter 1:19; "without defect," NIV). Being "above reproach" is an important theme in the Pastoral Epistles; "reproach" is found six times in this epistle (3:2, 7, 10; 5:7, 14; 6:14) and three times in Titus (1:6–7; 2:8). It means the person is "unrebukeable" (KJV; also see comments on 1 Tim. 3:2).

I find it fascinating that Paul insisted that Timothy foster piety, not until his death, but "until the appearing of our Lord Jesus Christ" (v. 14). The word translated "appearing" (*epiphaneia*) is the one from which we derive the English word *epiphany*. The apostle believed the next major event in God's plan was the rapture of the church (1 Thess. 4:13–18). Furthermore, he must have held to the opinion that it might come any day, since he implies here that it may take place before Timothy dies.[20]

That Jesus is coming back is the unambiguous teaching of the Bible (Acts 1:11 and many others). What we are not told is when. In Acts 1:7 Jesus said to the onlookers at His ascension, "It is not for you to know times or epochs which the Father has fixed by His own authority." In Mark 13:32 He told His disciples, "Of that day or hour no one knows, not even the angels in heaven, nor the Son, but the Father alone." If nothing else, we can learn from these verses that date setting is a foolish, and perhaps sinful, endeavor. We can be confident, however, that "He will bring [it] about at the proper time" (1 Tim. 6:15).

Starting with the second half of verse 15 and on through verse 16, Paul pens another one of his uplifting doxologies. God is "the blessed and only Sovereign."[21] Satan very much desires to be in charge of the universe, but the apostle leaves no doubt here that God alone is in complete and perfect control of everything.

The totality of God's sovereignty is reinforced by a pair of superlatives: "King of kings and Lord of lords." The idea is that of all those who have ever sat on a throne or in any other way have been bestowed with power, Jesus is far above them all (cf. Rev. 19:16). Jesus plainly declared in Matthew 28:18 that all authority had been given to Him.

Is it really true that God "alone possesses immortality"? What about the angels and human souls? They don't die. What Paul is emphasizing is

Jehovah's inherent immortality. Angels and the human soul will exist for eternity, but that feature is derived from God Himself. Another way to put it is that He is incapable of dying. What a wonderful thought that He will be with us and we will be with Him *forever!*

Notice the exclusivity the writer has stressed in verses 15 and 16: "only Sovereign," "who alone possesses immortality." The pagan deities of man's imagination do not have these qualities. They are not all-powerful, and there is even the possibility that they could die. Ours is the only true and living God.

Paul continues by declaring that God is unapproachable. Sinful people cannot draw near to Him, for He is holy. Only in Christ is a person worthy of being in His presence. The word "light" likewise implies His holiness and purity. It is often used in the Bible of goodness and wholesomeness. The psalmist wrote, "O LORD my God, Thou art very great; Thou art clothed with splendor and majesty, covering Thyself with light as with a cloak" (Ps. 104:1–2). And Jesus said to Paul, ". . . I am sending you, to open their eyes so that they may turn from darkness to light and from the dominion of Satan to God" (Acts 26:17–18). Many more could be listed, especially from John's writings.

"No man has seen or can see" (v. 16) the Almighty in His full glory. Not even the godly patriarch Moses was allowed to see God, for He warned him, "No man can see Me and live!" (Exod. 33:20). There's nothing left to do now but praise: "To Him be honor and eternal dominion! Amen." Such a God deserves our respect. Such a God should be in control. This passage is appropriately capped off with "Amen" ("So be it").

After this doxological detour, Paul returns to discussing wealth in verses 17–19, yet the people in question here are not exactly the same as in verses 9–10. Before, it was people who want to *become* rich. Here Paul is addressing those who *are* wealthy. The point is the same in both cases, however. To have one's thoughts centered on money leads to ruin of some kind.

These directives that Timothy is to pass on to that group of believers is laced with a play on the word "rich," which in some form is found four times in verses 17 and 18. What Paul is really doing is giving the proper definition of "wealthy"—in other words, the Lord's definition.

Observe that in verse 17 Paul clarifies "Instruct those who are rich" by adding "in this present world." Paul is contending that there are two ways to be well off: one is materially and the other is spiritually. For now he has the former in mind. He first tells them "not to be conceited." It is easy for those who are prosperous to get a big head. They start to think that they are clever businessmen or that God is mightily blessing them in spite of themselves.

This "that-person-is-rich-so-God-must-favor-him" mentality is vividly pictured in Matthew 19:23–25. "Jesus said to His disciples, 'Truly I say to you, it is hard for a rich man to enter the kingdom of heaven. And again I say to you, it is easier for a camel to go through the eye of a needle, than for a rich man to enter the kingdom of God.' And when the disciples heard this, they were very astonished and said, 'Then who can be saved?'"

Why were the Twelve so shocked at Jesus' statement? Because their logic worked like this: "Abundant possessions means Jehovah really likes this guy, and He saves only those people He likes." That is unbiblical reasoning. The Father is intimate with those who trust in His Son alone for their salvation. That someone is loaded with money does not necessarily prove that the Lord favors him. Some atheists are rich, and some Christians are poor.

The affluent can also fall into the trap of "fix[ing] their hope on the uncertainty of riches" (v. 17). This is foolish for two reasons. First, a person cannot buy his way out of *everything*. Second, wealth is uncertain. It might be here today but gone tomorrow. Putting one's hope in such an unstable commodity is irrational as well as foolish.

To avoid these pitfalls, wealthy individuals should instead place their hope "on God," because He is the One "who richly supplies us with all things to enjoy" (v. 17). We don't have to beg, scrape, and grab. Our loving Father abundantly meets our needs (cf. Matt. 14:20; Phil. 4:19). With just a few things? No! All things! To spoil us? No! For us to enjoy!

Verse 17 tells what the rich in this world should not do, and verses 18 and 19 tell what they should do. Christians need to be more concerned with being "rich in good works" than with being rich in stocks and bonds. Likewise, believers shouldn't have a reputation for being selfish and stingy but for being "generous and ready to share" (v. 18). This eagerness to give will result in a stockpile of true treasures "for the coming age" (v. 19 NIV).[22] "Lay up for yourselves treasures in heaven" (Matt. 6:20). To have these treasures means to participate in "all the joys and glories of heaven."[23] According to God's rules, the way to get is to give.

Not only will the generous have treasures in heaven, but they will also "take hold of that which is life indeed" (v. 19). The world says that the way to "live it up" is to possess lots of things. The Bible teaches that "life indeed" is obtained by doing things that are pleasing to the Lord.

The last two verses of 1 Timothy comprise one final admonition from Paul to his faithful coworker. Paul commands him to "guard what has been entrusted to" him (v. 20). The same word for "guard" is found in Luke 2:8 to describe the shepherds looking after their sheep. What Timothy is responsible for is God's revealed truth about Himself, sin, salvation, and His world. Certainly there is no more precious treasure than this.

Timothy must protect the truth from the attacks of the false teachers. Their two main weapons are "empty chatter" and "opposing arguments." The first expression is self-explanatory. What the troublemakers were teaching was of no substance; it was vanity. Paul also depicts it as "worldly." It was man's wisdom; it was not of God. The King James Version has it as "profane and vain babblings." Timothy is to avoid this nonsense.

The heretics were spouting "opposing arguments of what is falsely called 'knowledge'" as well. They didn't get anything right. Both their bold assertions and their blatant assaults on Christianity were wrong. These kinds of people are still around today. They think they are know-it-alls when in reality all they have is man's faulty philosophies. Like Timothy, we must be willing and able to defend the Lord's principles and precepts.

Identifying the "some" of verse 21 is difficult but most likely refers to the false teachers and their followers. It appears, sadly, that several in the church at Ephesus had been drawn in by the words of these charlatans. As a result, they "have missed the mark as regards the faith" (v. 21 NRSV). Their spiritual life is way off target.

The epistle ends somewhat abruptly with "Grace be with you." The "you" is plural, indicating that this letter of encouragement was not for Timothy alone; he was to share it with others. Probably it was read aloud in the house churches throughout the city. Imagine how the heretics squirmed in their seats!

But let's not allow all this speculation to detract from the power and beauty of that one word: "grace." O how the Lord is generous in dispensing it every day. We need grace to be saved (Eph. 2:4–9), and we need it to live the Christian life (Col. 2:6).

Study Questions

1. How do you understand the Bible's attitude toward slavery?

2. Do you believe the slave-master admonitions (vv. 1–2) can be applied to the modern-day employer-employee relationship?

3. Do you think it is significant that Paul put "envy" at the head of the list in verse 4? (See Prov. 23:17; Rom. 1:29; Phil. 1:15)

4. How do you understand verse 6: "But godliness actually is a means of great gain, when accompanied by contentment"?

5. Is verse 10 teaching that money is inherently evil?

6. Could you be content with just food and covering (v. 8)?

7. Are there things in your life from which you need to flee (v. 11)?

8. What does "fight the good fight of faith" (v. 12) mean to you?

9. In verse 13 Paul wrote: "I charge you in the presence of God." Are you keenly aware of the Lord's constant presence in your life?

Section II

2 Timothy

CHAPTER 7

The Goal Is Endurance
2 Timothy 1:1–18

Preview:

Second Timothy is the last canonical letter the apostle Paul wrote. Bible students come to this conclusion by way of verses such as 4:6, which speaks of his impending death. By contrast, in 1 Timothy 3:14 Paul tells Timothy that he expects to return to Ephesus soon. This first chapter of his final epistle could be summarized in three words: thanksgiving, endurance, and faithfulness. Thus Paul is picking up on his theme of encouraging his young friend to keep at his ministry despite the hardships.

Thanksgiving (1:1–7)

A number of parallels and similarities exist between the opening verses of the two letters to Timothy. The following chart specifies those correlations.

First Timothy	*Second Timothy*
"Paul, an apostle of Christ Jesus"	*"Paul, an apostle of Christ Jesus"*
"according to the commandment of God"	*" by the will of God"*
"Christ Jesus, who is our hope"	*"the promise of life in Christ Jesus"*
"to Timothy, my true child"	*"to Timothy, my beloved son"*

In these salutations, two distinctions in particular stand out. The first is Paul's parallelism of "hope" and "the promise of life" (cf. 1 Tim. 4:8, 10).

Christ's promise of eternal life brings hope. The rigors of this life will not inflict us forever. One day "He shall wipe away every tear from [our] eyes; and there shall no longer be any death; there shall no longer be any mourning, or crying, or pain; the first things have passed away" (Rev. 21:4).

The second distinction concerns the change from "my true child in the faith" to "my beloved son."[1] The former has more to do with Timothy being a genuine Christian (as opposed to the false teachers) and him being Paul's authorized representative. The latter ("my beloved son") is more intimate. It is the first of a number of verses that attest to the more personal nature of this letter.[2]

In verses 3 and following the great apostle elaborates on why he calls Timothy his "beloved son." This love is wonderfully expressed by the way he prays for his coworker. One can almost feel the passion coming through Paul's pen. His petitions for Timothy are not only deep, but frequent as well. Paul is so grateful for Timothy that he brings him before the Lord "constantly . . . night and day." What thoughts fill up your prayers?

Love for Timothy is further exhibited in verse 4. Their earlier departure was tearful, and Paul's joy will not be restored until they meet again.

Imbedded in verse 3 are the words "whom I serve with a clear conscience the way my forefathers did." Paul made similar statements in Acts 23:1 and 24:16 (see also 1 Tim. 3:9). What are we to make of this seemingly arrogant declaration? Paul does not believe himself to be perfect.[3] He is saying that he has been obedient to the Lord, and, if he has sinned, he has confessed it so as to maintain an intimate relationship with Jesus. How different the church would be if every Christian were this faithful!

Paul is grateful to have inherited such an attitude from some of his ancestors like Abraham, Moses, and David.[4] These men set high standards for themselves in living to the glory of God. This talk has reminded Paul of the godliness of Timothy's own immediate family (v. 5). Timothy has had the privilege of being under the pious influence of his mother and grandmother. What they cultivated in him was a "sincere faith." Paul's young associate was no phony. He served the Lord with pure motives.

Verse 5 also functions as the completion to Paul's thought begun in verse 3 ("I thank God . . ."). He is appreciative because ("for," v. 5) the Lord instilled this sincere faith in Timothy.

The apostle then appeals to this godly characteristic ("for this reason") in encouraging Timothy "to kindle afresh the gift of God which is in you" (v. 6).[5] His "fire" had not completely gone out, but Paul is here urging him to stoke the logs of his passion for Christ. It is understandable why Timothy might be a bit discouraged at this point. His mentor, Paul, was in jail and facing imminent death (2 Tim. 4:6). He had the additional stress of battling the heretics in Ephesus.

We aren't told exactly what this gift is, but we can safely assume it had something to do with church administration. Furthermore, the text maintains that the gift came about "through the laying on of [Paul's] hands." Although it is the Holy Spirit who distributes spiritual gifts (1 Cor. 12:11), apparently He occasionally used the apostles to do so. This activity was another manner by which the apostles' message was authenticated.[6]

Verse 7 is one of the better-known verses of 2 Timothy: "For God has not given us a spirit of timidity, but of power and love and discipline." It is indeed a powerful and stimulating verse on which to meditate.

Bible scholars are split as to whether Timothy actually had an apprehensive personality. We are jumping to conclusions, some say, when we deduce from this verse that this young pastor was intimidated to the point of not being able to stand up to the false teachers. In other words, Paul was merely *reminding* Timothy that "greater is He who is in you than he who is in the world" (1 John 4:4).[7]

The point is well taken, yet the more natural reading of this passage is that Timothy was prone to dejection and thus needed a large amount of encouragement. He has to be prodded "to fan into flame the gift of God" (v. 6 NIV), have his memory jogged that "God has not given us a spirit of timidity" (v. 7), and told to "not be ashamed" (v. 8).

First Corinthians 16:10 seems to substantiate this claim: "Now if Timothy comes, see that he is with you without cause to be afraid; for he is doing the Lord's work, as I also am." Don't get the impression that Timothy was cowering in a corner; it's just that confrontation was not his forte. Paul would not have left him in Ephesus if he thought Timothy couldn't handle the situation.

No Shame in Suffering (1:8–12)

Paul now comes to the "bottom line" of what he has been saying ("Therefore," v. 8). Timothy should have no qualms about boldly presenting the truth ("the testimony of our Lord"). After all, it is the truth! It doesn't matter what other people think about it.

He adds that Timothy shouldn't have any misgivings about the apostle's situation either. If you met someone who said that he had just been in jail, you would probably be taken aback. Even if that person wasn't violent, you would still place a stigma on him. It would be no different with Paul. Timothy may have felt some embarrassment knowing his mentor was incarcerated.

Note that Paul did not consider himself to be Rome's prisoner, but Christ's. He had done wrong in the eyes of men, but that didn't concern him, because he knew he was obeying the Lord.

Paul exhorts him not to concern himself with this matter. In fact, he invites his friend to join in the suffering! Has Paul gone mad? No. He is not suggesting that Christians intentionally inflict pain on themselves. What he is affirming is that a genuine follower of Christ will definitely experience difficulties, some quite harsh and horrible (cf. Matt. 10:25; Acts 14:22; 2 Tim 3:12).

The Doctrine of Suffering and Tribulation

In the world believers have much tribulation (John 16:33).

Believers are to "exult" in tribulation (Rom. 5:3).

Believers have tribulation in the body (1 Cor. 7:28).

Believers are to patiently endure sufferings (2 Cor. 1:6).

Believers are to be patient in afflictions (2 Cor. 6:4).

Troubles can be on "every side" (2 Cor. 7:5).

Afflictions are trials (2 Cor. 8:2).

Believers' sufferings are not in vain (Gal. 3:4).

Believers are to suffer for Christ's sake (Phil. 1:29).

Believers may endure grief and suffering wrongfully (1 Pet. 2:19).

Christ gave an example of suffering (1 Pet. 2:21).

Believers sometimes suffer for righteousness' sake (1 Pet. 3:14).

Christians are not rewarded if they suffer for their own wrongdoing (1 Pet. 4:19).

However, this is not just any kind of suffering. It is hardship experienced "for the gospel" (v. 8). Last, we note that in and of ourselves we can't bear up under the strain of persecution. It is solely "according to the power of God" (v. 8; "relying on the power of God," NRSV). The Lord pays special attention to those who are being afflicted for the cause of Christ, and will He see them through the anguish. He may not deliver them *from* the torment, but He will be with them *through* the torment (1 Cor. 10:13; 2 Tim. 3:11).

In verses 9 and 10, Paul launches into a beautiful doxology, with salvation being the first thing that comes into his thoughts. But wouldn't Timothy already know this? Of course he would. The apostle doesn't write these words to be informative; he pens them as an encouraging reminder to Timothy. How great is the Lord? Great enough to be willing to provide salvation for His rebellious children.

After rescuing us from hell, Christ "called us with a holy calling" (v. 9). The Father commissions believers and expects them to carry out their duties to and for Him.[8] The apostle refers to it as a "holy calling." This responsibility is not insignificant and temporary. It is vital and eternal. It is holy. I am not contending that every Christian is to be in a so-called full-time ministry, but everyone is to faithfully and boldly live for the Lord regardless of his or her occupation. We are Christ's witnesses whether we realize it or not, and whether we want to be or not.

God did this "not according to [that is, not based on] our works, but according to His own purpose and grace" (v. 9; cf. Eph. 3:11). A rendering that better captures the last part of that clause is "gracious purpose." He didn't make His decisions based on our good efforts. He did it for His own glory. That was His purpose. That is always His purpose. This choice was by His sovereign grace as well. That it was by grace means we don't deserve it. Life is not about us, it's about Him!

Verse 9 continues by declaring that this grace was granted to us. He has given us permission to serve Him. That's the equivalent of the president of the United States asking a person who never went beyond third grade to be the secretary of education. We are undeserving and unqualified, yet He lets us do it anyway!

One could perhaps paraphrase verses 8 and 9 in this way: "God saved you, Timothy, so it's not asking too much for you to suffer for the gospel."

The Lord did not make these determinations on the spur of the moment, but "before the beginning of time" (v. 9 NIV; cf. Eph. 1:4–6; Titus 1:2).[9] However, we did not know about them until Jesus came to earth. They were "revealed by the appearing of our Savior Christ Jesus" (v. 10). When Jesus came to earth He not only revealed God's plan, He also made death inoperative. Our bodies still die, but death no longer has any *eternal* effects on the believer. "Christianity is not based on philosophy or imagination but on a real historical Figure."[10]

Just as "purpose and grace" (v. 9) could be rendered "gracious purpose," so "life and immortality" (v. 10) can be understood as "immortal life." What a glorious truth we are reminded of here. Those who know Jesus as their Savior will never have to go through "the second death" (Rev. 2:11; 20:6, 14; 21:8) but will experience "immortal life."

Warren Wiersbe observes, "Paul was able to encourage people even when he was in a damp dungeon and facing death himself. Very little in the OT deals with the afterlife, so now Jesus has shed a great deal of light on death and the hereafter (1 Cor. 15:55; 1 Peter 1:4)."[11]

Some may read verse 11 and conclude that the apostle was bragging on himself here, whereas in reality he is showing humility. Paul did not set himself up to be a big shot; he was commissioned ("appointed") by the Lord to carry out this ministry.

To be specific, Paul was selected to three offices: preacher, apostle, and teacher. As a preacher, he was to proclaim the good news that the Messiah and Savior had come. As an apostle, he was to spread the Good News as far and wide as he was able. As a teacher, he was to instruct converts in the ways of the Lord. To put it another way, Paul had been appointed to exclaim the gospel (preacher), extend the gospel (apostle), and explain the gospel (teacher).

He goes on to firmly state that he is willing to suffer in the discharging of his duties (v. 12). He even adds that he is not ashamed of himself, his Lord, or his ministry. How is he able to do this? Because he "has become abidingly convinced of God's infinite power, tender love, and absolute faithfulness."[12]

As with much of this letter, Paul is again doing all he can to encourage Timothy. "Despite his own sufferings, Paul is not ashamed, and the reason he is not ashamed is as applicable to Timothy as it is to himself. Paul has placed his trust in the God who has saved him and appointed him to be an apostle, and despite the suffering he is still convinced that it was the right decision."[13]

Paul's Examples and Experiences (1:13–18)

In verses 13 and 14 the apostle returns to his emphasis on maintaining the integrity and purity of sound doctrine. He commands Timothy not to allow God's truth to be ruined by adding something to it, taking something away from it, or twisting it (cf. 2 Peter 3:16). Once again the conclusion is that the false teachers are distorting the words the Lord revealed to Paul.

Verse 13 also reminds Timothy *how* he is to fulfill his duties—with faith and love. William Hendriksen sums it up well: "Faith in God and his redemptive revelation, love toward him and the brotherhood is the spirit in which Timothy must hold on to the true doctrine."[14]

The same sentiment is expressed in verse 14, but different words are used. One can picture a sentinel standing watch over a cache of gold and jewels. That is the vigilance Timothy (and we) must maintain concerning an even more precious commodity—the Word of the Lord.

In verse 13 the source of "the faith and love" was Christ Jesus. Here, the third member of the Trinity is the necessary power supply. Timothy cannot protect the Word on his own. He needs to rely on the Holy Spirit, and He is never far away. In fact, He "dwells in us"!

Reference	Command	Object	Person
2 Timothy 1:13	Retain	Sound words	Christ Jesus
2 Timothy 1:14	Guard	Treasure	Holy Spirit

Verse 15 is both sad and shocking. It is sad because just when Paul needed the church, it abandoned[15] him, even after all he had done for them! Perhaps he had requested them to come to Rome to support him in his trial before Caesar.[16] It seems they fell into the trap about which the apostle warned Timothy (v. 8); they were ashamed to be associated with this great man of God. The false teachers may have played a role here. It's not impossible that they had so corrupted the thinking of the believers that they now doubted Paul's apostolic authority.[17] "He lied to us. Let him rot in jail!"

By "all" I do not believe Paul meant every single Christian in Asia.[18] Timothy, Prisca, and Aquila (2 Tim. 4:19), for example, were still loyal to him. Most likely "all" means those who were capable of doing something but didn't. Near the end of this epistle, he laments, "Only Luke is with me." (4:11). What a sad testimony.

If Timothy was already aware of this unfaithfulness, why would Paul write about it? Because the grace of God that helped Paul through his circumstances would see Timothy through his ordeal.

What is shocking is that Paul would name names. Many today would find that just outright unkind. We need to remember, however, that Paul is writing under the inspiration of the Holy Spirit. What's more, if someone is advocating a concept that is *clearly* unbiblical (which automatically means it is not a minor issue)[19] and is unrepentant, then, according to Matthew 18, he must eventually be brought before the church. There is nothing wrong with exposing people who promote heresy (cf. Josh. 7). The purity, veracity, and integrity of God's Word are at stake.

The question now is, why were Phygelus and Hermogenes singled out by Paul? Were they the only two among the "all" (v. 15) that Timothy knew personally? Were they the two worst offenders? Were they in the best position to help Paul but failed to do so? Perhaps all of those factors come into play.

Those are negative examples for Timothy. Now Paul gives a positive example. In verses 16–18 we are introduced to a man named Onesiphorus, a man
who was a pleasant contrast to the defectors. Consider for a moment everything this passage tells us about him.

He had made the long journey from Ephesus to Rome,[20] a trek that took
several weeks at least. Once he arrived in the imperial capital he still had the
difficult task of locating his friend. That Onesiphorus may not have been
familiar with this large city coupled with the fact that many of the Christians
had been driven out by this time (about AD 66 or 67) made for an arduous
search.

Furthermore, Paul was in a place most people would find horrendous—a
stinky, rat-infested dungeon. This loyal friend went there anyway because he
"was not ashamed of [Paul's] chains" (v. 16). He didn't visit Paul just once
either, but "often" (v. 16).

The apostle wrote the word "refreshing" in describing Onesiphorus's ministry. He may have brought Paul food and water, and perhaps some portions
of Scripture, yet just his very presence must have been an encouragement to
the elderly prisoner. Would the people around you describe you as refreshing?
Last, we are informed that Onesiphorus had rendered "services" (plural) in
Ephesus.

Paul expresses his gratefulness by twice asking for the blessing of mercy
on Onesiphorus (vv. 16, 18). In verse 16, however, the request is couched in
a way that has generated some discussion. Why does the apostle bless the
house of Onesiphorus and not Onesiphorus himself?

Some Bible students speculate that Onesiphorus may have died, but other
interpretations are possible. Since Onesiphorus would be away from his family for a long period of time, perhaps Paul was asking the Lord to watch over
them during Onesiphorus's absence. Too, verse 18 specifies him personally
("the Lord grant to him"). "That day" is primarily utilized in reference to the
day believers will "appear before the judgment seat of Christ" (2 Cor. 5:10).
Paul could never return the favor, but God could.[21]

Study Questions

1. Do you fervently pray for others as Paul did (v. 3)?

2. What is your spiritual heritage like? What heritage are you
   passing on (vv. 3, 5)?

3. Does verse 7 motivate you? How?

4. What things would be different if God called us based on
   our works (v. 9)?

5. Are you convinced, as Paul was (v. 12), that God will take good care of you?

6. Is sound doctrine (good theology) important for the church? to you?

7. What do you think of Paul naming names in verse 15 (cf. 2:17)?

CHAPTER 8

The Goal Is Diligence
2 Timothy 2:1-26

Preview:

This chapter is similar to the previous one in that Paul helps Timothy through the hardships of ministry as well as addresses the matter of the heretics. He makes use of a series of illustrations to demonstrate that life is tough regardless of one's occupation. In the second half of the chapter, he gives Timothy additional advice on the minister's personal conduct.

Suffering Servants (2:1-13)

An old adage says, "Whenever you see a 'therefore,' find out what it's there for." Paul has been telling his young friend that the ministry is tough, but God is good. He concludes this part of his pep talk by emphasizing that we cannot serve the Lord effectively in our own strength. He writes, "be strong in the grace that is in Christ Jesus" (v. 1).

Note that Paul does not just say "in Christ Jesus," but "in the *grace* that is in Christ Jesus."[1] Without God's unmerited favor (the meaning of "grace"), we could never survive this life, much less the ministry. Also notice how personal and tender Paul is here: "my son." With the concern of a loving father, Paul wants to see Timothy do well.

Another concern of the apostle is that Timothy pass on the teachings that Paul had given him[2] (v. 2; cf. 1:13). If the body of truth revealed by God were not properly taught to the next generation, Christianity would rapidly lose its power to influence the world to any significant degree. Timothy was not to entrust this doctrine to just anybody. He needed to select men loyal to Christ.

"Faithfulness negatively consists in [these men] not losing, neglecting, ignoring, or falsifying (like the false teachers mentioned in this letter) what Paul has said, and positively consists of their 'handling accurately the word of truth'" (2:15).[3] They must also be men "who will be able to teach others also" (v. 2). As this is a requirement for elders (1 Tim. 3:2), they should be the ones instructed to pass along God's truth. This, among other reasons, is why it is so crucial to select church leaders biblically.

In the next verse (v. 3), Paul again invites Timothy to "suffer hardship with me." The first time he did it was in 1:8, and in both verses it is a command. "Such faithfulness to God's truth would inevitably involve Timothy in suffering, even as it had Paul. Thus without varnishing Timothy's prospects the mentor once again called his protégé to share in hardship or suffering."[4] From this point to the end of verse 6, Paul uses three illustrations in explaining the rigors of serving Christ—the athlete, the soldier, and the farmer.

The first of these, found in verses 3b–4, draws one's thoughts to the military ("as a good soldier of Christ Jesus"). This illustration can be summed up in the phrase "Stay focused." Believers must be constantly on guard against the distractions of the world and the impulses of our self-centered nature. Entertaining a sinful thought, even for a moment, may lead to ruin (Mark 4:19; James 1:15).

Christians have to deal with everyday events, but we should not allow them to engross us. Our goal and motivation is to "please the one who enlisted" us, namely, Christ. It is no easy task to maintain this concentration on holy matters. It requires the power of the Holy Spirit.[5]

The second illustration has to do with sports competition in accordance with the rules (v. 5). Paul often draws his metaphors from the world of athletics (1 Cor. 9:24–27; 1 Tim. 1:18; 4:7; 6:12; 2 Tim. 4:7). At first glance this word picture seems strange. Was Paul troubled that Timothy was going to "break the rules," or is there something else here?

The answer may lie more with *preparing* for an athletic event rather than *competing* in one. A Greek athlete was obliged to prepare several months before the games began and then swear to Zeus that he had properly made himself ready.[6] Whatever the case, attributes such as diligence, self-control, discipline, and the like are involved.

It is good that at this point Paul mentions a positive aspect of serving Christ, since he has been speaking a great deal about suffering.[7] One day faithful believers will "win the prize" (literally, "crown"; "victor's crown," NIV). That "God is not unjust so as to forget your work and the love which you have shown toward His name" (Heb. 6:10) has been a source of great comfort and encouragement to many a weary worker.

The "hard-working farmer" is Paul's third and final illustration of the Christian life. That phrase—"hard-working farmer"—seems redundant, doesn't it? What farmer doesn't labor long and hard? The answer is, "The one with the empty stomach!" His enjoyment of his produce is a well-deserved compensation and incentive. The Christian, too, can enjoy the "fruit" of his labor. Seeing people trust Christ and then grow in Him is an unparalleled pleasure.

Paul's point is well taken with these illustrations. The Christian life is hard work. Followers of Christ who are not satisfied with their levels of holiness should ask themselves if they are devoting enough time to private and corporate worship, prayer, and personal Bible study.

Steps to Personal Holiness

Believers are called to be holy (saints) (Rom. 1:7).

Believers are to live by the power of the Holy Spirit (Rom. 15:13).

Believers are made holy (sanctified) in life by the work of the Spirit (Rom. 15:16).

Believers in their final state are to be presented holy and blameless (Eph. 1:4).

The Lord's desire is that His church be holy and blameless (Eph. 5:27).

Believers are to live holy because God is holy (1 Pet. 1:16).

The apostle now implores Timothy not just to read over this letter but to take it to heart, to genuinely ponder what it is saying (v. 7). He isn't dwelling on suffering to discourage Timothy. On the contrary, he does so to help Timothy (and us) brace for the arduous days ahead. The result of this meditation will be that "the Lord will give you understanding in everything." Paul is not declaring that Timothy will know absolutely everything, but that he will have sufficient wisdom to deal with the problems in the Ephesian church.

In his mulling, Timothy must be sure to "remember Jesus Christ," the One who set the example of persevering under adversity (cf. 1 Peter 2:21). Compared to what He went through, our suffering is very slight (cf. Rom. 8:18; 2 Cor. 4:17). What else is Timothy to remember? That Jesus is "risen from the dead" and is a "descendant of David" (v. 7). Some scholars believe these expressions were a part of an early creed.[8]

The term "Christ" would remind Timothy that Jesus is the Messiah who has finally come. That He rose from the dead is a reminder that He suffered on the cross for our sins. That He is from David's seed recalls His humanity and His royal status. Jesus is both Savior and King. When Timothy feels like quitting, he needs to contemplate these things.[9] Furthermore, these truths are the essence of Paul's gospel. By "my gospel" (v. 8) the apostle does not mean that the Good News originated with him, but that it is the one he proclaims; it is the true gospel (cf. Gal. 1:6–7).

Paul continues his admonition into verse 9. The great apostle himself is right now experiencing much unpleasantness and discomfort. He is "bound as an evil-doer"[10] in a Roman jail, not exactly a luxury hotel room. He is there for preaching the very gospel he has been writing about in this passage.[11] By contrast, God's message is not confined, nor can it be confined. It will continue to penetrate people's hearts regardless of the situation in which His servants find themselves.

Why is Paul willing to put up with all of this? "For this reason . . . for the sake of those who are chosen" (v. 10). He is very much aware that the eternal destiny of many people depends on getting the gospel spread as far as possible as quickly as possible. The "chosen" are God's elect (*eklektos*).

In the second half of verse 10, Paul becomes more specific as to why he is willing to endure hardship for the elect: "that they also may obtain the salvation which is in Christ Jesus." Notice that Paul doesn't stop with "obtain the salvation"; he adds, "in Christ Jesus." "And there is salvation in no one else; for there is no other name under heaven that has been given among men, by which we must be saved" (Acts 4:12). Certain realities of our salvation are evident now, but Christians can also look forward to "eternal glory." How wonderful to be in the presence of the Lord forever!

Paul moves from prose to poetry in verses 11–13.[12] This series of "if" clauses was likely part of an early hymn or creed. The first two lines have to do with loyalty to Christ, whereas the last two concern disloyalty to Christ.[13] The way all four "if" clauses are constructed in the Greek indicates that the statements are assumed to be true for the sake of argument. However, that does not necessarily mean that the "if" should be translated "since" in every case.[14] By contrast, the reader is assured up front ("It is a trustworthy statement," v. 11) that the consequences ("live," "reign," "deny") are unavoidable. No exceptions are stated.

To determine the meaning of the first clause ("if we died with Him"), we must figure out what Paul meant by "die." Did he mean physical death, or was he using it in some figurative sense? Because the tense of the verb is past (aorist), it seems unlikely that the apostle had physical death in mind. Not a few scholars have noticed the similarities between verse 11 and Romans 6:3–8.[15] If that affinity was intentional, then the sense of the verse is, "Since baptism identifies us with His death, it is logical to assert that we will also be a part of His resurrection ("live with Him"; future tense).[16]

To identify with Christ in His death means it is as if we were there, receiving the death that we deserve for our sins. All who have "died with Him" can know with absolute certainty that they will be with their Savior forever. Hence, this first line (v. 11) has to do with conversion.

The next line is, "If we endure, we shall also reign with Him" (v. 12). This promise is more to the point. Timothy needs to dwell on the fact that living for Christ now is difficult, but one day he will have some ruling function in Christ's kingdom (cf. Rev. 3:21). All Christians can take heart that the pain and anguish of this world will some day come to an end.

Those thoughts are encouraging. Now come the warnings. The remainder of verse 12 declares, "If we deny Him, He also will deny us." Both instances of the verb "deny" are future tense. People who claim to be Christians but really aren't will eventually be exposed. They will not endure and will deny Christ at some point (cf. Titus 1:16). Jesus will then later (at the Great White Throne perhaps, Rev. 20:11) deny ever knowing them (Matt. 7:23). Christians can deny Christ, but it will not be for long. Peter denied Him (Matt. 26:70) but later repented (26:75) and was restored by the Lord (John 21).[17]

Praise the Lord that at those times when we are faithless, "He remains faithful" (v. 13; cf. Heb. 13:8). We know this with certainty because God cannot act against His nature—and He is a faithful Being (1 John 1:9). The Lord is not fickle; He can be trusted to follow through on His promises (including the ones about judgment!).

As we approach verse 14, some questions come to the fore right away. Paul instructs Timothy to "remind them of these things." Does "them" allude to the genuine believers or to the false teachers? What is meant by "these things"? The "them" more than likely refers to the saints under Timothy's ministry since the heretics will not listen to reason anyway. The most logical antecedent to "these things" are the warnings of the immediately preceding passage (vv. 11–13). Reminding the congregation of these things will help them not to falter when they are confronted about their faith.

Paul goes to great lengths to demonstrate the seriousness of this issue. First he "solemnly charge[s]" Timothy to do something about this problem. Then he adds that Timothy is to do so "in the presence of God" (v. 14). All we are told is that the issue has to do with a fruitless argument about words. Timothy and his associates must have been feuding over the definitions of certain words with the unorthodox troublemakers. A reasonable assumption is that the latter were trying to change the meaning of certain key terms to fit their theology.

Paul's Charges to Timothy

Do not sharply rebuke an older man (1 Tim. 5:1).

Honor widows (1 Tim. 5:3).

Do not lay hands on anyone too hastily (1 Tim. 5:22).

Instruct the rich not to be conceited (1 Tim. 6:17).

Guard what has been entrusted to you (1 Tim. 6:20).

Remind believers not to dispute over words (2 Tim. 2:14).

Preach the Word (2 Tim. 4:1–2).

Paul was thus telling Timothy to keep away from the false teachers because the confrontations were doing more harm than good. In fact, they were destructive ("the ruin of the hearers," v. 14). He stresses this again in the next chapter: "avoid such men as these" (3:5).

Unbiblical doctrine should not, indeed cannot, be tolerated. Some Christians today think that it is all right to let a "little bit of disagreement" into the church, but when a major teaching is on the line, that decision is fatal for the Christian community. Consider this: would a person want even one tiny cancer cell in his body?

Timothy is additionally commanded to "be diligent to present yourself approved to God" (v. 15). The Greek word translated "be diligent" is rendered "make every effort" in 4:21.[18] The idea is to give it your all; strive to do your best. The goal and purpose of this industry is to please the Lord. Each Christian should not go about his ministry (whether it is "full-time" or not) worried about what people think of him and his ministry. His primary thought should be to make sure he is "a workman who does not need to be ashamed." Duane Litfin observes, "Paul had spoken of shame before men (2 Tim. 1:8, 12, 16); far worse is shame before God."[19]

The expression "handling accurately the word of truth" is intriguing and has generated much debate. "Handling accurately" is one word in the Greek, and it literally means "to cut straight."[20] The KJV has it as "rightly dividing." It is probably a figure of speech whose meaning has been lost to us. It may be that Paul's point is that Timothy needs to be very careful in how he interprets and teaches the Bible ("the word of truth"). The false teachers have wandered from the truth (v. 18; cf. 2 Cor. 2:17). Timothy is to cut it straight. "Not only are we to make an all out effort at pleasing God; we are also to handle His word with utmost care and respect. The servant of God must treat with great reverence the vocal chords of God Himself, lest God's message to man be muffled by the ineptness of His messenger."[21]

Positively, Timothy is to "be diligent." Negatively, he is to "avoid worldly and empty chatter" (v. 16). This picks up Paul's reprimand not to "wrangle about words" (v. 14). Getting into arguments over words is "useless" (v. 14) and will result in "further ungodliness" (v. 16). He does not mean that the definitions of words are unimportant; he is contending that neither side will be persuaded and that the animosity between the two parties will likely intensify.

This sentence does not end with verse 16 but continues on into verse 17. Another awful consequence of these disputes is that "their talk will spread like gangrene." What a vivid picture! Empty chatter is like a disease that gradually eats away at the church's testimony and ministry until it is essentially gone. Unbiblical doctrine must be cut out of the body of Christ just as a diseased foot or hand is cut off from the body.

Paul begins to talk about two of the heretics in the second half of verse 17: Hymenaeus and Philetus. Nothing is known about Philetus. This Hymenaeus is most likely the same one Paul "delivered over to Satan" along with Alexander (1 Tim. 1:20). Almost certainly these are the ringleaders of the unorthodox sect.

Relative to the truth, they are way off track (v. 18). The Greek word for "gone astray" (*astocheō*) does not mean that the person inadvertently wandered off the path, but that the person purposely strayed from the truth.[22] These deviant teachers had mangled one of the key doctrines of biblical Christianity: the resurrection.[23]

To say that the resurrection has already taken place is to repudiate the doctrine of a bodily resurrection. The Ephesian Christians know their loved ones have not bodily risen, and therefore the errorists must be talking about a spiritual resurrection. By default, then, they deny there is such a thing as physical resurrection (since they claim it has already happened). I noted earlier in this commentary that one aspect of the false teachers' belief system is that flesh is evil and only spirit is good. That there is a spiritual resurrection but not a physical one is the logical outcome of this line of thinking.

The false teachers also may have distorted some of Paul's statements on the resurrection, such as Ephesians 2:6, which reads, "[God] raised us up with [Christ], and seated us with Him in the heavenly places, in Christ Jesus." That kind of "cafeteria" theology is evident even today. One's beliefs should not be founded on only select passages, having picked and choosen just the verses one likes. That almost always results in false doctrine. It is vital that *every* relevant passage be considered in trying to develop a theological statement.

Paul would agree that there is a spiritual resurrection, yet he also clearly taught a bodily resurrection. In fact, he taught that this belief is the keystone to biblical Christianity. In 1 Corinthians 15:13 he wrote, "If there is no resurrection of the dead, not even Christ has been raised" (see v. 16 also).

You can understand why some believers in Ephesus would be upset. If the false teachers are correct, then Jesus did not rise from the dead, and therefore Christianity is a fraud! For this and other reasons, the false teachers must be stopped.

Even though some people were distraught by this situation, Paul assures them and Timothy that the Lord cannot be defeated. "Nevertheless, the firm foundation of God stands" (v. 19). The apostles, the resurrection, the truth of the gospel, Christ Himself, and the doctrine of election are some of the suggestions that have been put forth as to the identity of this "foundation."

However, the best answer seems to be "the church," which is of course made up of "those who are His." Its "firm foundation" can even withstand the onslaught of all evil forces ("the gates of Hades," Matt. 16:18; 1 Tim. 3:15).

We know it will continue to stand firm, because it has "this seal" (v. 19). This word denotes a "signet" or an "inscription." In ancient times a scroll or other document would be sealed with wax and some impression would be stamped on it (cf. Matt. 27:66; Rev. 5:1, 7:2). Doing so would give the document authority, protection, and authenticity, as well as indicate its owner. The firm foundation will stand because no one can break God's seal.

The foundation is embossed with two sayings (cf. Rev. 21:14), which serve as two proofs (one divine, one human) that God's seal cannot be violated.[24] The first, "The Lord knows those who are His," is loosely based on Numbers 16:5. The opponents had caused some to doubt their salvation, but the Lord is perfectly aware of who His true children are, and He will never let them go. Another reason Paul was lead of the Spirit to write this quote may be that it is not always obvious who is saved and who isn't (false teachers?).

The second saying encourages holy living. "Let everyone who names the name of the Lord abstain from wickedness." After studying 2 Timothy, the student gets the idea that the heretics were not clean-living people. They assumed the flesh was inherently evil anyway, so why not live it up. Genuine Christians should be known for their morality and integrity.

To get his point across, the apostle gives an illustration in verses 20 and 21 having to do with the various pots and urns commonly found in an ancient Near East household. They are distinguished from one another by their material (gold, silver, wood, earthenware) and by their function (used for an honorable or dishonorable task). A pot used to remove waste (dishonorable task) will not be used to cook a meal (honorable task).

Who Does God Use?

Matthew (Levi) the tax–collector who wrote the Gospel (Mark 2:14)

Lowly fishermen (John 1:35–51)

Saul (Paul) who had violently persecuted early believers (Acts 9:1–22)

A husband and wife team—Aquila and Priscilla (Acts 18:1)

A great host of just ordinary Christians (Rom. 16:1–16)

An older man (Simeon) and a widow (Anna) who witnessed that Jesus was the Christ child (Luke 2:25–38)

Timothy—half Jewish, half Gentile—who was taught godly things from his childhood (2 Tim. 3:14–15)

Perhaps what the apostle is saying is that there are different kinds of people in the church, and their true value depends on how "dirty" they are, not on which material they are made of. Even a "gold" believer (however that is defined) becomes useless if he allows sin to contaminate his life. On the other hand, believers who stay away from wickedness and evil ("cleanses himself from these things," v. 21) can be used for noble purposes. The other good news is that, unlike a pot, a fallen Christian can be restored to honorable service. First John 1:9 reads, "If we confess our sins, He is faithful and righteous to forgive us our sins and to cleanse us from all unrighteousness."[25]

By "these things" (v. 21) Paul may have had in mind not only those things he had already brought up ("worldly and empty chatter," "wickedness"), but also some things he is about to mention ("youthful lusts," "foolish and ignorant speculations," "quarrels").[26]

Undefiled saints are "sanctified, useful to the Master, prepared for every good work."

Sanctified . . . has the basic meaning of being set apart. A Christian is sanctified, set apart, in two ways. Negatively, he is set apart *from* sin. Positively, he is set apart *for* God and for His righteousness. Just as the vessels in the tabernacle and temple were set apart from all mundane uses and dedicated solely to God and His service, so are those believers who are vessels of honor in the church. Their supreme purpose as Christians, the purpose from which all duties derive, is to serve God. For that they keep themselves pure.[27]

All followers of Christ should be open to whatever the Lord has in store for them. The word "prepared" has within it the connotations of eagerness, willingness, and readiness. Readiness not only encompasses a pure lifestyle, but also a working knowledge of the Scriptures (cf. 2 Peter 3:18).[28]

John Stott writes of the full impact that this passage should have on us. "It would be difficult to exaggerate the privilege which the apostle here sets before Timothy. . . . No higher honour could be imagined than to be an instrument in the hand of Jesus Christ, to be at his disposal for the furtherance of his purposes, to be available whenever wanted for his service."[29]

A few more comments are in order about the statement "cleanses himself from these things." Notice the personal responsibility involved. Christians have a duty not to associate with the ungodly aspects of our society. This includes everything from the more obvious sins (bank robbery, murder, etc.) to the more subtle ones (the unbiblical beliefs of a certain group or movement), anything that would contaminate one's soul.

The most effective way to shun iniquity is to run away from it. "Now flee from youthful lusts" (v. 22) commands the great missionary. Like Joseph of old, we should get as far away from sin as humanly possible (Gen. 39:12). This verse is very similar to 1 Timothy 6:11, "But flee from these things, you man of God; and pursue righteousness, godliness, faith, love, perseverance and gentleness."

However, don't get the idea that Paul is speaking to those under twenty-five years of age alone when he mentions "youthful lusts." Sinful desires afflict believers of all ages. It's just that they are at the height of their evil influence during adolescence and early adulthood. Too, lust is not limited to sexual matters. People can and do crave power, money, and an assortment of other things.

While we are fleeing vices, we must be pursuing virtues. Paul specifically lists "righteousness, faith, love and peace."

Paul encouraged Timothy to follow hard after righteousness, an open rectitude in attitude and action. He was to show faith—a sincere confidence in God—and love—a growing affection for others. He was to seek peace—a genuine fellowship and harmony with other Christians.[30]

In his dealings with the troublemakers, Timothy needs to keep these commendable qualities in the back of his mind for himself and for all who are standing for the truth.

Verse 23 very much parallels verse 16. Here is further instruction as to how Timothy should cleanse himself (v. 21). Paul does not mean speculations in general, but the ones the opponents are spewing. Those are characterized as being "foolish and ignorant." Their teachings are not based on the Bible, but are drawn from their corrupt minds (and not "from a pure heart"). They are simply guessing. Just as "worldly and empty chatter" results in "ungodliness," so "foolish and ignorant speculations . . . produce quarrels."

How, then, is Timothy to handle all this? By politely listening to the speculations? No! He is to refuse them, have nothing to do with them (so NIV).

Paul then flatly states, "the Lord's bond-servant must not be quarrelsome" (v. 24). How unbecoming it is for a Christian to have a cantankerous disposition. Whatever we say or do reflects on Christ because we are His servants. We belong to Him. We are bonded to Him. Let us never forget that every time we sin, it affects others. Christians are hurt and non-Christians lower their assessment of the Lord.

Moreover, don't miss the fact that this verse indicates that we have God's authority to do what we do. We are the *Lord's* bond-servants.

The qualities that should mark all believers are kindness, ability to teach, patience, and gentleness (vv. 24–25). "Kindness," as with "love," does not prohibit a person from being firm. Oftentimes the kindest thing to do is forcibly stop a person from destroying himself. Not being "able to teach" well does not make you a bad Christian. Certainly this is a requirement for being a leader in the church (1 Tim. 3:2), but having a degree of deficiency in this area is no reason to sit around and do nothing for the Lord. We are responsible to develop the skills we do have and to increase our knowledge of the Word as far as our mental capacities allow. "Patient when wronged" carries the idea of not becoming resentful or bitter. "Gentleness" (v. 25) means we serve Christ with meekness and humility. These words are not difficult to understand; the difficulty comes in implementing them in our lives, making them a part of who we are.

If Timothy and his flock do find themselves in a confrontation with the errorists, they are not to squabble over "foolish and ignorant speculations" (v. 23), but they are to graciously yet firmly straighten out their thinking (v. 25). Note that heresy is not to be tolerated. Paul wasn't encouraging Timothy to put up with it, but to correct it with truth from God's Word. These instructions imply that Paul has not given up on the opponents (and their followers) either. The possibility for repentance still exists.[31]

The desired result is for the false teachers to repent and come "to the knowledge of the truth." "The goal is always remedial, never punitive, when dealing with brethren (cf. 2 Thes. 3:15). The purpose must always be to edify

Christ's body, not tear it down"[32] Galatians 6:1 is likewise germane: "Brethren, even if a man is caught in any trespass, you who are spiritual, restore such a one in a spirit of gentleness; each one looking to yourself, lest you too be tempted."

Let's look again at the phrase "if perhaps God may grant them repentance" (v. 25). It teaches that it is God who brings about repentance. It is our part to pray for people and show them from the Bible where they are wrong, but it is God's part, and no one else's, to convict and change their hearts. In addition, Paul is not declaring that they *will* repent, only that they *might*. We want them to, but we can't know for sure.[33]

A second hoped-for result from this correction is that "they may come to their senses" (v. 26) as the prodigal son did (Luke 15:17). The heretics' beliefs are not rational. They need to mentally wake up and realize the error of their ways. In doing so, they will free themselves "from the snare of the devil" (cf. John 8:32).

The very last part of verse 26 shows the extent of Satan's influence on a believer.[34] Instead of doing God's will, Timothy's deviant opponents were aligned with the will of the devil. Besides being in hell, I cannot imagine a more horrible existence.

Study Questions

1. What do you think of Paul virtually commanding Timothy to suffer (v. 3, where the verb "suffer" is an imperative)?

2. What are some examples of getting entangled "in the affairs of everyday life" (v.4)? What about Christians being involved in politics?

3. Does the fact that salvation is eternal (v. 10) mean that a believer cannot lose his salvation?

4. What do you think it means to "deny Him" (v. 12)?

5. Was it appropriate for Paul to publicize the names of two of the false teachers (v. 17)?

6. In what ways can a Christian cleanse himself (v. 21)?

7. Are you prepared for every good work (v. 23)?

8. What does it look like to pursue righteousness, faith, love, and peace (v. 22)?

9. Do you believe a Christian can be demon possessed (v. 26)? What passages do you give to support your answer?

CHAPTER 9

The Goal Is to Expose Sin
2 Timothy 3:1-17

Preview:

In this chapter Paul discusses the past, the present, and the prophetic. He starts at the end—that is, he speaks of the ungodly actions and attitudes that will typify the last days. He then leaps way back to the days of Moses. His point in all of this is not so much to give a history lesson as it is to highlight a lesson from history. That lesson is that there will always be people who oppose the truth. Another feature of this chapter is the apostle's ongoing encouragement to Timothy to remain steadfast in the present.

Looking Ahead and Looking Back (3:1-9)

The beginning of chapter 3 comes as a jolt. Seemingly out of nowhere Paul starts telling his young friend Timothy about the future.[1] The word "but" gives us a clue as to what is going on. Paul, in some form or fashion, is contrasting what he has just written with what he is about to pen.

At least two purposes for verses 1–5 can be suggested. First, Timothy needs to recognize ("realize this," v. 1) that he can't do it all. In other words, don't be discouraged if it looks like you're not making much progress. People will be rebellious and evil until Christ returns. Second, he should take heart because things could be worse; in fact, they will be as we approach the end (cf. v. 13). Our problems don't seem to be quite so overwhelming when we keep in mind that the situation could be worse. There is always someone else who has a bigger crisis.

The apostle then lists some nineteen traits that will mark people in the end times,[2] none of which are flattering. This is not to say that these wicked attitudes and actions are not present today. It is probable that the false teachers fit into these categories in some way or another. The "last days" are highlighted because the world will become more and more corrupt as the time of the Lord's return approaches.[3]

"Lovers of self" is justifiably the first on the list because it is the root that turns out all the other bad fruit. Our selfishness causes us to put our efforts into pleasing ourselves and minimizes our concern for others.[4]

A first consequence of self-love is greed, an abnormal quest for money. This craving is sparked by our desire to please ourselves, and we need funds to do that. Next, Paul mentions "boastful" and "arrogant" (v. 2). These two words might be distinguished by noting that "boastful" has to do with bragging, whereas "arrogant" describes a person's demeanor and disposition. For all intents and purposes, it is impossible to stunt the growth of pride in one who is wrapped up in himself.

The Greek word for "revilers" is *blasphēmos*, from which we get the term *blasphemer*. Paul uses this word in 1 Timothy 1:13 to describe what he used to be. It means speaking against God, making slanderous remarks about Christ. It goes without saying that being "disobedient to parents" is not a modern development. The problem is addressed at least as far back as Deuteronomy 21. There, children who persisted in their rebellion were executed by stoning (Deut. 21:18–21).

Men and women who are selfish are almost always "ungrateful," the next vice on the list. Psalm 69:30 declares: "I will praise the name of God with song, and magnify Him with thanksgiving." We dishonor the Lord when we don't show our appreciation for all He has done for us. The last descriptive term in verse 2 is "unholy." This is not just wickedness. It is an active revulsion of the things of God.

Not surprisingly, most people in the last days will be "unloving" (v. 3)— that is, they won't love others, but they greatly love themselves. The word actually means they lack normal human affection. They are quite callous. Paul also portrays them as "irreconcilable." Another way to translate this word is "unforgiving." They have no desire to seek peace in their relationships.

It's bad enough to be known as a gossip; it's even worse to be known as a "malicious gossip," one who purposefully spreads spiteful rumors. "Without self-control" is a direct antithesis to a fruit of the Spirit given in Galatians 5:23, self-control. It encompasses more than just acting like a madman. In a list such as this one, the major stress is placed on moral failure.[5] Nevertheless, it is fitting that "brutal" follows, a word that can be defined as "untamed" or "savage."

"Haters of good" is a near synonym to "unholy." They want nothing to do with matters that are pure, noble, and right (cf. Phil. 4:8). This outlook on life is diametrically opposed to one of the qualifications for a spiritual leader, "loving what is good" (Titus 1:8).

Paul commences verse 4 with "treacherous." This word can have the meaning of "traitor," as in Luke 6:16 ("Judas the son of James, and Judas Iscariot, who became a traitor"), or "betrayer," as in Acts 7:52 where Stephen uses it to condemn the Sanhedrin. Interestingly, the literal meaning of the following word, "reckless," is "falling forward." It describes a person who rashly rushes headlong through life, caring little about the consequences.

"Conceited" is nearly identical to "arrogant." When the former is applied to the troublemakers, it may suggest they are infatuated and bedazzled with the authority and power of their teaching.[6] In the second part of verse 4, Paul explicitly sets up a contrast. He laments that in the last days men will be "lovers of pleasure rather than lovers of God," a suitable summary of this entire passage. That this tumor is already beginning to grow on the body of Christ is sad and deplorable. We want to be entertained rather than educated; we want to be fed by a spoon rather than dig with a spade; we want to ease our pain rather than evangelize the unsaved.

In some incredible way, the personages just depicted still manage to put on "a form of godliness" (v. 5). The word for "form" can also mean "appearance" or "semblance." In the situation at Ephesus, the opponents masquerade as very spiritual people and do it well enough to attract a following. Their behavior gives them away, however. A person cannot claim to be teaching God's truths yet live out the devil's lies. This kind of lifestyle and testimony is merely an empty shell, not having any power to influence others for the good.

Various passages in the New Testament warn committed believers about being in the presence of people who reject sound doctrine or behave in wicked ways. Second Timothy 3:5 is one such passage.[7] The chances are much greater that a group of unbiblical men and women will have a negative affect on you than you having a positive affect on them. This is not to say we are to avoid them to the extreme. We need to spend some time with them showing them from Scripture the error of their ways (cf. 1 Cor. 5:9–11).

Verse 6 expounds upon one of the sleazy maneuvers of the religious charlatans. The NIV vividly portrays them as men who "worm their way into homes and gain control over weak-willed women." These women are further described as "weighed down with sins," "led on by various impulses," and (from verse 7) "always learning and never able to come to the knowledge of the truth."

What exactly was taking place in these encounters is a matter of speculation, because no other details are revealed. It may be that these were young and wealthy widows who were vulnerable to the charms of the heretics. They were "weighed down" with past sins and were still struggling with being alone. Then these spiritual-sounding men come along to help these at-risk women—for a price, of course. Furthermore, it is not impossible that sexual immorality was part of the scheme.

Avoiding the Wicked and Those Who Teach Error

Believers are to avoid all those practicing gross apostasy (2 Tim. 3:1–9).

Elders are to silence those who teach heresy (Titus 1:10–12).

Believers are to shun foolish controversies (Titus 3:9).

Believers are to reject and warn against factious men (Titus 3:10).

The unruly are to be admonished (1 Thess. 5:14).

The undisciplined and lazy are to be avoided (2 Thess. 3:6–15).

Believers are to shun grossly immoral people (1 Cor. 5:1–13).

Believers are not to have in their homes those who deny the true teachings about Christ (2 John 1:9–12).

That they were "never able to come to the knowledge of the truth" implies that the religious frauds were dishing out platitudes that would supposedly relieve the guilt these women had, but they weren't teaching them the precepts of God's Word. This passage may shed some light on other portions of the Pastoral Epistles. You may recall 1 Timothy 5:11–13 where Paul discusses the delicate issue of dealing with "younger widows" in the church. Notice his use of "learn": "They also learn to be idle, as they go around from house to house; and not merely idle, but also gossips and busybodies, talking about things not proper to mention" (1 Tim. 5:13).[8]

Once more Paul connected false teaching with moral deficiency. Their carnality and immaturity rendered them easy targets for the false teachers (cf. Eph. 4:14). Out of a so-called "openness to learn" they evidently embraced as a fad whatever new heresy came along. Their problem was that they could not recognize the truth when they saw it.[9]

False Teaching Leads to Immorality
Leads to idleness, gossip, being busybodies, unmentionable sins (1 Tim. 5:13)
Leads to the seduction of the naïve (2 Tim. 3:6)
Leads to never finding the truth (2 Tim. 3:7)
Leads to gross carnality (Titus 1:10–13)
Leads to myths (lies), human reasoning, and a departure from truth (Titus 1:14)

A biblical example of resisting the truth is presented in verse 8. It is not known how Paul knew the names of the Egyptian magicians who contended with Moses (Jannes and Jambres), but he was probably familiar with them from Jewish oral or written traditions. The names appear nowhere else in the Bible.[10] Homer Kent well observes, "Jannes and Jambres withstood Moses by imitating his works. So these apostates in Christendom are imitators of true religion."[11]

Jannes, Jambres, and the troublemakers touch on three points. All "oppose the truth," are "men of depraved mind," and are "rejected as regards the faith" (v. 8). It's not that these men are indifferent to the truth; they intentionally speak against it. You may know someone who won't change his mind even when confronted with the facts. "Depraved" means "corrupted," "ruined," or even "destroyed." The particular Greek verb used here (*kataphtheirō*) is a participle in the passive voice, which indicates that their minds were being ruined and they really didn't even realize it. No doubt Satan was the one behind this corrupting influence. One of his favorite tactics is counterfeiting. He likes to spread ideas that seem to match up with the truth but, in reality, are false.

"Rejected" also has an interesting definition. It has to do with testing something, finding it deficient, and thus discarding it. It is translated in 2 Corinthians 13:5 and 6 as "fail the test." In other places it is rendered "disqualified" (1 Cor. 9:27), "worthless" (Titus 1:16; Heb. 6:8), and "unapproved" (2 Cor. 13:7). Therefore, to be labeled as "rejected as regards the faith" proves that the teachings of the opponents are false and unbiblical.

The silver lining on this dark cloud of heresy is that their foolishness will soon be exposed (v. 9). Just as Jannes and Jambres were eventually shown to be fakes, so also these false teachers' doctrine will be shown to be absolutely bogus. In fact, it "will be obvious to all." Paul's hope, then, is that their followers would "come to the knowledge of the truth."

Persecution by the World (3:10–12)

In this portion of Scripture it seems at first that Paul is bragging on himself. He commends Timothy for following his teaching, conduct, purpose, and so on, and then mentions all the suffering he has endured for the Lord. But the great apostle is not being conceited here. His purpose is to instill boldness and hope in Timothy, a purpose that is evident throughout the Pastoral Epistles.

Paul now stresses the contrast ("But," v. 10) of character between Timothy and the false teachers. The "you" in verse 10 is singular. "Follow" is defined as "to conform to someone's belief or practice by paying special attention."[12] Dr. Luke used this word to express how he did his research for his gospel: "having investigated everything carefully from the beginning" (Luke 1:3). Paul had such an intimate relationship with Christ that he could humbly declare: "Be imitators of me, just as I also am of Christ" (1 Cor. 11:1; cf. 1 Cor. 4:16, Eph. 5:1). That is what Timothy was doing.

The root word for "teaching" (*didaskalia*) is encountered fifteen times in the Pastoral Epistles and means "instruction, doctrine." That Paul brought up this word this often clearly suggests it is an important matter. Directly on its heels is "conduct." This term has to do with "manner of life" (KJV) or "way of life" (NIV). It is appropriate for "teaching" and "conduct" to be listed together, because what we believe has a direct impact on our behavior.

The Greek word for "purpose" is an unusual word in that it can also be translated "consecrated" or "sacred." In this verse it pertains to "Paul's resolve, his single-minded commitment to Christ."[13] "'Faith' begins the list of specific virtues that flow from correct doctrine and characterize a proper way of living. Timothy likewise is encouraged to pursue faith (cf. 2 Tim. 2:22)."[14] Mounce continues by remarking that although the original has "the faith" (as in Jude 1:3 and other places), this occurrence "refers not to creedal faith but to 'trust.'"[15]

Two of the last three virtues in verse 10 are "patience" and "perseverance." These two terms are similar but not identical. The former describes a person who is not easily irritated, and the latter a person who is not easily discouraged.[16] Paul and Timothy were both familiar with people and circumstances that tested these qualities.

This list would be incomplete if it was lacking "love" (*agapē*), but how can we define love? We can comprehend it more fully by demonstration than by definition. "For God so loved the world that He *gave* . . ." (John 3:16, emphasis added). Paul held such a great love for the Lord that it was reflected in his love for others, friend and foe alike.

The list continues into verse 11 where "persecutions and sufferings" are mentioned. During the first missionary journey, Paul and Barnabas were kicked out of Pisidian Antioch, and nearly killed in Iconium, and in Lystra Paul was left for dead after being stoned (Acts 13–14). Of these three places, Timothy would have been most familiar with Lystra, his hometown (Acts 16:1–3). And this is only a partial list of Paul's woes (see 2 Cor. 11:23–27)!

The now aged apostle had been through tremendous adversity, yet he knew that God was with him through it all. The Father did not immediately remove Paul from the difficult situations, he still had to endure them. But the Lord made sure Paul was able to "finish the course" (2 Tim. 4:7).

Paul then encourages Timothy with this reminder: "All who desire to live godly in Christ Jesus will be persecuted" (v. 12). These words echo Jesus' admonition to His disciples in John 15:18–20, "If the world hates you, you know that it has hated Me before it hated you. If you were of the world, the world would love its own; but because you are not of the world, but I chose you out of the world, therefore the world hates you. Remember the word that I said to you, 'A slave is not greater than his master.' If they persecuted Me, they will also persecute you."

This may sound more like distressing news than encouraging news, but this is what Paul is saying: "Timothy, you need to get ready for times of hardship. You've already had some, but more will come. But remember this: the Lord will be with you as He was with me." Christians today who are not being persecuted need to ask themselves: "Am I living godly in Christ Jesus?" It's one thing to *look* godly in Christ Jesus; it's another to *live* godly in Christ Jesus.

The Power of the Word (3:13–17)

This last section of the chapter returns to the depressing but true prediction given in verse 1: society will become worse, not better. Paul uses four expressions to characterize the increasingly ungodly populace (v. 13), of which the unorthodox teachers are prototypes.[17] First, "evil men." All people are evil by nature, but the *expression* of that evil is what will intensify. Second, "imposters." This word is found in no other place in the New Testament. It originally meant "magician" or "sorcerer." It took on the connotation of "imposter" from the fact that a magician tricks people into believing something that is not actually true. Perhaps the author was still thinking about Jannes and Jambres.

Third, "deceiving." This word fits in nicely with the above discussion. Sadly, some people deliberately fool others, usually for fame or monetary gain. Of course. what is most significant here is that people's eternal destinies are at stake. Fourth, "being deceived." The false teachers know they are pulling the wool over other people's eyes. What they don't know is that they too are being deceived. Satan progressively blinds their minds to the truth.

Again, this warning is not given to dishearten us but to help us. We need to face the fact that religious charlatans "will proceed from bad to worse," and to be forewarned is to be forearmed.

For the third time in this letter (cf. 2:1, 3:10), Paul makes plain the distinction between Timothy and the heretics ("You, however . . . ," v. 14). They will keep on being deceived, whereas Timothy needs to hold firmly to what he has received. "Continue" actually means to "remain" or "abide." He not only learned these "things"; he later became convinced of their validity. People can know something but not believe it. Many know *about* the gospel, but they don't believe it is true or don't believe it applies to them. Timothy wasn't that way. He was absolutely persuaded that what he had read and heard about was the truth.

Paul then gives the two factors that convinced Timothy. One was that Timothy trusted the apostles who taught him ("knowing from whom you have learned," v. 14). "Whom" is plural and most likely includes Paul and his associates, but may also refer to Timothy's mother and grandmother (cf. 2 Tim. 1:5). The second factor comes from verse 15: "from childhood you have known the sacred writings."[18] The Old Testament alone contains enough wisdom that when Timothy heard the gospel, he immediately knew that Jesus was the Messiah and that one is saved by faith in Him.

This is a helpful reminder to parents that children who have hidden God's Word in their heart are better equipped to meet the rigors of adulthood than those children who have not been exposed to Scripture.

Verses 16 and 17 are some of the most significant in all the New Testament. In no uncertain terms they declare the Source (and thus the authority) of the Bible we possess today. Along with 2 Peter 1:21, these two verses form the basis for our belief in the inspiration and inerrancy of the Scriptures. The Greek word behind "inspired" is a confluence of two words that literally means "God-breathed" (*theopneustos*). God wrote the Bible, not men, and since God cannot make mistakes, it is impossible for there to be errors in it.[19]

This inherent power (cf. Heb. 4:12; 2 Pet. 3:5) makes the Bible "profitable," meaning it is "valuable," "useful" (NIV), or "beneficial." Paul lists four things for which it is profitable. The first is "teaching," the Greek word found some fifteen times in the Pastoral Epistles. Such repetition clearly affirms the importance of instructing believers in the ways of God. Our souls will deteriorate without ingesting the meat of His Word (cf. Heb. 5:12–13).

It seems at first that "reproof," "correction," and "training in righteousness" all mean the same thing, but there are distinctions among them. "Reproof" is the act of admonishing a believer who has strayed from the teachings of the New Testament, whether in word or deed. "Correction" is showing him how to get back on course. "Training in righteousness" is needed to keep him on course. If we know of a wayward brother or sister, the Lord expects us to "restore such a one in a spirit of gentleness" (Gal. 6:1).

The ultimate goal here (in addition to glorifying God) is so "the man of God may be adequate, equipped for every good work" (v. 17). All Christians have the responsibility to prepare themselves for any and every ministry God may have for them. To be "adequate" and "equipped," we must be involved in personal Bible study, maintain a quality prayer life, and participate regularly in private and corporate worship.

Study Questions

1. Do you think we are living in the last days?

2. What does it look like to "avoid such men as these" (v. 5)? Are there some you should be avoiding but are not?

3. Concerning verse 12, ask yourself: Am I being persecuted? Am I living godly in Christ Jesus?

4. Does the fact that the world will get worse and not better (v. 13) influence your beliefs and behavior in any way? If so, how?

5. Does it matter to you that the Bible is inspired? Why or why not?

6. Are you willing to rebuke a fellow Christian (v. 16)? Have you ever had to do so?

7. To what extent are you "equipped for every good work" (v. 17)?

CHAPTER 10

The Goal Is to Keep the Faith
2 Timothy 4:1-22

Preview:

One can almost sense the pain in Paul's words in this final chapter. He was cold. Many had deserted him. He was without the Scriptures. He was about to die. Nevertheless, we see no self-pity. In fact, he was still ministering to Timothy. Additionally, he had no regrets. He had boldly and faithfully served the Lord for some thirty years. The man who had been the most adamant persecutor of the church became its most ardent proclaimer. How a believer finishes says more about him than does how he began.

Preach the Word (4:1-5)

This last chapter of 2 Timothy is staid. Paul becomes even more serious as he winds down his letter. The opening clause sets the tone: "I solemnly charge you in the presence of God and of Christ Jesus." Each successive word is like the blow of a hammer. "I"—the greatest missionary the church has ever had. "Solemnly charge"—he doesn't just charge Timothy, he does so with a very somber deportment. It's as if Paul wants Timothy to take an oath.[1] "In the presence of God and of Christ Jesus"—not just any witnesses will do. The presence of the first two members of the Trinity tells us this is a serious and important matter.

The second half of verse 1 is about as heavy as the first, for in it Paul reminds us that God is going "to judge the living and the dead" (cf. Rom. 14:9). Some of that judging will take place when Christ returns to establish His thousand-year kingdom on earth (cf. Rev. 20). Keeping in mind that our walk and our work will be evaluated someday by the Lord of the universe should motivate us to watch our step (cf. Titus 2:12–13). The Scriptures nowhere teach that this judgment of both the living and the dead will happen all at once. This judgment for those living will transpire at the Rapture, when the Lord Jesus comes to take His church home to Himself. Then He will give rewards at the judgment seat of Christ. All believers will be rewarded, having the counsels of the inner heart revealed, and then every child of God will have his or her just praise from the heavenly Father (1 Cor. 4:5).

The judgment that falls on the dead is not for rewards but for condemnation. It will happen right after the one thousand years of the Davidic reign of Christ on earth, called the Millennium (Rev. 20:5). Timothy was charged "in the presence of God and of Christ Jesus" in light of the fact that He is to be the final Judge of all men, first the living and then the dead. The Christ should always have these thoughts in view, and they need to be continually kept in mind. Life is short, and it will soon pass for everyone, or the Rapture will take place, by which the believer is suddenly taken home. These facts make for an all-important priority about morals and about character.

So what is the content of this charge? Paul finally gets to it in verse 2: "Preach the word." This command is not as simple and obvious as it first appears. I've heard pastors virtually preaching the newspaper. What a travesty! A biblical sermon is based upon and thoroughly saturated with Scripture. Addressing matters that are not explicitly noted in the Bible is fine, but they should not occupy a significant part of the homily. Some believe that to "preach the word" has only the gospel in view. The verb *kērussō* signifies to proclaim as a herald. But the idea here can be more encompassing to include the teaching of the entire Word of God. This seems to be by what Paul says in the rest of verse 2.

The importance of this command cannot be overemphasized. God communicated the Bible to us to provide nourishment for the souls of His children (among other reasons). Nothing else will work (psychology, politics, emotional stories, etc.). The Bible is the only piece of literature in the world that can change people's lives, for it "is living and active and sharper than any two-edged sword, and piercing as far as the division of soul and spirit, of both joints and marrow, and able to judge the thoughts and intentions of the heart" (Heb. 4:12). That's the what; now for the how.

The very end of the previous chapter (3:17) stated "the man of God" should "be adequate" and "equipped for every good work." The current passage goes on to say that preachers and teachers must "be ready in season and out of season." What in the world is Paul talking about? He likely means the pastor-teacher should be prepared at all times to give instruction from the Word—whether he feels like it, whether it's convenient, whether it's popular.

To "be ready" actually means to stand by, to be at hand. Though this injunction seems to be an exhortation with a specific reference to verbal proclamation, it would certainly include the general duties of the pastor's service. The minister must seize upon every opportunity without pay or regard for the wishes of someone else. Whatever the conflict, the minister of the gospel must be ready under every circumstance or with any conflict to commit himself to the Lord and then to give forth the truth.

"Reprove, rebuke, and exhort" also hark back to the end of chapter 3 ("for reproof, for correction, for training in righteousness," 3:16). For the veteran missionary to stress these aspects of the ministry makes it clear that they are not incidental, but vital. As unpleasant as it is, Christians must be confronted about their sins and transgressions. That is not a popular notion among American Christians today, but the New Testament orders us to do it.[2]

Ministers of the gospel are not only to show other believers where they have transgressed (reprove), but also to tell them to stop (rebuke), and then we are to come alongside them to help them get their lives straight with God again (exhort). No matter what is called for in reproof or rebuke, the minister of the gospel must be up to the task, and in a sense, disregard the feelings of the one who is in rebellion. He must not reprove with irritability or indignation, but try as he can to muster up forbearance, with the readiness and diligence to speak and teach the Word of God with as much gentleness as possible. Instruction must point out error but then give correction and new direction. The Scriptures must be rightly used for the profit of the listener. Teaching should always go with negative reproof and exhortation.

In carrying out these duties, as already explained, Timothy or any pastor should exercise "great patience" (v. 2). Christian maturity does not develop in a few days; it takes years. Keep that in mind the next time you become frustrated with a fellow believer. "Instruction" is another part of this process. It is not enough to *tell* a wayward Christian to cease sinning; he needs to be *shown* from the Scriptures the necessary steps.

Why all this instruction? Isn't encouragement enough? Paul anticipates that question and answers it in verses 3 and 4. "For [or 'because'] the time will come when they will not endure sound doctrine." This word "doctrine" is from the same Greek root word as is "instruction" in verse 2.

The impact of these words is more keenly felt when one recalls Paul is now speaking of followers of Christ, not of the false teachers. They won't want to hear about sin, judgment, and the holiness of God. They will turn from the truth (v. 4) and turn to popular and positive preachers "in accordance to their own desires." "Desires" is translated "lusts" in 2 Timothy 2:22 and Titus 3:3

(and other places). All they will wish for is to listen to "myths," stories, and tales. (For more on myths, see comments at 1 Timothy 1.)

The verb "accumulate" (v. 3) is in the active voice, meaning that the turncoats will aggressively pursue speakers who can satisfy their "itching ears" (NIV, KJV). How Christians need discernment—and then to act on it! Paul may have had in mind the Athenians who liked to hear new ideas and then proclaim them as if they were their own original thoughts. It is unfortunate when congregations choose pastors on the basis of the fact that they will tell them what they want to hear and not on the fact of the proclamation of the truth. How paradoxical that weak sheep should choose their own shepherds who cannot bring them along any further than they are at present in their spiritual condition.

When a church slips away from the truth, the people will end up wanting to listen to teachers who will suit their own fancies. The mind thirsts for something to feed upon, but if the mind has been led astray, it will swallow any and all lies! What Paul said would all come to pass after the postapostolic era. Doctrine became twisted, human leadership prevailed over the teaching of Scripture, the miracles of the saints mesmerized the common people, and theological and ecclesiastical myths ruled the sheep. The neglect of the Word of God brings on superstition and false doctrine. There is no end of heresy and the neglect of the true gospel.

Paul commands Timothy to stand out from the crowd ("But you," v. 5) and concentrate his efforts on fulfilling his ministry. Four imperatives are found in this one verse. The first is "be sober." Paul is not talking about drunkenness (though of course the Bible does speak against it; Prov. 20:1; Eph. 5:18).[3] Nor is the apostle telling his young friend to go around with a sour face all day, since that would contradict Philippians 4:4: "Rejoice in the Lord always; again I will say, rejoice!" What Paul *is* stipulating is for Timothy to keep a level head. Don't get all bent out of shape when the pressure builds. The Greek word *nēphō* means to be sober, literally free from intoxicants, and it is used in the New Testament exclusively in the metaphorical and illustrative sense. It conveys the thought of freedom from excess. It indicates stability over against extreme. The point here is set in contrast to the fickleness of those who gravitate to that which is new or novel (v. 3).

Paul next exhorts Timothy to "endure hardship." The difficulties have come and will come. Timothy should prepare himself to bear that burden. The third imperative is "Do the work of an evangelist." It would be easy for Timothy to be sidetracked by these other problems and eventually come to the place where he was doing very little witnessing.[4] That's a charge to all of us! The fourth and final command is for Timothy to fulfill his ministry.

"Don't give up, Timothy. Carry out your duty." The young minister was to stay on track with the work he began in his association with Paul. Yet he was also to continue in his pastoral ministry. A teacher of God's Word cannot cease or take a rest in the work of the gospel. "To fulfill" actually means to bring to full measure the work assigned!

Bring On the Crowns (4:6–8)

There is a significant change in the tone and content of the letter at this point. Up until now, Paul has been addressing Timothy directly with admonitions and instructions, but now he writes once again about himself: his past (v. 7), his present (v. 6), and his future (v. 8).

The wording of verse 6 sounds strange to our ears: "I am already being poured out as a drink offering" (cf. Phil. 2:17). Duane Litfin explains it thus: "This refers to the libation connected with the daily offerings of the lambs (cf. Num. 28:4–7)."[5] Paul understands this process to have "already" started. The last part of verse 6 is more direct: "the time of my departure has come." That Paul senses he will be executed in the near future[6] explains the strong words to his young friend and coworker. Timothy is the one who must pick up the mantle. Tradition says Paul was beheaded in Rome about AD 67 or 68.

But Paul can joyfully look back on a life of service for the Lord. As he often does, he couches his description of the Christian life in athletic terms ("I have fought the good fight, I have finished the course"). Twice in his first letter Paul told Timothy to "fight the good fight" (1 Tim. 1:18, 6:12). There, as here, it is a "good" fight because we are doing it for the glory of God. It is very easy (especially in Western countries) for believers to forget we are in a spiritual battle against evil forces (cf. Eph. 6:12). And we should not look for any cease-fire until Christ returns.

The original readers would have immediately picked up on the phrase "I have finished the course." Again the imagery has to do with sports. This is a "course" as in "racecourse." Paul has accomplished all the tasks laid out for him.

Most important, Paul neither compromised his beliefs nor was he disloyal to the King ("I have kept the faith," v. 7). "The faith" in this context refers to that body of truth revealed by God (cf. Jude 1:3). How many of us will honestly be able to say, "I have kept the faith" at the end of our lives?

How Paul must have looked forward to receiving that "crown of righteousness" (v. 8)! There are two possible interpretations of this expression. First, the crown (*stephanos*) *is* righteousness. Christians will receive their righteousness in full measure upon their arrival in heaven. Second, it is a crown for righteousness. Believers who have remained loyal to the Lord will be awarded this special crown.

I tend to favor the first view; otherwise it makes it look as if Paul is bragging (which he is not). Whatever the case, this kind of prize won't wither and blow away as did the wreaths given to the Olympic champions. Too, recall that near the end of chapter 3 Paul noted that "All Scripture is . . . profitable . . . for training in righteousness" (3:16).

Rewards for Believers

Rewards are built on the foundation of Christ (1 Cor. 3:10–13).

Rewards that are fleshly will be consumed (1 Cor. 3:14–15).

Works done in the Christian life will be recompensed at the judgment seat of Christ (2 Cor. 5:10–11).

All believers will appear before the judgment seat and give an account for what is done in this life (Rom. 14:10–12).

Believers are to hold fast to the truth to receive a "full reward" (2 John 1:8).

That this crown is "laid up" means it is "on reserve," or "stored away." [7] The verb *apokeimai* is found in Luke 19:20 of coins wrapped up in a napkin. It is used illustratively of a hope for the future (Col. 1:5). In this present verse Paul is mentioning again his references to the Greek Olympic games where the victor receives a crown or laurel of leaves that dry up and fade away. Paul is speaking of an imperishable crown of righteousness, that is, one that is rightly adjusted and a reward, for faithful Christian service. The article before "crown" makes the word definite and implies certainty and exactness in the honor given by the Lord.

Back in verse 1 the apostle had identified the Lord as the One who will "judge the living and the dead." Here in verse 8 he calls Him "the righteous Judge." Jesus will never make a mistake in His judgments. We can be sure He won't give in to political pressure and that His rulings will always be perfect. We will receive exactly what we deserve—no more and no less.

Paul will not be the only one rewarded "on that day" (cf. 1:12, 18).[8] Christ will give a crown to "all who have loved His appearing." By this expression Paul means that true Christians will have a longing for Jesus to come back. By contrast, those who don't know Jesus as their Savior will be stricken with fear when they see Him.[9]

Closing Personal Remarks (4:9–22)

Paul often finishes off his letters with notes about specific individuals, and 2 Timothy is one such instance.[10] He mentions twenty-four proper names in this section: seven place names, two women, and fifteen men.

The urgency of verse 9 cannot be missed. Paul did not begin, "Timothy, if you have time . . ." He wrote, "make *every* effort to come to me *soon*" (emphasis mine). Later, in verse 21, he makes the same plea: "Make every effort to come before winter." In verses 10–13 he explains why Timothy needs to come as soon as possible. To me this is one of the saddest passages in the entire New Testament.

Verse 10: "For Demas, having loved this present world, has deserted me and gone to Thessalonica." Demas had been a traveling companion of Paul's as we know from Colossians 4:14 and Philemon 1:24. He loved worldly matters more than he loved Christ's return (v. 8). People do not fall in love with something or someone overnight. It takes time. Demas must have considered doing this during the last few months. There are no indications that Demas was an apostate believer who walked away from his Christianity. But he must have been driven by cultural and worldly desires or comfort. It was good that he departed, because he would not have been good for the church.

The word "deserted" is a strong one. Demas did not approach Paul and explain what was going on. He simply bolted, and at a time when the apostle greatly needed some support and help. Thessalonica, a city on the northwest shore of the Aegean Sea, may have been his hometown.[11]

Crescens and Titus do not fall into this category. They apparently had been dispatched by the Lord to Galatia (perhaps the modern-day region of France and northern Italy) and Dalmatia (the area now known as Croatia, Bosnia, and Herzegovina), respectively. Nothing else about Crescens is revealed in the New Testament. Titus of course is the recipient of the third Pastoral Epistle.

Incredibly, Paul informs us that "only Luke is with me" (v. 11). It is awful that after all Paul has done for the Lord and for others that the good doctor alone is there to comfort and encourage him. Some were in the Lord's will, but what about the others? Were they ashamed of Paul?

Timothy is to run some errands on his way to Rome. First, he is to meet up with Mark and bring him along. This is the John Mark who (1) wrote the second gospel, (2) was Barnabas's cousin (Col. 4:10), and (3) had deserted Paul (and Barnabas) on the first missionary journey (Acts 15:38).[12] What a turnaround! He had once again become faithful to the Lord and useful to Paul (v. 11). Mark apparently had been to Rome, so it seems from this verse.

He was also considered useful to the apostle for ministering. This is in contrast to the fact that years before Mark had made the decision to leave Paul and Barnabas on the first missionary trip. The Lord had need of Mark again and had put him in contact with Paul only in his later years of service.

(Verse 12 will be passed over for the moment.)

Too, Timothy is to "bring the cloak which I [Paul] left at Troas with Carpus, and the books, especially the parchments" (v. 13). All of these items would have been expensive; maybe they were gifts from those supporting Paul's apostolic ministry.[13] A cloak was a heavy outer wrap made of thick wool and provided extra warmth during the cold weeks of winter. Paul desired the warmth and comfort of God's Word as well. Some have suggested that Paul's coat was some kind of ecclesiastical vestment, but that is not true. The cloak was needed because of the winter weather. The apostles are never said to wear some special churchy garments for their ministry. This is imposing on history something that has no factual support behind it.

Troas was on the eastern shore of the Aegean Sea about 150 miles north of Ephesus. Nothing is known about the man Paul visited, Carpus.

Third, Paul's young colleague was to be on the lookout for "Alexander the coppersmith" (v. 14). To identify him in this manner must mean that more than one Alexander was mutual to Paul and Timothy. Because Alexander was a common name, it is impossible to determine which one is referred to here. It could be the Alexander of 1 Timothy 1:20, one of two men whom the apostle had "delivered over to Satan."[14] When, where, and how he attacked Paul is not disclosed. If indeed this Alexander is the one mentioned in 1 Timothy 1:20, he was fired up with fierce indignation against Paul's discipline.

Note the modifiers selected by the writer in assessing the danger of this man. He did Paul "*much* harm" (v. 14), and he "*vigorously* opposed our teaching" (v. 15; emphasis mine). Some take the occasion here to be about Paul's defense that is cited in verse 16. If Paul is writing about the Alexander of Acts 19:33, and if he was a Jew, he was probably of the strict sect of the Pharisee party. This would answer why he was so bitter against Paul, because he too had been a Pharisee! Nevertheless, Paul wants Timothy to avoid him, not seek revenge against him. God will see to that (Num. 32:23; Rom. 12:19). The last portion of verse 14 is an allusion to Psalm 62:12 ("Lovingkindness is Thine, O Lord, for Thou dost recompense a man according to his work").

Lest Timothy be concerned about how the work in Ephesus might suffer in his absence, Paul reassures him by stating in verse 12: "Tychicus I have sent to Ephesus." Tychicus is frequently linked with Paul (Acts 20:4; Eph. 6:21; Col. 4:7; Titus 3:12).

Paul's story does not become any more cheerful in verse 16. The word for "defense" is *apologia*, from which we get the word *apologetics*, a defense of the faith. There are two possible meanings of "first defense." One is his first Roman imprisonment. The second suggestion is more probable, as Gordon Fee makes clear: "Most likely my first defense refers to the present captivity and the Roman juridical practice of a *prima actio*, a preliminary hearing before the emperor or a magistrate, roughly comparable in purpose to a grand jury hearing. This would then be followed by the actual trial."[15]

Another theory about verse 16 is that Paul is speaking of his first defense, which was his appearance before the imperial Roman tribunal that was related to his last trial. One charge may have accused him of somehow taking part in the fire at Rome (AD 64), and the other charge may have focused on treason shown by hostility to the various social customs of the nation. Paul was then seen as weakening imperial authority. In any case, his friends were abandoning him. He was following in the steps of his Master, Christ!

Again Paul's nonretaliatory attitude is evident toward those who deserted him: "may it not be counted against them" (v. 16).

Actually, there was one other person who didn't forsake him—the Lord (v. 17). "Paul's courage in proclaiming the gospel was not dampened by the weakness of those around him. The secret to his ministry was his dependence on the strength of God (Phil. 4:13; 1 Tim. 1:12)."[16] Two good things came out of this difficult situation. All the Gentiles heard the gospel, and Paul was "delivered out of the lion's mouth." The occasion Paul is speaking about is found in Acts 27:23 where an angel stood by him. God more than made up to him for the fact that men deserted and left him. Men were unfaithful, but the Lord was not! The verb "strengthened" is often used to convey that the grace and power of Christ was bestowed (2:1; cf. Eph. 6:10; Phil. 4:13; 1 Tim. 1:12). The Lord gives sustaining strength and comfort with spiritual power to His servant and still does even today, to those who trust Him and walk in His will.

Not every Gentile heard the Good News, but, just as in his first arrest, Paul, ever the evangelist, took advantage of the audience he had with some high-ranking Romans and preached to them (cf. Acts 24, 26). From Rome the gospel could potentially reach the ears of hundreds of thousands of people.[17]

Scholars debate the meaning of lion's mouth. As literally as we should take the Bible, an actual lion may not be in view here. Roman citizens, such as Paul (Acts 16:37), were normally not executed in that manner. Others suggest that the lion's mouth refers to death, the emperor, the empire itself, and even Satan (cf. 1 Peter 5:8). The Greek church fathers suggest the lion in this verse is Nero. Josephus gives a parallel idea to this in writing about the announcement to Agrippa of the death of the emperor Tiberius as if a lion had died. Because there is no article before "lion," it is doubtful that Paul is referring to him. The same may be said of Satan. He is more than likely not suggesting him either. The apostle Paul is simply using a common illustration and expression indicating deliverance from peril about to fall upon him. Whatever the case, he was protected from some potentially fatal event.

In verse 18 he expresses his continued confidence in the Lord and again looks to the future. Not even "every evil deed" can thwart Christ's plan to bring His choice servant into the kingdom. Believers should have the same attitude toward death as Paul does here, and when they do, together they will shout with him: "to Him be the glory forever and ever. Amen." This great hymn and doxology is about Christ (see Rom. 9:5; Rev. 1:6). The phrase implies that glory is to be ascribed to Him eternally. It should be rendered "unto the ages of the ages." This is also used in many other places in the New Testament (Gal. 1:5; Phil. 4:20; 1 Tim. 1:17; Heb. 13:21; 1 Pet. 4:11; 5:11). "Amen" can mean "so be it" or "let it be." It is also used of Christ in Revelation 3:14, since His coming to earth is the final and ultimate purpose of God in redemption. The Lord many times used the word to introduce new revelation from the mind of God. In John's gospel "amen" ("truly, truly") is repeated twice, such as in 3:3, 5, 11.

The apostle first met Prisca and Aquila (v. 19) while on his second missionary journey (Acts 18). They had resided in Rome and Corinth but were now (apparently) settled in Ephesus. A second personal greeting in verse 19 goes out to "the household of Onesiphorus." This family was blessed before by Paul back in 2 Timothy 1:16–18. They must have been very dear to the aged apostle for him to write about them twice. Concerning Prisca and Aquila, the same order of the wife mentioned before the husband is in Acts 18:18, 26 and Romans 16:3. It has been suggested, though without proof, that Prisca was of a higher social rank than her husband. Her name may have been from an established and honored Roman family. Sometimes the diminutive, Priscilla, is used (Acts 18:2, 18, 26).

Both Erastus (Acts 19:22)[18] and Trophimus (Acts 20:4, 21:29) were traveling companions of Timothy, and Paul brings news of their whereabouts (v. 20). Erastus must have been a native of Corinth (Rom. 16:23). He may be the same companion of Timothy mentioned in Acts 19:22. The statement here in 4:20 seems to show that Paul had been traveling about since his first imprisonment. The question that naturally arises from this verse is: "Paul, why did you leave Trophimus sick at Miletus? You have the power to heal (Acts 20:10)!" Two answers are given.

First, miraculous gifts are not for show or entertainment. The Holy Spirit gave them as a way to authenticate the message of Jesus and the apostles (Luke 5:24).[19] In other words, Paul could not perform a miracle on a whim. Second, it is not always the Lord's will for a believer to be healed. In 1 Timothy 5:23 we are told that Timothy had "frequent ailments." Many godly people today live with pain and disease.

Paul's use of the gift of healing was not simply directed by his own desire. Those who had the gift of healing were acting as the Lord's ministers, and their power was controlled by their Master, not by their own personal wishes. The healing was accomplished by trust in the Lord, but faith healing was not practiced as some kind of "magical" art.

In verse 21 the apostle again pleads with his dear friend to "come before winter." Once the winter cold set in, it was nearly impossible to do any traveling. The names Eubulus, Pudens, Linus, and Claudia obviously meant something to Timothy, but we know nothing about them.

Paul ends his letter with two benedictions. The first is directed at Timothy (the "your" is singular). This does not mean that Timothy had wandered from the Lord, but that He would see him through the difficult times ahead (Paul's death, confrontation with the defectors, etc.) just as He had been with Paul (vv. 17–18).[20]

I surmise that the second blessing is to be bestowed on all (especially the Christians in Ephesus) since the "you" is plural. Like two bookends, "grace" is found at the beginning (1:2) and end of 2 Timothy—that attribute of God without which none of us would be here.

Study Questions

1. Paul wrote that a "time will come when they will not endure sound doctrine." Instead, Christians will want "to have their ears tickled" (v. 3). Has that time come for you? If so, what can you do about it?

2. Also regarding verse 3, does the fact that a preacher is popular mean he is biblical in his teaching?

3. What do you do to resist the allurement of the world (v. 10)?

4. Most of Paul's friends had abandoned him (v. 16). Do you know someone in a very difficult situation whom you could support and encourage?

5. In verse 18, Paul expresses the proper Christian view of death. Does your view of death measure up to his?

Section III

Titus

CHAPTER 11

The Goal Is Elder Leadership
Titus 1:1–16

Preview:

In this chapter Paul warns Titus to be alert to certain moral characteristics of the Cretans (1:12). With this in mind, he shows an understanding of human nature, even of the way some Christians act because of their cultural backgrounds. The apostle also expressed concerns about Judaizers who were harming the churches (v. 10). To counter the effect of heretical teaching, it was important to have leaders who were doctrinally sound. The same applies today; without these mature men in place, churches will flounder and fall into the chasm of false teaching. Families will be destroyed and lives ruined spiritually.

Paul's Greeting to Titus (1:1–4)

When Paul was driven to his knees by his encounter with Christ on the Damascus road (Acts 9:1–9), he rose to his feet a humble bond-servant of God and of Jesus (Rom. 1:1). Other apostles felt the same, such as Peter (2 Pet. 1:1), James (1:1), Jude (1:1), and John (Rev. 1:1). Since the Lord Jesus is very God, Paul had no problem considering his servitude as equal to both the Father and Christ (Rom. 1:1). Believers in the Lord are not by compulsion the servants of men (1 Cor. 7:23), but they are to be the slaves of Christ first and foremost (Rom. 6:16).

The word apostle (*apostolos*) comes from two words, *apo* ("from, away from") and *stello* ("to stand aloft, put up, make ready"). *Apostolos* came to refer to one sent forth, an envoy, an emissary, or messenger representing a master, mediator, king, teacher, or even philosopher. The stress often falls on the one who gives his authority to the one whom he sends and whom he takes into his service.[1]

In the narrow sense, Paul as an apostle was in the same category as the twelve apostles (2 Cor. 12:11–12). In a wider sense, Silas, Timothy, and others were also called "apostles of Christ" with a certain level of authority (1 Thess. 2:6). Titus was in the latter category (2 Cor. 8:23).

"For" (*kata*) is better translated "with reference to"; that is, he was appointed to be an apostle *with respect to the faith of* those whom God had chosen or "in order that" they might be led to believe the gospel. God had chosen them to salvation, but he intended that it should be in connection with their believing. He had appointed Paul to be an apostle that he might go and make known to them the gospel. Those "chosen" or "elect" (*eklektos*) have been sovereignly called of God unto salvation.[2]

"God's elect . . . refers to those whom He has chosen and with regard to whom He has a certain purpose. . . . To summarize, Paul is saying that one object of his apostleship was that, through his instrumentality, those chosen of God should believe."[3]

The word "knowledge" (*epignōsis*) is a compound noun from *epi* ("upon") and *gnōsis* ("knowledge") giving it the fuller sense of "knowledge intensified." The thought is "the knowledge of truth is designed to lead to godliness."[4] "The (truth) with a view to godliness."[5]

"Godliness" is a word that can mean "piety, fear of God, devout, worthy of reverence, venerable." The Greek root carries the thought of stepping back from something or someone, to maintain a distance. From this came the metaphorical idea of trepidation, with the intention of shame, wonder to something approaching fear.[6]

The thought continues into verse 2 (and the sentence does not actually end until verse 4.) A better translation for "hope" would be "anticipation." This is not, "Well, I *hope* I will have eternal life," as if it were a wish, but it is of a certainty and a longing for eternal life promised by the Lord! The preposition "in" could also be read, "'Resting on' . . . from the single Greek word *epi*. But it is better to understand this word as 'with a view to,' as in Ephesians 2:10."[7]

What did the apostle have in mind when he wrote of a promise made long ago? The last part of verse 2 can be translated "before eternal times." That is, before God created the world, in eternity past, He had purposed to save us.

Eternal life is certain also because of the Lord's attribute of truth. Jesus said, "I am . . . the Truth . . ." He cannot lie! The statement that God "cannot lie" is actually an adjective (*apseudēs*) from two Greek words, the negative *a*, and the word for lie, *pseudēs*. He is "the unlie-able God" or "the cannot-lie

God." "We human beings lie, and the Cretans were notorious liars (v. 12), but God never lies. Indeed, he cannot, because 'he cannot disown himself', that is, contradict his own character"[8] (see Num. 23:19; 1 Sam. 15:29; 2 Tim. 2:13; Heb. 6:18). Our salvation is based on a promise given by the God who cannot lie!

The "but" of verse 3 shows the contrast from the past. He promised then, *but* now He has revealed. "Manifested" means "to make visible, to bring to light, make known, reveal." At the right season of time, the gospel was made known. The past tense would seem to mark a specific moment at which this truth was brought forth and made evident. God is the author of time and history. He had a plan of redemption that arrived at just the right moment according to His timing.

With "word" Paul seems to be specifically referring to the message of the gospel. By using the singular noun *logos* ("word"), he sums up this good news into a total package of revelation that includes all that is made known about Christ and the redemption He now provides for humanity.

Paul alone was given the full understanding of the gospel, in a certain exclusive doctrinal way. Through him the message of the cross of Christ was systematized and placed into a doctrinal formula. The apostle seems to stress this by using the personal pronoun *egō* ("I").

The apostle had a unique relationship to the gospel. He was divinely commissioned to the gospel through the commandment from God. His ministry was not a matter of his own choosing. He makes it clear that he was set apart from his mother's womb and was called through God's grace to reveal His Son (Gal. 1:15). Earlier in the Pastoral Epistles he wrote of "the glorious gospel . . . with which I have been entrusted" (1 Tim 1:11) and "for which I was appointed a preacher and an apostle and a teacher" (2 Tim 1:11). Though Paul has been given strict orders to share the cross of Christ with the world, it is a commission driven by love. The responsibility of presenting Christ in the gospel is now entrusted to us.[9]

In this verse God is called "our Savior" (*sōtēr*). This word has the thought of "deliverer, rescuer, helper, protector." Often the Greek gods, such as Zeus, Apollo, Poseidon, and Heracles were called soters. Even philosophers and statesmen were sometimes labeled with the same term. Caesar was known as the "soter of the world," and Augustus was called the "soter of humankind."[10] What a slap to the world at that time to likewise call the God of Israel *Sōtēr,* and His Son as well, with the same description (v. 4). The ancient world did not mind passing the word around to supposedly ruling deities and reigning kings, but the New Testament will use the word in an exclusive fashion, proclaiming that there is no other way of finding spiritual and eternal deliverance.

Sōtēr is used six times in Titus, more than in any other New Testament writing. Three times it is applied to God (1:3; 2:10; 3:4) and three times to Christ (1:4; 2:13; 3:6). "God our Savior" is used also in Jude 1:25 and "my Savior" is found in Luke 1:47.

"Titus" (v. 4) is a Latin name, though he was Greek by birth. He is one of the least known figures in early church history. The first reference to him is found in Galatians 2:1 where Paul mentions that he and Barnabas had brought Titus to Jerusalem. Here Paul makes it clear that he led Titus to the Lord and into the common faith. Titus probably accompanied Paul on his missionary journeys, but this younger man did not come into prominence until his contact with the Corinthian church.[11]

The expression "true child" could also be rendered "genuine, legitimate" child. Titus is Paul's genuine child in the fellowship of the faith. By this he means he gave spiritual birth to this younger man who was added to the fraternity of believers in Christ. As to the details of his conversion, we have no information.

Though "grace" and "peace" were common expressions of greeting in letters in Paul's day, they are not used as empty words of courtesy by the apostle. These are benedictions and blessings, wishes for Titus coming directly from God the Father and the Lord Jesus. This greeting is similar to Paul's words in 1 Timothy 1:2 and 2 Timothy 1:2.

Grace is God's unmerited favor, and Paul desires that the Father bestow favor upon Titus because of the thankless task he must perform spiritually there on the island of Crete. "Peace" theologically would have to do with the peace that the believer experiences from becoming reconciled with God through Christ. But experientially, as in this verse, it has to do with an inner calm, an assurance that no matter what comes, God is not far away. The child of the Lord can trust Him regardless of the circumstances.

This grace and peace originate from God the Father and His Son Jesus. The doctrine of the Trinity is again hinted at. Before, (vv. 3–4) both are described as "our Savior." "The Son has brought to us salvation from the Father, and the Father has bestowed it through the Son."[12] Now both are identified as the Ones sending forth the spiritual blessings of grace and peace. If Jesus was a mere man, He would in no way join in such blessing and gifting along with God the Father.

Paul's Charge Concerning Elders (1:5–9)

From what is said next, one gets the idea that Paul was with Titus on Crete for evangelism purposes. Many believe this would have been a journey undertaken after Paul's first Roman imprisonment. "From what follows, one can sur-mise that the two were successful in evangelizing various cities on the island but did not have time to return and strengthen the believers by setting the churches in order and seeing that elders were elected. . . . Therefore, Paul left Titus to 'set in order what remains and appoint elders in every city, as I direct-ed you' (v. 5b)."[13]

"For this reason" (v. 5) might be translated "For this gracious reason," or "With this kind intention." Paul had a distinct purpose for Titus, a man whom he thoroughly trusted. Titus had the full confidence of the apostle who knew this younger leader could carry out the task of getting the churches on Crete organized.

"Might set in order" is one word in the Greek, meaning "to set limits upon" with the further thought of "to make right, improve, set on the right path."[14] What he was to set in order was "what remains," or "the many things that are left." Titus, acting as a chief elder and underapostle, had the authori-ty to straighten out many issues. It must be remembered that many who had come to Christ were pagan and had no idea of how the churches on the island must be run. Though where the Gentiles had some contact with the Jewish communities, they had some conception, even as unbelievers, of who the God of the Old Testament was. But now the new dispensation of the church was beginning. The synagogues would be hostile to the new faith found in Christ.

Added to his task of clearing up many issues was the job of appointing elders. Some in the Baptist persuasion think that only one elder in each church would be appointed. The single pastor would have almost the sole responsibility for the congregation. But this is not the case. There were many churches on the island, and there would be a plurality of elders in each assem-bly.

The idea for "elder" (*presbuteros*) comes from both the Old Testament rulership of the community and from the practices of even the pagan world. All societies, communities, and villages in the ancient past were elder ruled. Older wise men, who had much experience in life, were brought into the inner circle of leadership. Rarely was this an elective office but a position appointed by other elders. They would be the ones responsible for the teach-ing ministry and spiritual health of the congregation. "Titus was now acting as an apostolic agent (cf. Acts 14:23) in Paul's absence. His authority in the Cretan church[es] was an extension of Paul's own. Such authority ended with the close of the Apostolic Age."[15]

Plural appointments were taking place in the many cities and villages on Crete. This had to be done with much care because problems were certainly beginning to grow. Paul would want only the most responsible men appoint-

ed. "In Crete the business of organizing the various churches was far from finished, and undue haste in appointing men to office was contrary to Paul's
principles (1 Tim. 3:6; 5:22)."[16] Again, Titus was invested with full apostolic
authority ("as I directed you").

Now Paul lays out the qualifications of such men to Titus (v. 6). This list
is almost identical to what the apostle wrote to Timothy (1 Tim. 3:1–7). There
he addressed the list specifically to the "overseer" (*episkopos*), one who guards
or watches what is coming, who evaluates and gives approval or warning. The
word is closely related to the work of a shepherd. "According to 1 Pet 2:25
Christ is the shepherd and *overseer* of souls."[17] In 1:7 Paul shows that the elder
and overseer is the same person but with two descriptions. "Elders . . . are synonymous with overseers or bishops. . . . The former term connotes their dignity, and the latter their function . . ."[18]

(For the meanings of "husband of one wife," "having children who
believe," "not addicted to wine," "not pugnacious," "not fond of sordid gain,"
and "hospitable," see comments on 1 Timothy 3.)

The words "not accused of dissipation or rebellion" apply to the children,
not to the elder. The elder's offspring should not be in such moral defiance as
to bring negative light on him or the work of Christ. As already mentioned,
some commentators do not think the children have to be Christians, but they
must be under control, relatively ethical, and not in moral or civil rebellion.

"Dissipation" in ancient Greek carried the thought of being a "desperate
case" or "past recovery," even "unsaveable." It also implied "moral abandon-
ment."[19]

"Rebellion" describes one who moves up and away from what is pre-
scribed and ordered. It can refer to those who are "unrestrained, not made
subject, and certainly insubordinate."[20] It is not impossible that there was a
unique problem on the island of Crete with unruly teens and young adults.
Paul is concerned that such attention would destroy the witness of such young
churches. Yet the apostle's injunction stands for guiding all congregations
everywhere.

"Being wild and disobedient" (NIV) would place the children of the elder
in a state of anarchy against both home and civil authorities. This certainly
could not be tolerated.

In Acts 20, Paul called the elders of the church of Ephesus together and
reminded them that they were made "overseers" by the Holy Spirit "to shepherd" the church (v. 28). In these verses we see the same group of leaders
described by two important pastoral nouns, "elder" (sometimes called "presbyter") and "overseer" (sometimes called "bishop"). They are then responsible "to pastor" the Ephesian congregation.[21]

Verse 7 describes the elder as "God's steward." He belongs to God, and thus He is the One to whom the elder is accountable. A steward is a manger. An elder is to properly handle what the Lord has given him. These thoughts suggest "that the steward of such a Lord should conform to the highest ideal of moral and spiritual qualifications."[22]

Though the standards are high for the men who will spiritually lead the church, John Calvin warns that to expect perfection in human flesh is unrealistic. "[Paul] does not mean one who is exempt from every vice, (for no such person could at any time be found,) but one who is marked by no disgrace that would lessen his authority."[23]

"Self-willed" can mean "stubborn, arrogant." The word is found only here in the New Testament and often can mean "self-complacent, assuming, imperious."[24] The opposite is the virtue of being gentle, kind, and gracious that is found in 1 Timothy 3:3.[25]

"Quick-tempered" carries the thought of being inclined to anger. "The pastor-teacher cannot be hot-headed. He cannot explode with unjust rage. Caution: Neither should the pastor-teacher be effeminate. He must occasionally stand up in righteous indignation when believers harm each other with gossip and other sins. He must speak out forcefully against heresy and evil. The Reformers displayed proper moments of anger against evil."[26]

By using the contrast "but," Paul stresses the virtuous characteristics of verse 8 over the vices in the last two verses.

The elder is to love "what is good." This means he is to support that which is right and just. He should be commending all that is good, in public, in private, and certainly in the assembly of believers. "[This] may apply to any thing that is good. It may refer to good men, as included under the general term *good*; and there is no more essential qualification of a bishop than this. A man who sustains the office of a minister of the gospel should love every good object and be ever ready to promote it."[27]

"Sensible" (*sōphrōn*) is a compound word from *sophos* ("wisdom, wise") and *phroneō* ("to think, reflect, set the mind"). "To be sensible," then, is to "think wisely, soundly, use common sense." Some see the word referring to self-restraint or expressive of mastery of self. It could refer to "that self-command which wisely regulates pleasures and passions."[28] (See 1 Tim. 3:2.)

"Just" may "refer to his character, that 'he lives a righteous life.' Or it may refer to the way he treats others, that 'He provides justice to everyone.' This man will be fair to all. He will give you an honest hearing and he can be counted on to do what is right."[29]

"Devout" is related to holiness and sanctification but more. He must be conscious of how he walks with the Lord and pleases Him. He is aware of his piety and spiritual devotion to his God. "He is faithful in all his duties to God."[30]

"Self-controlled" (*egkratēs*) is a compound word from *en* ("within") and *kratos* ("power, authority, might")—hence, to have inner strength and discipline. Paul is not talking about self human effort as if moral strength is innate. Lasting discipline has a higher purpose and meaning for the Christian in contrast to the world. The apostle is not advocating a form of modern "self-help" as if we are the moral captains of our own ships. He teaches clearly that all spiritual and moral virtue comes from God. Here, he is advocating "having the inner strength that enables [the elder] to control his bodily appetites and passions, a virtue listed in Galatians 5:23 as one quality of the fruit of the Spirit."[31]

Self-control comes last in this list of Christian virtues, as it does in the fruit of the Spirit. This is an appropriate ending, "covering everything which has preceded it."[32]

"Holding fast" (*antechomenon*) is a compound of two words, *anti* ("against") and *echō* ("to have, hold, possess"). The first meaning is "to hold against."[33] The second usage is "to hold out, stand against." "*Holding to* correctly suggests the notion of withstanding opposition. Having care of it, making it his business."[34]

Paul is concerned that the elder stand firm doctrinally and not depart from what has been committed to him. He should "constantly be keeping to, and not letting go" of the teaching of biblical truth.[35] This will be one of the main tasks of the elders. They are first and foremost responsible for the doctrinal integrity of the congregation. They are in charge of keeping error at bay. The chief purpose of the elder is "principally for the sake of teaching; for the church cannot be governed in any other way than by the word."[36] The Word whose doctrine makes it so reliable and worthy of confidence and faith. . . . The expression is compact and unites in one concept: the Word—its doctrine—its trustworthiness; the Word—its great contents—its supreme quality. Every elder is to be a man who holds solidly to this Word, who knows it, makes it his whole stay."[37]

The "faithful word" may be translated the "truthful word." It is a singular concept, as is "teaching." This probably includes the fact of the inspiration of the entire new revelation of the cross of Christ and the salvation found in Him. Paul envisions this as a whole. Yes, thousands of truths are revealed with the coming of Jesus. But the apostle here seems to place those truths all into One!

In other letters, Paul writes against those who advocate "a different doctrine," not agreeing with sound (healthy) words, "those of our Lord Jesus

Christ" (1 Tim. 6:3). But he also writes of the *word* as a single unit. He speaks about the "word of the Lord (2 Thess. 3:1), of those who are sanctified by the word of God (1 Tim. 4:5). He urges Timothy to "preach the word" (2 Tim. 4:2) and praises those who labor in the word (1 Tim. 5:17). As well, Paul ties in what he as an apostle taught the Thessalonians, not as the word of men, but what it truly was, the word of God (1 Thess. 2:13). He makes exhortation to faith and Christian living "the teaching" that he connects with the substance, "the doctrine."[38]

Throughout this section Paul has used the present tense. He may be implying that such vigilance, teaching, and exhorting must be continual and never cease.

The word "'able' here means equipped, in terms of knowledge and commitment, to carry out one's responsibility as an elder/overseer."[39] Evil forces constantly come against the truth. The elder will be empowered by holding fast the faithful Word. This is the means God uses to create strong elders who then have power from above because they are standing on what God has said and not on their own devices. If the elder fails to obey in teaching what the Lord has laid down, he becomes an "airy, uncertain man."[40] The elder "must himself be sound in doctrine, and fully persuaded of the supreme claims of the truth."[41]

When the apostle writes "sound doctrine," he uses the present participle of *hugiainō* ("to be healthy").By using a participle, Paul is saying that this doctrine, by its very nature, is healthy and produces healing results. With the participle "The emphasis is upon sound (*hugiainō*) doctrine; . . . and is to be contrasted with the sickly, unpractical teaching of false teachers."[42]

"Refute" has a wide range of meaning. The noun can be translated as "rebuke, censure, conviction, correction."[43] In the majority of passages used in the New Testament the word "designates fatherly or divine correction and punishment for the purpose of improvement. . . . The intellectual aspect of refutation appears in Titus 1:9."[44]

In the context, this refutation must be applied apparently against Jewish converts ("the circumcision," v. 10) who are confused and mislead believers. Known as Judaizers, they believed a person had to become a Jew before he could become a Christian. They must be reproved "severely that they may be sound in faith" (v. 13). These are "Jewish church-members (cf. Acts 10:45; Gal. 2:12), [who] belong to the class of futile talkers and mind-deceivers. They probably regarded their circumcision as a mark of superior excellence, entitling them to be heard and looked up to by others."[45]

These Jewish members are said to be "those who contradict" (*antilegō*). The word is a compound verb from *anti* ("against") and *legō* ("to speak").

These are continually going about speaking against what Paul and others are teaching that is sound and trustworthy. The apostle goes on and writes strong words against them in verses 10–11.

The task of teaching truth is unending. The church cannot let its guard down. Paul warned the Ephesian elders that after his departure, "savage wolves will come in among you, not sparing the flock" (Acts 20:29). He added that from their own company men would arise who would "draw away the disciples after them" (v. 30). Such a doctrinal war would never cease. He urged the elders to "be on the alert" (v. 31), and he reminded them that he spent three years warning and urging. He did not stop in admonishing them even with tears to be awake for trouble (v. 31). "Christian truth needs not only defense against attacks, but also clear exposition. Effective presentation of the truth is a powerful antidote to error."[46] "The pastor ought to have two voices: one, for gathering the sheep; and another, for warding off and driving away wolves and thieves. The Scripture supplies him with the means of doing both; for he who is deeply skilled in it will be able both to govern those who are teachable, and to refute the enemies of the truth."[47]

Problems in the Local Church (1:10–16)

In these verses Paul is more specific as to what is happening there on the island of Crete. He will prepare Titus in some detail about what he is to expect. The apostle apparently heard reports and speaks justifiably with righteous indignation, because he sees many being turned away from the truth (v. 14). He reserves some of his strongest language for verses 15–16. He argues that their consciences are defiled (v. 15) and says that they are detestable, disobedient, and worthless for any good deed (v. 16).

In verse 10, Paul uses three very unflattering descriptions of those bringing trouble to the churches. By what he says in the rest of the verse, he notes that they are Jews who probably boast in their knowledge of the Old Testament and continually contradict New Testament truth. The apostle calls them "rebellious," a word he used in verse 6 to describe wayward children of potential elders.

They are also "empty talkers," which is one word in the Greek that can also mean "independent, undisciplined, disobedient,"[48] or even "spoiled" (as with the youngsters mentioned in verse 6). They want to be heard and try to have their way in the congregation. They would rather talk than practice their Christianity.[49] Every church has these kinds in its midst. They never seem to settle down. They act contrary to what others readily accept.

The third word is "deceiver." The only other place the word is used is in Galatians 6:3 where Paul uses it as a verb and writes of those who deceive even themselves. It carries the thought of "mind-deceivers."[50]

The apostle has little patience with those who are "of the circumcision," because they should have more spiritual common sense. Archibald Robertson adds, "Jews are mentioned in Crete in Acts 2:11. Apparently [they were] Jewish Christians of the Pharisaic type tinged with Gnosticism."[51] "Rebuke is especially needful with Cretan heretics, in whom the Jewish strain is disagreeably prominent. Alike in their new-fangled philosophy of purity, and in their pretensions to orthodoxy, they ring false. Purity of life can only spring from a pure mind; and knowledge is alleged in vain, if it is contradicted by practice."[52]

Paul orders Timothy to silence the unorthodox teachers (v. 11). The reason Paul is so concerned is that they were upsetting "whole families." Entire households were being turned upside down doctrinally and spiritually. The churches on the island of Crete were in terrible turmoil, and Paul wanted it stopped. "There was, indeed, grave cause why these men should be put to silence; the mischief they were doing in Crete to the Christian cause was incalculable."[53]

Biblical Directives to Confront Error

The "teaching" elders must teach, exhort, and refute when challenging error (Titus 1:9).

False teachers must be silenced (Titus 1:11).

Reproof should lead to soundness in the faith (Titus 1:13).

Instruction is meant to correct ungodliness and worldly desires (Titus 2:11–12).

Foolish controversies and false doctrine are to be shunned (Titus 3:9).

Pastors today are often afraid to confront error. They believe they have but a passive role, or they think they might be "unspiritual" to show righteous indignation toward those causing trouble. Too, many leaders are simply fearful of the congregation. "What would happen if church members left and we lost numbers because they were confronted?," they reason.

With "for the sake of sordid gain" Paul gets to the heart of the problem. Money or compensation must have somehow been part of the motive of the Jewish Christians who were causing problems. "Sordid" means "repulsive, shameful" (cf. 1 Cor. 11:6; 14:35; Eph. 5:12). It is a word that implies the lowest of motives. These Jewish Christians were in some way making money by giving contrary opinions to the religious teachings of Paul. They were being subsidized through giving spiritual advice. Avarice is a destructive plague in those who teach.[54] "The majority of deceivers would soon stop if their evil work produced no financial profit. Modern history has some notorious examples where great sums were secured by the leaders and shared in by their lieutenants. The Cretans had a bad reputation for heeding itinerating prophets who worked for profit."[55]

By using the word "prophet," Paul is not implying that this person is a prophet in the biblical sense, but that he is simply a philosopher or wise man in the Greek religion or culture. "Liar" is easy enough to understand. "Evil beasts" signifies that the Cretans were untamable, uncontrollable, and unpredictable. "Lazy gluttons" actually can be translated "idle stomachs," referring to those who are given over to luxurious feasting and who do no work.

The "prophet" Paul refers to is Epimenides (according to some of the church fathers), a native of Phaestus or Cnossus on Crete. Epimenides lived around six hundred years before Christ. He gave a strong indictment that his own people, saying that they were full of lies and were ferocious in character. To deceive and lie became known as "playing the Cretan." The "characteristic was so notorious, that it was the subject of frequent remark; the very expression here used of it is also found in a hymn to Zeus by Callimachus."[56] Though the charge may not fit all Cretans, it was an accepted general description of how the population behaved. Because the description became "a kind of byword and reproach to the island, it was to be expected that the noxious qualities would not be long in making their appearance in the Christian church."[57]

The apostle will not tolerate such behavior in the new churches developing on Crete. He will instruct Titus to "reprove them severely" in order to turn things around (v. 13).

"Testimony" (v. 13) is that which can be seen and not doubted. What Paul is saying cannot be challenged, for everyone could see the fact of it. A testimony becomes an outward demonstration of what is actual. The generalization about the Cretans was true, no matter how much pain was caused expressing the fact. Titus had to face this, and so did the people. Paul is applying this ugly but truthful description to the Jewish believers who were living out such a wasted life. They were using the habits of the island to feed off of their own Gentile and Jewish brethren in the faith who were apparently terribly gullible as new believers.

But Paul knew God could change things, if even progressively and by sound rebuke. Cretans were in Jerusalem and accepted Jesus when the gospel was presented by Peter (Acts 2:11). They were born again by the transforming power of the Holy Spirit. "The elders Titus was to appoint (5–9) were themselves Cretans, who were certainly not liars, but teachers of the truth."[58]

It still must be recognized, however, that all sins that are part of the old nature are not always eradicated at the moment of conversion. That could certainly be said of the Jewish believers Paul refers to. They carried into their Christian experience sins that were part of their culture but that would also harm others.

"For this cause" is a phrase used eight times in the New Testament. It is stating the grounds for what follows. "Since matters stand this way, something has to be done."

"Therefore," or "for which cause," introduces the action demanded by this situation. Titus must continue to "rebuke them sharply," dealing incisively with the danger, like a surgeon cutting away cancerous tissue.[59]

"Reprove" (same word as "refute" in v. 9) is a present tense imperative that may imply that this correcting may have to take awhile and be ongoing. Old habits are hard to break. Though the deceiver may not improve quickly, the rebuke should be sharp and certain. The reprover is to "cut off, be abrupt, rugged, and sharp" with his words and actions.[60] "It is necessary to appear rude sometimes for safety, if the house is on fire and life is in danger."[61]

Note that Paul says "sound *in the faith*" (emphasis mine). They are already believers in the Lord. But *within* that faith, the apostle wished that they would be free from the disease of sin.

We note the positive purpose of all truly Christian rebuke. Paul's aim was not to humiliate the Cretans for being gullible, but to rescue them from error and establish them in the truth.[62]

Paul is trying to break the cycle of the Jews who paid more attention to tradition than they did to biblical truth, both Old and New Testaments. To be "paying attention to" (v. 14) implies the giving of one's assent as well as one's attention.[63]

The Jewish "myths" probably are references to the books written between the testaments, such as the Jewish Apocrypha scrolls. (For more on these myths, see comments at 1 Timothy 1.)

More than likely the traditions the Lord referred to when encountering the Pharisees and scribes encompassed these human elements—"the commandments of men." For example, the Pharisees always washed before eating, "thus observing the traditions of the elders" (Mark 7:3). They badgered the Lord and asked Him why His disciples did not follow the traditions they observed (v. 5). Christ answered and called them hypocrites and quoted Isaiah 29:13: "In vain do they worship Me, teaching as doctrines the precepts of men" (v. 7). The Lord then accused them of setting aside the commandment of God "in order to keep your tradition" (v. 9) and noted that they also invalidated the word of God "by your tradition which you have handed down" (v. 13). This was in reference to the fact that the Pharisees were living by tradition and unbiblical ritual that they thought made them holy. Christ urged His audience to see through such religious practices that were not from God.

In Paul's great personal testimony given in Galatians 1, he admits that before being born again, he was well known for his "former manner of life in Judaism" (v. 13) and as well was "extremely zealous for my ancestral traditions" (v. 14). But by the time he began to pen his New Testament letters, the great apostle saw the dangers of following what was not true.

These human regulations caused the new Christians on Crete to "turn away from the truth," away from the simple message and truth of the new life in Christ. The Greek is such that it could be translated "Turn *themselves* away from the truth."[64] They consciously moved away from the truth. In virtually identical language, Paul wrote to Timothy not "to pay attention to myths and endless genealogies, which give rise to mere speculation rather than furthering the administration of God which is by faith" (1 Tim. 1:4; cf. 2 Tim. 4:4).

"Pure" (v. 15) basically means "clean." The Greek word is *katharos*, from which we get the English word *catharsis*. Most references in the Gospels allude to the purification from leprosy. Leprosy was a serious illness in the Old Testament that caused those inflicted to be isolated from the camp (Lev. 13–14). Outside the Gospels, however, the thought spills over to spiritual or moral cleanliness or lack of the same.

Here in 1:15 Paul lays down an abiding principle when he writes, "To the pure, all things are pure." He is again repudiating the ascetic and legalistic practices of the false teachers. They are "men who forbid marriage and advocate abstaining from foods" (1 Tim. 4:3). Years earlier, however, Jesus Himself had "declared all foods clean" (Mark 7:19; cf. Acts 10:15). Thus the apostle is here affirming that those of us who are "pure" (spiritually redeemed and cleansed) need not be concerned about dietary restrictions, because "all things are pure."

By contrast, people who are "defiled" (that is, the "unbelieving") are impure in every aspect of their being. "Defiled" carries the idea of being impure and stained. It is an old word that is used to describe coloring or staining in the dyeing of cloth. It is used only five times in the New Testament. John 18:28 gives a perfect illustration as to how the Jews used the word: As the Jews led Christ from the hearing with Caiaphas to Pilate's headquarters, they refused to enter the Praetorium "in order that they might not be defiled, but might eat the Passover." They were concerned about ceremony and ritual. Morally, they were unclean and devious. But Paul goes further when considering defilement. He is concerned about genuine spiritual defilement, not simply some ritualistic and religious display of outward false piety

"Mind" refers to the thinking and calculating aspect of humans. "Conscience" is a compound noun from *sun* ("together") and *eidos* ("knowledge"). The conscience is an accumulation or gathering of knowledge that should bring about right action.

To "profess" (v. 16) something is to call it what it is, to authenticate it, to affirm it, to acknowledge it, or to confess to it. By using a present tense, the apostle emphasizes that these people are long on speech and are good religious talkers. They continually and loudly profess that they indeed know God!

Although these people outwardly make a claim to knowing God, they are so self-deceived tha they fail to recognize that those around them observe their actions and do not believe their testimony ("by their deeds they deny Him"). They act as if God is "a metaphysical abstraction, out of all moral relation to human life."[65]

In these final words, the apostle is full of righteous indignation at these false teachers, who are by their acts and by their teachings destroying the work of the gospel on Crete. On one hand, they put forth such piety. On the other, they are liars, fakes, and deceivers. No doubt they had to continually contradict what Paul had taught. Here He uses the strongest, most cutting words against them.

"The one participle ["being"] also substantiates and amplifies the nouns. Being detestable . . . being disobedient . . . being worthless."[66]

"Detestable" means "horrid, abominable." The corresponding (Greek) noun is translated "nausea, sickness, filth, nastiness,"[67] and it is used in Matthew 24:15 and Mark 13:14 to describe the image of the Beast that will be set up in the temple.

By using "disobedient," Paul is virtually saying that these false prophets have no intention of being convinced and obeying the truth. As such, they are absolutely "worthless for any good deed." They are not even qualified to do *one* good thing for the Lord!

In Titus 2, Paul announces what good deeds genuine followers of Christ can and should do.

Study Questions

1. Why is it important for an elder to be "above reproach" (v. 6)?

2. Why does Paul talk about an elder's children in verse 6?

3. Which character trait mentioned in verses 6–9 do you need to work on first?

4. How does your church handle rebellious people (v. 10)?

5. Describe the actions and attitudes you should have in dealing with any false teachers that might come into your church.

6. What steps can you take to make sure sound doctrine is being taught in your church?

7. In light of verse 16, how can we know if a person is a genuine believer?

CHAPTER 12

The Goal Is Defending Sound Doctrine
Titus 2:1–15

Preview:

In this chapter we gain a glimpse of how Paul gives instructions to the flock. His own way of teaching is revealed, and it is both doctrinal and practical. The apostle believed in instructing the aged, both men and women. He wanted instruction to filter down to young women with children and to young men. This included exhortations also to Christian servants. Here Paul places the responsibility for this chain of instruction on the shoulders of Titus who was left in charge of the newly formed churches. Paul uses the words "encourage," "teaching," and "doctrine" frequently in these verses. He uses verbs as well to impress Titus that the believers must "adorn the doctrine of God our Savior in every respect" (v. 10).

Speaking Sound Doctrine (2:1–10)

Paul introduces a contrast with the very first word of chapter 2. "But as for you, in contradistinction to those I have just mentioned."[1] This charge is aimed directly at Titus. Paul uses the emphatic personal pronoun "you" to get his attention. He knows this younger man is up to the task, and he lays the responsibility to mature these assemblies right in his lap.

Titus was Paul's brother in the ministry (2 Cor. 2:13). Earlier he had called him his "true child in a common faith" (Titus 1:4).

In this charge (Titus 2:1), "Titus was to be as active in teaching positive truth as the heretics were in teaching evil."[2] He is to teach "things which are fitting" or "suitable." By using "things," Paul broadens the doctrinal spectrum to include a variety of teachings and instruction. This is in contrast to the deceivers' teachings of "things they should not" (1:11) be proclaiming. His goal is to bring about maturity and change in the lives of the congregations. The Cretans were deep in paganism, and their journey out of it would be long and difficult.

"Fitting" is better translated "suitable." Originally the word meant "to stand out, be conspicuous" or to be "conspicuously fit" to do a task.[3]

The apostle desires to hear that "sound doctrine" is going forth. He uses almost the same phrase in 1:9, and in 1 Timothy 1:10 and 2 Timothy 4:3. Here in the Pastorals, he uses "sound" "in the metaphorical sense in reference to Christian doctrine. . . . Christian teaching is thus characterized as correct or reasonable in contrast to false teachings, which deviate from received doctrine."[4]

"Doctrine" often emphasized military regulations or discipline, specific directives, and instructions.[5] It came to represent logical and clear instruction, objective presentation of fact. Paul incorporates the word into his lexicon of important words to indicate how truth should be presented. Accordingly, it should not represent simply cold facts without application. The apostle sees God's Word in doctrinal form reshaping lives and creating spiritual maturity.

Apparently the more mature men in the church had many things to learn in the way they lived. Paul used this same word about himself when he was probably around sixty ("the aged," Philem. 1:9). The word is also used of Zecharias, the father of John the Baptist, who questioned the angel about his becoming a father. He said, "I am an old man, and my wife is advanced in years" (Luke 1:18). "In ancient Greek literature the word sometimes was used of men as young as 50."[6] It must be remembered that these believers were coming out of a pagan society. They had lived as they pleased in an immoral lifestyle.

"Temperate" should better be translated "sober." It is an adjective that warns against abusing wine. The verb is often used in the sense of sober watchfulness in regard to spiritual issues and in having sound judgment (1 Thess. 5:8; 1 Pet. 1:13). Second Timothy 4:5 reads, "you, be sober in all things."

"Dignified" describes how the old men are to carry themselves. In a pagan society there was a lot of pushing and shoving in order to survive. But Paul wants these men to live above the way the culture acts. The word can mean "august, venerable, reverent," or mean that one has "integrity, dignity."[7] The older men are to rise above the circumstances of living in a rough society. They should not cave in and live as others who have no guidelines.

"Sensible" carries the thought of "being of sound mind," walking "disciplined, reasonable." Often we forget that Christianity is meant to help the believer in areas that even go beyond morality, though biblical morality is also certainly in view. The apostle wants the same thing for younger women (v. 4) and the younger men as well (v. 6). Some have seen in this word "the renunciation of worldly passions."[8]

"Sound in faith" means that the faith of the older men should be continually robust and active. As older men they are to be leading, setting the pace of trust toward God. (See also 1:9, 13; 2:1.) The Word of God is virile and strong, and if presented as such, it should speak to the people's needs. If men are godly, the women and children are blessed. When men, in this context especially, older men fail, women and children suffer.

"Love" here is the word *agapē*. "Perseverance" is two Greek words, *hupo* ("under") and *menō* ("to abide, remain"). The thought is that one is to shoulder up and remain secure even though under persecution or pressure. Charles Ellicott has this to say about this "healthy" triad of faith, love, and perseverance: "In respect to these "three" they must be healthy, sound. The faith must not be adulterated with superstitions—the love must be chivalrous, not sentimental. . . . The patience must be no mere tame acquiescence in what seems to be the inevitable, but must be brave, enduring, suffering—if suffering comes—for the Lord's sake with a smile on the lips."[9]

"Likewise" (v. 3) the apostle wants the teaching of sound doctrine to spill over to the older women as well. Though men are to be the head of their wives in position within the family (Eph. 5:22–24), in terms of the spiritual relationship before God, all stand as equal. All have their individual, personal walks with the Lord. Therefore, the older women are to mature under the teaching authority of the Word just as the men are.

"Reverent" is a compound word from *hieros* ("holy") and *prepō* ("to stand out, to be conspicuous, to be fit").[10] The women are to carry themselves, and be seen, as godly women. They are not to conform to what the other women in the culture are doing. John Calvin believed that women often want to hold on to their youth and dress like young women. They demean their own maturity and attempt to dress culturally fashionable or even flirtatiously. Though there is nothing wrong with a woman adorning herself with pretty clothes (Prov. 31:22), a line may be crossed that signals sensuality. Lemuel, the writer of Proverbs 31, reminds the godly woman: "Charm is deceitful and beauty is vain, but a woman who fears the LORD, she shall be praised" (v. 30). Paul may have had this passage in mind when he penned his words here in Titus.

The phrase "malicious gossips" is practically redundant since it is not possible to be a gossip and not be malicious. The Greek word Paul uses here for "malicious" is *diabolos*, a word sometimes used to describe the devil. It is a compound from *dia* ("through") and *ballō* the verb "to throw." A gossip is one who throws accusations against someone. The believer is not to give place to *diabolos* (Eph. 4:27), but instead is to stand against his cunning (Eph. 6:11). Unfortunately, malicious gossips will be around until the end of the world (2 Tim. 3:3). Though men can certainly gossip, Paul twice uses this word *diabolos* to describe a specific sin of women (1 Tim. 3:11; Titus 2:3).

Paul was also fearful that the women would become "enslaved to much wine." "Enslaved" has the idea of "to be given over to, to have been entrapped." In the Cretan culture, women as well as men could be addicted, but it seems to have been a sin that especially gripped females.

Women have tremendous power in the home setting in which they are able to impart to the children what is noble and right by "teaching what is good." Women mold and shape their children in godly ways and attitudes. In modern times, very little moral instruction is given in many homes. The loss of motherhood in the modern generation cannot be recaptured unless the older women teach the younger (v. 4).

The older women are to be so molded by sound doctrine that they can turn around and teach the younger women. Paul here is describing a trickle-down effect from the older to the younger. The older woman has had rich experiences as a mother and wife. But now the practical lessons she has learned are tempered and shaped by the power of biblical truth, not simply by human trial and error.

"Encourage" doesn't fully grasp the idea here. The Greek word is used only here in the New Testament and means "to make sane, to restore to one's senses, to discipline."[11]

Aged women should be an example to younger women in the teaching and practice of all that is pure and good. It is impossible to exaggerate the value of the influence of one good woman.[12]

The Greek words behind "younger women" have the idea of fresh dough or anything that is fresh or youthful. "'Younger' is a positive adjective literally meaning 'new' or 'fresh' and probably suggests a reference to the newly married."[13] Younger men also come into this new relationship with attitudes and sins fostered by the culture. Both sexes will struggle to make a binding relation. It will not be easy, and Paul knows this. But more than likely before their conversion, the young couple had strained relations that were torn and buffeted by the world. But by now submitting themselves to God's ways, there is hope for a meaningful and satisfying marriage, as the Lord intended.

Godliness for the Next Generation

Sound doctrine strengthens old men in the faith (Titus 2:1–2).

Sound doctrine strengthens older women in the faith (Titus 2:3).

Older women then are to encourage younger women in order to strengthen the home (Titus 2:4–5).

Young men are to learn how to be "sensible" in the faith (Titus 2:6).

Young men are to learn how to be subject to their elders (1 Pet. 5:5).

Elders are to pass down the teaching of the Word to faithful men (2 Tim. 2:2).

Paul gets specific in where he wants this instruction to go ("to love their husbands"). He desires that younger women are "brought to their senses" in learning how to get along with their husbands. Interestingly, he does not use *agapē*. It may be that the apostle knows that many marriages start with burning love but must be sustained by another form of affection and caring. The apostle uses the noun *philandrous*, a compound from *philos* ("affection, befriend, caring"), and *anēr* ("man" or "husband"). It is used only here in the New Testament. Since "to be" is present tense, Paul is saying that the young women are to be learning how to care for their husbands. This is an ongoing process and experience. "Love is the first and foremost basis of marriage, not so much the love of emotion and romance, still less of criticism, but rather of sacrifice and service. The young wives are to be "trained" in this, which implies that it can be brought under their control."[14]

Much of what was said about "to love their husbands" can be said about "to love their children." This phrase also is governed by the present tense of "to be", it is one word in the Greek (*philoteknous*) and is a compound word found nowhere else used in the New Testament. *Teknos* is the Greek word for child, and by using *philos*, Paul seems to be stressing cultivating how to understand and properly care for one's offspring. He could certainly be going beyond what is natural and be referring to developing qualities that go farther than what is normal. "It may seem strange for older women to be called upon to teach younger women to love their husbands and children. But this is put into perspective when we realize that Christians are constantly being taught in the New Testament to love, whether it be God or fellow Christians and neighbors (here the closest neighbor)."[15] With a bit of humor, A. T. Robertson remarks, "This exhortation is still needed when some married women prefer poodle-dogs to children."[16]

Paul continues writing (into v. 5) about what he wants to happen in the lives of younger married women. The list continues, and it is meant to be extremely practical. The apostle wants them to be "sensible." Being sensible or discreet signifies "an ability to govern all our affections and passions. Discretion is but one piece of the fruit."[17] Then he adds "pure" (*hagnos*), which is related to the word *hagios* ("holy"). The apostle uses *hagnos* five times in his epistles. He writes of *pure* things (Phil. 4:8) and keeping oneself *pure* (1 Tim. 5:22). John writes of the purifying effect of seeing Christ when He comes. "We know that, when He appears, we shall be like Him, because we shall see Him just as He is. And everyone who has this hope fixed on Him purifies himself, just as He is pure" (1 John 3:2–3).

"Workers at home" in Greek is simply the one word *oikourgous*, which is a compound noun from *oikos* ("house") and *ergon* ("work, task"). The woman is to expend her energy at home, maintaining a nest and a safe haven for both her husband and children. This is culturally not correct in modern times. Nevertheless, most husbands want to see their home and children protected and taken care of by the loving nurturing that only their wife can give. "Mothers who work at home usually find it a more absorbing pleasure than 'going about from house to house' (1 Tim. v.13)."[18] "Their attention, moreover, must be concentrated on their own families. Hence, not only must they be chaste but also workers at home (see on 1 Tim. 2:10 and especially on 1 Tim. 5:13). The two virtues quite obviously are related. Now, while performing their tasks in the family, these young women must take care that the constant strain of domestic duties does not make them irritable or cruel."[19]

"Kind" is actually the Greek word *agathas*, which is better translated "good." Paul does not dwell on the full implication of this word in the context. The range of what is considered as good is broad, and, as all the virtues he has enumerated, it comes from the sound teaching of doctrine (v. 1). With heavy cares at home, it may be difficult for young women to show forth patience. Yet their "goodness (or kindness) should shine through."[20]

The verb *hupotassō* ("being subject to their own husbands") is a compound from *hupo* ("under") and *tassō* ("to attach") and is a present middle participle. It may read, "being continually submitting themselves" to their own husbands or "placing themselves under the authority" of their own husbands. Wuest translates the word as "obedient" as used "in a military connection of a general arranging soldiers under him in subjection to himself."[21]

"Dishonored" is the stronger word *blasphēmeō* ("blasphemed"). It can also be translated "to be slandered, accused wrongfully." What the believer does can cause a reviling or disparagement of the Word of God. Though the Scriptures are "not at fault," the enemies of the Lord would love to cast blame at biblical

Christianity itself. "So she's a Christian," they would love to spit out in a mocking voice. Carried away by their newfound faith, some young wives may have thought homemaking was no longer important. "Such failure in everyday tasks would, of course, be bitterly charged on the religion of Christ, and the gospel would run the danger of being evil-spoken of, even in other than purely pagan circles."[22] If the home is neglected, practical Christian doctrine is spoiled and wasted. Truth must find its way into all aspects of our lives.

It is possible that "in all things" in verse 7 goes with this one clause here in verse 6, but more than likely it does not. It has been asked, "Why does Paul have only this one line of command to give to young men"? At first glance, the answer seems to be difficult to find. One suggestion is that in New Testament times, young men were bound by a cultural code to listen to and obey, and they were not to go beyond the boundaries set for them by the elders of either the church or the village. For them to live and act sensibly covers a multitude of instructions already given by Paul. In other words, they would be expected to follow the examples of the older men as given in verse 2. The Greek word for "sensible" is used in various forms by the apostle extensively in the Pastoral Letters (1 Tim. 2:9, 15; 3:2; 2 Tim. 1:7; Titus 1:8; 2:2, 4–6; 2:12).

Since these men are young, they are still pliable, they are not yet hardened spiritually and morally. They are ready to listen and follow instructions. These young men should have well-governed minds and be steady in their behavior. They are at the age when they should discover personal self-control and learn to avoid temptations. Peter advises young men, "Be subject to your elders; and all of you, clothe yourselves with humility toward one another, for God is opposed to the proud, but gives grace to the humble" (1 Pet. 5:5).

Verse 7 begins, "in all things." What is the apostle referring to? It seems as if he is summarizing how Titus is to behave before the new believers on Crete. Paul's lists of qualities in the verses above could be extended with additional spiritual examples of how he wants the people to live. But more important, what he seems to be saying here is that Titus can show the people how they are to walk before the Lord and before each other. A living example is worth a thousand words. "Doctrine will otherwise carry little authority, if its power and majesty do not shine in the life of the bishop [such as with Titus], as in a mirror. [Paul] wishes, therefore, that the teacher may be a pattern, which his scholars may copy."[23]

Paul tells Titus to "show yourself to be an example." "Titus was to confront them not only with spiritual words but with a spiritual life that corresponded to those words. Even the most forceful and compelling counsel will fall on deaf ears if the one who gives it fails to live by it."[24]

Whatever circumstances may manifest themselves, doctrine must never be compromised ("with purity in doctrine"). Twisting the truth (cf. 2 Pet. 3:16) is an affront to God. Often doctrine in the Pastorals refers to the apostolic Christian teaching as an entire body of spiritual information (1 Tim. 1:10; 4:6, 16; 6:1, 3; 2 Tim. 3:10; 4:3). It is the doctrine that is in accordance with true religion, as Paul speaks of the new revelation (1 Tim. 6:3) and contrasts the false teaching put forth by demonic powers (1 Tim. 4:1). Doctrine is to be sound (1 Tim. 1:10) and good (4:6). "The image of the storm or wind in Eph 4:14 (cf. also Jude 1:12f.; Heb 13:9) is intended to portray the unreliability of human teaching in contrast to the truth of faith (v. 15)."[25]

Too, Titus is to be an example of dignity. This word pictures someone who is worthy of respect or who carries himself with stateliness or composure.[26] In the Pastorals it refers to respectful behavior. An overseer is to see to it that his children have respectful behavior (1 Tim. 3:4), and the wives of deacons are to present themselves in the same manner (v. 11). The same is expected of elderly men (Titus 2:2) and of the whole Christian community (1 Tim. 2:2). Here in verse 7 the word is probably applied directly to how Titus is to teach doctrine. It has to do with the manner of his instruction. He is "to combine purity of motive, soundness of matter and seriousness of manner" in his delivery.[27] His teaching of truth to these new congregations is not to be taken lightly.

With verse 8, Calvin believes the apostle has just shifted his emphasis to how Titus will relate to the average person in ordinary life and familiar conversation. On a daily basis, Titus still is to carry a certain representation of his position in Christ. He is to represent the Master in ordinary conversation during the normal transactions of life.

The word "speech" is in the singular; the implication is that Paul's presentation is a whole, a unit of expression. It is not simply words but one's entire deportment that others hear, and see. Others, such as Patrick Fairbairn, disagree and believe that Paul is still talking about how Titus is to present himself as he teaches.[28] "Sound" is used figuratively, and as used by the apostle before, implies that the speaking (or teaching) is to healthy. (See 1 Tim. 1:10; 2 Tim. 4:3; Titus 1:9; 2:1)

Paul adds that the speech is to be "beyond reproach," an expression that could be translated "not according to that which is known." Titus should so speak that no one could find anything to blame him for. He must therefore choose his words carefully and watch the manner of what he says and what he does.

In his public ministry of teaching Titus must show an integrity, seriousness, and soundness of speech that cannot be condemned. Paul was always concerned lest those who oppose be provided ammunition for their attacks.[29]

Paul uses "opponent" in the sense of the one who is hostile, contrary, and coming against the believer and what he is teaching. The world hates the gospel and detests also those who put forth spiritual truth. The lost are always finding fault and seeking cause to show the weaknesses of Christianity. The minister of the Word must be sure of not only his doctrine but his style and even the verbal "phrases" he uses in speech.

As a result, they will have to rethink their opinions regarding Christianity ("be put to shame"). The opponent will be "either feeling personally ashamed of his own conduct or made to look foolish because he is shown to have no case."[30]

Notice that Paul does not say the evil speaking would be against Titus but against *us*. "The antagonism is directed not against Titus as an individual but against him as a disciple of Christ; hence, really against Christ himself and all his messengers."[31] "Concerning teachers of the Scriptures, their purity and sincerity of motive and aim must be apparent in their teaching; and their speech in public and private must be pervaded by a dignified seriousness, that the adversary of the truth may be put to confusion by the power of the word and the evident sincerity and enthusiasm of the preacher."[32]

That Paul dedicates two verses (vv. 9, 10) to the subject of bondslaves may indicate that a spirit of rebellion had arisen among some of the Christian slaves. They may have reasoned that, since Christ was their new Master, they owed no loyalty to another. These bondslaves were probably household servants and not slave captives from other nations who lived a miserable existence. Whichever, as new believers in Christ, they had a responsibility not to resist and to serve honorably in the position they found themselves.

Though the apostle does not deal with the issue of a rebellious spirit in his discussion of slaves in Ephesians 6:5–8, he writes on the issues of attitude and heart service rather than simply giving the master eyeservice (v. 6a). They need to consider themselves "as slaves of Christ, doing the will of God from the heart (v. 6b). Servants are "to be satisfied and contented with such things as they have, and in their state and condition as servants, and cheerfully abide in the calling wherein they are called."[33]

"To be subject" is the same as in verse 5. This is one of Paul's most important words. He uses it to remind believers that they are subject to government authorities (Rom. 13:1), to those laboring for the gospel (1 Cor. 16:16), to one another (Eph. 5:21), and to Christ (v. 24). Wives are to be subject to husbands in the domestic order (v. 22). Peter also addresses the theme of subjection and says believers are to subject or submit to every human ordinance (1

Pet. 2:13); servants are to submit to masters (v. 18); the younger are to submit to the elder (5:5); and Christians are to submit to one another (5:5). He adds that angels, authorities, and powers are also made subject to Christ (3:22).

In 1 Timothy, Paul distinguishes between those slaves who had Christian masters and those who did not (1 Tim. 6:1–2). Here he does not make that distinction ("to their own masters in everything"). Paul balances the issues of human respect with the issues of obedience. Care, honor, and reputation play a key role in all he says on the issue.

Leviticus 25 gives sound rules for the treatment of slaves. If he is a countryman who has had to sell himself into slavery to survive economically, he is to be treated with respect as a stranger or traveler, with kindness. He is not to be subjected to a common "slave's service" (v. 39). He is to be treated simply as a hired hand (v. 40) and released in the year of Jubilee if it comes while he is in the service of the Jewish master (v. 41). The overall general rule is that a fellow Israelite must not be sold as slaves (v. 42), and, "You shall not rule over him with severity, but are to revere your God" (v. 43). Though Moses' arguments in the same chapter are not the same for the treatment of slaves taken from "pagan nations," he in no way advocates cruelty to them because they were not Israelites. In fact a good case could be made from the context that they were to be treated with equal consideration and kindness.

After addressing the issue of slaves and their conduct, Paul flips the coin over and writes equally important guidelines for those who are masters and have slaves (Eph. 6:9; Col. 4:1). He reminds them that they have a Master in heaven who shows no partiality. They are to render good to those in their keeping and give up threatening words. "Grant your slaves justice and fairness" (Col. 4:1). In two little often forgotten verses in Philemon, the apostle lays the groundwork for the end of slavery, at least within the Christian community. He writes to the slaveholder Philemon about his runaway slave Onesimus who came to Christ through Paul's witness. The apostle urges Philemon to take Onesimus back without penalty. He asks him to receive him "no longer as a slave, but more than a slave, a beloved brother, especially to me, but how much more to you, both in the flesh and in the Lord. If then you regard me a partner [in the faith], accept him as you would me" (vv. 16–17).

"Masters" here is the Greek word *despotēs* from which we get the English word "despot." The word "denotes that as owners they had complete authority over their slaves."[34]

Slaves are always to be pleasant ("well-pleasing"). The word comes from a Greek verb that may be translated "to accommodate, be agreeable, to satisfy." The focus is on the conduct. They are to give satisfaction to their masters with goodwill while rendering service.[35] They are to "please them well in all things."[36]

Christian slaves are not to talk back ("not argumentative"). The apostle is writing that Christian slaves are not to be characterized as those who go about challenging and defying their masters. They are not to be contradicting.[37] Paul seems to be concerned about Christian slaves' witness to the non-Christian world. They will be viewed as new spiritual creatures, whose circumstances may be the same but whose way of relating has drastically been altered. Or, they may reflect the same old bitter attitude, though claiming to be followers of Christ. Though difficult, the apostle wants slaves, who may be physically mistreated, to show new hearts and minds to their owners. "So either we give no evidence of salvation, in which case the gospel-jewel is tarnished, or we give good evidence of salvation by living a manifestly saved life, in which case the gospel-jewel shines with extra luster. Our lives can bring either adornment or discredit to the gospel."[38]

Paul continues his instructions to slaves into verse 10. As slaves, they must see themselves in a better light since they now have a higher spiritual calling in Christ. In this sense, the apostle is lifting them above the way they see their station in life. They have a calling to serve the one true God and His Son, the Lord Jesus Christ. "Even slaves should not think their example a matter of indifference: their religion exalts and beautifies them."[39] People do not ennoble Christianity, but Christianity ennobles them.

The verb "pilfering" means to "set apart, separate," but in the bad sense "to embezzle" or covertly misuse for oneself.[40] In the Greek it is written in what is called the middle voice and thus may be translated "stop stealing [from your master] for your own use." Household slaves in New Testament times were of business managers who had the opportunity to take money, food, jewelry, or other valuables they were entrusted with. "When Christians do such things, their actions not only are unethical and damage their employer financially but also are unspiritual and do damage to the Lord's name and to their testimony."[41]

The "but" brings out the contrast in how the slave is to act now as a believer, in opposition to how he may have behaved. This "good faithfulness" must extend to all areas of the slave's living and serving. "Faith" (or "fidelity") is here not to be taken in the active sense as a confidence that the slaves place in their masters, but in the passive sense as a confidence that their masters may have in the slaves. Christian slaves are always to show themselves worthy of being fully trusted by their masters in everything that serves their masters' interests.[42]

The result is "that they may adorn the doctrine of God our Savior in every respect." "Adorn" here means to "put in order" or "decorate." It may also imply "to make attractive" or "do credit to."[43] The apostle is expressing what he wants to see come out of the way these slaves are relating as Christians to their masters. "God deigns to receive an 'ornament' from slaves, whose condition was so low and mean that they were wont to be scarcely accounted men."[44]

"The doctrine of God our Savior" is an unusual expression in the New Testament epistles. In using it, Paul seems to be placing all Christian truth under this entire phrase. He is not simply writing about the teaching in regard to God, but also about salvation. "He is our Savior!" Note also the similarity of what the apostle says here with 1:3, where he says he was entrusted according to the commandment "of God our Savior." "God our Savior" is not a Trinitarian formula. See 1 Timothy 1:1 where Paul uses the same expression but separates it from "and of Christ Jesus." "Not Christ, but the Father is meant: in that place (1 Timothy 1:1) the distinction is clearly made."[45] In a very real sense, however, the Father is our Savior as well as the Lord Jesus. Many verses attest to this (1 Tim. 2:3; 4:10; Titus 1:3; 2:13; 3:4; 2 Pet. 1:1; Jude 1:25). The Father planned our salvation, and Christ was obedient unto death to secure its blessings for us (Phil. 2:8). "The Father has sent the Son to be the Savior of the world" (1 John 4:14).

The slave then is to be an ornament "in all things, as remembering that it is the doctrine of God our great Preserver, and of Jesus Christ our blessed Savior."[46] Though Paul's statement does not have a Trinitarian concept in view, Gill still writes, "Christ is our alone Savior, and he is truly and properly God, and so fit and able to be a Savior; and the Gospel is his doctrine, not only what he himself preached, when on earth, but it is a doctrine concerning him; concerning his Deity, and the dignity of his Person, and concerning his office as Mediator, and the great salvation [comes] by him."[47]

Living Sound Doctrine (2:11–15)

The "for" of verse 11 is indicating a conclusion and a summary. It "connects vv. 11–14 with what has been brought before us already in this chapter; all the pillars of exhortation in vv. 2–10 are based upon these concluding verses."[48] All the moral injunctions Paul has so far discussed come from the fact that God has revealed His matchless grace in the salvation provided by the Lord Jesus. Such a giving of favor is found in no other religion on earth. It is certainly a fact not experienced in Greek or Roman theology. "This summary of 'the teaching' presents the salvation purchased and won for all men, but as one that changes their whole lives from ungodliness to good works. . . . 'For' reaches back through the whole chapter."[49] This summary speaks not only to slaves, but also to all levels and classes of Christians. This grace admonishes all to practice good works.

Living What We Believe

Keep the faith and have a good conscience (1 Tim. 1:19).

Men: Pray, living holy live, without wrath and dissension (1 Tim. 2:8).

Women: Practice good works and live godly (1 Tim. 2:10).

Elders: Be above reproach (1 Tim. 3:2).

Deacons: Be men of dignity (1 Tim. 3:8).

Have hope in the living God (1 Tim. 4:10).

Honor older men, women, and widows (1 Tim. 5:1–16).

Slaves, give honor to your masters (1 Tim. 6:1–2).

Retain the standard of sound words (2 Tim. 1:13).

Do not be argumentative (2 Tim. 2:14).

Follow the example of Paul in living (2 Tim. 3:10).

Endure hardships (2 Tim. 4:5).

Sound doctrine should change lives (Titus 2).

Believers are to be subject to rulers and authorities (Titus 3:1).

Shun foolish controversies (Titus 3:9).

Be ready to forgive and accept a brother back into the fold (Philem. 1:16–17).

The "grace of God" brings about the salvation through Jesus. But the apostle may also be pointing out that grace equally promotes a new way of living. "The grace of God is His unmerited favor toward men expressing itself in active love."[50] "There is the necessity for right conduct [in] the all-embracing scope of the saving grace of God, which has visibly appeared as a call to repentance, a help to amendment of life, and a stimulus to hope. Christ's gift of Himself constrains us to give ourselves wholly to Him."[51]

"Appeared" is *epiphainō*, from *epi* ("over") and *phainō* ("to shine, appear"). From this word comes the English word *epiphany*. The meaning is "to shine over, to appear over." It is in the past tense; this grace has already been given and has arrived. "The illumination of God's gracious work is complete." "Become visible, to become clearly known."[52] "It means that the plan of salvation has been revealed to all classes of men; that is, that it is *announced* or *revealed* to all the race that they may be saved."[53]

"Salvation" is an adjective modifying and qualifying "grace." Verse 11 may read "Saving grace has appeared to all men." The question is raised, "Is this salvation being offered to all people or simply all classes of people?" Or, "Is salvation provided for all classes of people and applied to only the few who are elect?" Good expositors have wrestled over this passage for generations without completely reconciling the meaning. One's theology comes into play here and causes the reader to fall on one side or the other. Some argue that since Paul focuses on different age groups and the different sexes in the previous verses, and then focuses on slaves, he is addressing the fact that Christ died for all kinds of people. If this is so, the apostle is not making a universal statement but is pressing his point concerning types of people.

The doctrines of predestination and election are absolute truths in Scripture. There is nothing innate in anyone that commends that person to God, not even foreseen faith, as some attempt to argue. The depravity of the human race is absolute. No one can come to God unless that man or woman is awakened by the work of the Holy Spirit. It therefore seems to be no violation of these teachings if the provision of salvation is sufficient for all but applied only to the elect. There is no violation of these points if Paul argues for the provision of salvation for all. But the fact that salvation is provided for all simply adds to the culpability of people. They cannot argue with God, "But I was not of the elect! There was no way I could be saved since I was not chosen!" Instead, the lost will stand before God and all their thoughts will be revealed. "Though not chosen, I did not want You. My heart was hardened, and I only wished to run from You."

Some object and argue for a limited atonement, one that is applied only to the elect and is in no way available for the nonelect. Able scholars present both sides, and some even argue that the issue is not clearly stated in this verse: "Whichever interpretation be adopted, the sense here will not be essentially varied."[54] God "'is God our Savior, who will have all men to be saved' (1 Tim. 2:3–4). Sadly not all men will be saved, 'for all men have not faith' (2 Thess. 3:2)," and, "God's grace has not in fact yet appeared to all men, but it is laden with salvation for all."[55] Paul "does not mean individual men, but rather describes individual classes, or various ranks of life."[56] "In a word, the salvation-bringing grace of God is without respect of persons; it is unfolded to men indiscriminately, or to sinners of every name."[57] "Aged men, aged women, young women, young(er) men, and even slaves . . . , *for* the grace of God has appeared bringing salvation to men of *all* these various groups or classes."[58] "This is to be understood of all sorts of men, of every nation, of every age and sex, of every state, and condition, high and low, rich and poor, bond and free, masters and servants; which sense well agrees with the context."[59] "Paul is prompted to affirm the universal availability of salvation through Christ."[60]

Some teach the doctrine of double predestination. God elected to salvation, they say, but He also predestined to damnation. The Scriptures do not teach this. In fact, Romans 9:22–23 makes it clear that God waits patiently for the "vessels of wrath prepared for destruction," but they will not come to Him. But He has made "known the riches of His glory upon vessels of mercy, which He *prepared beforehand for glory*" (italics mine). Salvation and judgment of course are inscrutable and difficult doctrines and are beyond our comprehension.

However, the Bible clearly states that God chose His own before the foundation of the world (Eph. 1:4). Yet Scripture makes equally clear that those who do not believe are responsible and guilty for their rejection of Christ (cf. John 3:17–20). Paul and Peter also concur that God "desires all men to be saved and to come to the knowledge of the truth" (1 Tim. 2:4), and that the Lord is patient, "not wishing for any to perish but for all to come to repentance" (2 Pet. 3:9b). As taught by Calvin and the Reformers, depravity, predestination, and election are scripturally verifiable. Concerning the atonement, or the application of salvation grace, it is not that people are actively excluded by God,[61] as John makes clear in his second letter: Jesus "is the propitiation for our sins; and not for ours only, but also for those of the whole world" (1 John 2:2). Nevertheless, the other side would argue that this propitiation is sufficient to save the whole world but applied only to believers.

"Instructing" (v. 12) is the word from which we get *pedagogy* and *pedagogue*. The word is also related to the Greek noun *paidion*, meaning small child. The overall idea carries the connotation of "teaching like that done with a small child." The noun *paideia* can also mean "reprimand, discipline," with the thought of teaching that reins in a wayward person or brings about inner control of a rebellious offspring. God disciplines us as sons (Prov. 3:11), and that produces the "peaceful fruit of righteousness" (Heb. 12:11). "As in [the Old Testament] wisdom literature, sonship and discipline are 'viewed as a divinely ordained training process.'"[62] With the present participle, Paul is implying that this is an ongoing happening that causes us to reach a stage of denying ungodliness. This teaching personifies "grace" as guiding believers in the things that come from sound doctrine (v. 1). "It comprehends the entire training process—teaching, encouragement, correction, discipline."[63] "Instructing" qualifies "grace" "and further indicates the purpose accomplished by the appearance of [that] grace."[64]

"To deny" sounds rather weak, limited, and not very assertive. However, the Greek word translated "deny" is a strong word meaning "to refuse, to renounce." In Classical Greek it carries the thought of "to disown, to decline"[65]

"Ungodliness" describes all forms of atheism and even false religion that is dead. It refers to "living without regard to any Divine Being, or according to our own erroneous and superstitious conceits and opinions of him."[66] It must be remembered that believers in Christ may live like atheists and even in their actions look like the lost. Paul said this of the Corinthians when he wrote, "You are still fleshly. For since there is jealousy and strife among you, are you not fleshly, and are you not walking *like mere men?*" (1 Cor. 3:3, italics mine). The apostle warned the Ephesians, "Do not participate in the unfruitful deeds of darkness, . . . for it is disgraceful even to speak of the things which are done . . . in secret" (Eph. 5:11–12).

"Worldly desires" actually means lusts spawned by the world or the popular culture. "'Worldly' means that the desires are connected only with life in this cosmos and seek their satisfaction in nothing higher."[67] By using the plural, Paul indicates that these may be many and varied temptations that the believer in the Lord may fall for and embrace. *Desires* conjures up the idea of the lowest form of tugs and temptations that draw people into dark, forbidden, and heinous activities. These lusts trap the body and soul and are difficult to overcome. The apostle John writes, "For all that is in the world, the lust of the flesh and the lust of the eyes and the boastful pride of life, is not from the Father, but is from the world" (1 John 2:16). Here in the Pastoral Epistles Paul continues his discourse on lust and speaks of "foolish and harmful desires" (1 Tim. 6:9) and "youthful lusts" (2 Tim. 2:22), which believers are to deny and flee from. Only by the gospel and by the grace it dispenses can a child of God have victory. "Grace disciplines us to 'renounce' our old life and to live a new one, to turn from ungodliness to godliness, from self-centeredness to self-control, from the world's devious ways to fair dealing with each other."[68]

The gospel insists upon the inseparable connection between creed and character, doctrine and life. It is a discipline, enforcing self-restraint in a world where sin is the normal state of things, and enabling us to live soberly, righteously, and godly, as a constant reproof to the world's sin, and an example and stimulus to all who are striving to conquer the world spirit.[69]

"To live" is better translated "that we might, ought live . . ." "Believers should be carrying out their physical existence in this manner . . ." Grace must be living and active in the experience of the child of God who faces terrible temptations.[70] The positive side to all this is that we should "live sober-mindedly and righteously and godly in the present eon."[71] "Sensibly" can be translated "soberly, self-controlled, with reasonableness, or self-discipline."[72] The word and its various forms is used sixteen times in the Pastorals. It is one of Paul's favorite concepts. In this verse, such self-control and reasonableness "do not mean mere accommodation to one's civic environment, but are coupled rather with anticipation of the parousia."[73] The *parousia* ("the coming") can refer in context to the rapture of the church or the second coming of the Lord to reign in the Davidic millennial kingdom. Here the verse that follows is referring to the Rapture.

"Righteously" in a popular sense may mean "to live right." But there is more involved in the word in the New Testament. "Righteousness" theologically refers to being "legally acquitted." Christ's substitutionary sacrifice effects this work, and the redeemed are "declared righteous." This means to be more than simply without sin. Imputed or reckoned to us is the very righteousness of the Son of God! Believers fare "justified (made righteous) by faith apart from works of the Law" (Rom. 3:28). And, "to the one who does not work, but believes in Him who justifies the ungodly, his faith is reckoned as righteousness" (4:5). Peter writes that Jesus "died for sins once for all, the just for the unjust, in order that He might bring us to God" (1 Pet. 3:18a).

In 2:12 Paul is referring to living righteously, living out the new position believers have in Christ. Christians are to live justly as those who have been declared positionally justified through faith in Christ. "God's grace requires of us a life of truth and strict justice in all our dealings with our fellow men."[74]

"Godly" is the opposite of ungodliness mentioned here in the same verse (see above). From the positive perspective, living *godly* means to live with a devotion for the Lord, to have true piety, reverence, and respect for Him alone who "is the proper Object of worship."[75] Paul wants the believers to have godliness as a genuine attitude of the heart and mind toward God. Sometimes Christians treat God with a certain lightness and familiarity that fails to show proper respect. This is not to say that the child of God should move in the other direction that promotes a stiff formalism. The Lord is after our hearts. He desires communication and fellowship with His own. But He still should be given a proper worship that is not false or rote. "Godly" refers to "a godly manner, according to the word of God, and agreeably to the will of God: and in all godly exercises, both public and private, and to the glory of God."[76]

"In the present age" literally reads, "in the present course of things."[77] The apostle is speaking of his times, his generation, and his era. Each generation of Christians must live godly in the period of history in which God has placed them. The evils of today may be a little different than the past, but the child of God must walk according to the Word of God and the injunctions set forth in it. Some generations are destined to suffer greatly. Others face waves of error and false doctrine. But these words of Paul remain firm and are as applicable to us today as when the apostle wrote them. "The Lord has appointed the present life for the trial of our faith."[78] And "these are the duties which we owe in the present life."[79]

Verse 13 is clearly a Rapture verse. Paul wants us to be looking for His coming in glory. Since the rapture of the church is the next event on the divine timetable, this is more than likely the meaning.

The doctrine of the rapture of the church is not necessarily proven by any one passage of Scripture. It is built on the evidence gleaned from many references. For example, Paul commended the Thessalonians because they were both serving the "living and true God" (1 Thess. 1:9b) and waiting "for His Son from heaven" (v. 10a). He adds that Jesus' coming "delivers us from the wrath to come" (v. 10b), which would of course be the Great Tribulation. In 1 Thessalonians Paul writes of the "we" and "us" who may be around "until the coming of the Lord" (4:15). The Lord Himself will descend from heaven with a shout (v. 16), "and the dead in Christ shall rise first. Then we who are alive and remain shall be caught up together with them in the clouds to meet the Lord in the air" (vv. 16b–17). He adds, "For God has not destined us for wrath, but for obtaining salvation through our Lord Jesus Christ" (5:9).

"Looking" (v. 13) has the sense of expecting or waiting with great anticipation. The New Testament usage is "to take up, receive, welcome, wait for, expect."[80] Also, "to receive favorably, to admit to, receive hospitably."[81] Here with the present tense the word means "an ongoing welcoming and expectation." "Primarily," it can mean "to receive [something] to one's self."[82] This "looking for" then is "an ongoing process of greatly anticipating and welcoming to one's self the appearing" of the Lord.

The words "instructing" in verse 12 and "looking" here work together and may read, along with verse 11, "The grace of God has appeared . . . *instructing us* [that we might live sensibly] . . . [as we are] *looking for* the blessed hope." This "describes the glad expectancy which is the ruling and prevailing thought in the lives of men looking for their Lord's return."[83]

"Blessed hope" is better translated the "joyous anticipation." There is no question about this anticipation. It *is* going to come about, and it produces within the believer a great joyousness that looks forward to ultimate redemption. "Those now being trained by God's grace eagerly anticipate the eschatological future. Having renounced their sinful past, they live disciplined lives in the present and look eagerly to the future (cf. 1 Thess 1:9, 10)." This "waiting for" in verse 10 shows that they are looking for this blessed hope, the personal return of Jesus, and that this waiting is the proper attitude of believers, "ever ready to welcome the returning Lord."[84]

"Appearing," which is often translated "brightness," is the same word as "appeared" in verse 11. "Glory" is the Greek word *doxa* and can mean "reputation, honor, radiance, even reputation."[85] Some versions render the passage "glorious appearing," but the more literal "appearing of the glory" is better and points to Christ's glorification now in heaven. "His glory shall appear!" The article "the" is not in the Greek text, but the Greek actually places "the blessed hope and the appearing of the glory" under one article. Thus, it should read, "the blessed hope, even the appearing of the glory" or "the joyous anticipation, that is, the glorious appearance!" This implies that the reference is to one event viewed from two aspects. "For believers, it is indeed the blessed hope and the longed-for consummation of that hope."[86] The appearing or epiphany of the glory of Jesus Christ, shall at last arrive. Then he who in his own person is 'our God and Savior' . . . will come in all his glory, . . . which shall transcend all that we are able to imagine.[87]

"Our great God and Savior, Jesus Christ" is a remarkable phrase in Paul's letter. It strongly supports the fact that Christ is *very* God, and it is an outstanding and important testimony to the doctrine of the Trinity. This passage "furnishes an important proof of the divinity of Christ."[88]

Kenneth Wuest argues that the god and savior of the Roman empire was the emperor himself, who was seen as the savior of the world and the state. He also was worshiped as the god in the state religion. The Christian's God and Savior is Jesus Christ.[89] Paul was making a protest against emperor worship.

The "for" in the phrase "gave Himself for us" (v. 14) carries the thought of "on behalf of, in place of, for the sake of, instead of." Jesus gave Himself on the cross and took our place under the wrath of God. The apostle has in mind the great substitionary atonement passage, Isaiah 53, in which the prophet writes of the coming death of the Messiah: "He was pierced through for *our* transgressions, He was crushed for *our* iniquities" (v. 5, italics added).

Paul repeats this idea of substitution often: Christ "who gave Himself for our sins" (Gal. 1:4); "The Son of God who loved me, and delivered Himself up for me" (Gal. 2:20b); "Christ also loved the church and gave Himself up for her" (Eph. 5:25); and, Christ "gave Himself as a ransom for all" (1 Tim. 2:6).

"Redeem" is the word that refers to giving a ransom, especially for the release of prisoners of war, slaves, and debtors. It is the "price of release" for the liberation of a prisoner. Generally, the release is determined by law or the "right of the sovereign."[90] Jesus actually gave Himself as the ransom price. He was willing to pay the debt of our sins before the sovereign God. Christ made it clear to His disciples that "the Son of Man did not come to be served, but to serve, and to give His life a *ransom* for many" (Matt. 20:28; Mark 10:45, italics added).

Jesus would not only redeem His own "from every lawless deed," but He would "purify" this redeemed people. "Purify" is used figuratively by the apostle (2 Cor. 7:1; Eph. 5:26; also Heb. 9:14) of moral and religious cleansing "and therefore means 'cleanse or purify' from sin."[91] "Redeem" has to do with the removal of the Christians from the power or control of sin.

Verse 14 continues by stating that Christ died to "purify for Himself a people for His own possession." "Possession," a single word in the Greek and used only here in the New Testament, carries the force of "chosen, elect,"[92] or "a selected people."[93] "A people over and above, occupying a position separate and peculiar, like one's. . . . special treasure."[94] The redeemed then are Christ's special property, chosen and elect, and belong to Him.

"To be zealous" means to have zest, show a passionate commitment, in this case, for good works. Out of a gratitude for Christ, living out principles of truth and love, "and with a zeal for the glory of God, and the honor of his Gospel," believers need to strive to serve the Lord with their whole lives and with all their abilities.[95] "Christ purifies his people with this very purpose in mind, namely, that it shall be a people for his own possession 'with a zest for noble deeds,' deeds which proceed from faith, are done according to God's law and unto his glory (cf. I Peter 3:13)."[96]

R. C. H. Lenski summarizes the verse: "Jesus 'ransomed us from all lawlessness,' i.e., paid the price to buy us free and take us away from all lawless living (ungodliness and worldly lusts, v. 12) 'and cleanse us for himself as a people select, zealous for all excellent works.'"[97]

"These things" refers to all the commands Paul has given in the verses above. He wants to make sure they are repeated over and over, with full reasoning power and conviction. The Church is a body of Christians who have different problems and who do not mature at the same pace. As well, all believers do not face the same temptations or issues. Exhortation is a continuing process by the elder leadership.

"Speak" is the most common word for simply "talking" or "telling." Paul wants this to be an ongoing process that continually reminds the saints of what he has cautioned about. It might be translated "keep on telling."

"Exhort" is the common word *parakaleō*, which should probably be translated "counsel." It is a favored word used by the apostle, and in its noun and verb forms, it is used nine times in the Pastorals (1 Tim. 1:3; 2:1; 4:13; 5:1; 6:2; 2 Tim. 4:2; Titus 1:9; 2:6, 15) and sixty-four times in Paul's other letters.

"Reprove" is the strongest and most forceful of these three commands. It is often translated, "to rebuke, correct, censure, punish, convict." "It designates fatherly or divine correction and [even] punishment for the purpose of improvement."[98] (See 1 Tim. 5:20; 2 Tim. 4:2; Titus 1:13). Many pastors are reticent to correct those in the assembly who are wayward. They are fearful of the sheep. They argue that if they speak out, the immature sheep will seek other pastures. But their job is to oversee what is happening with the flock. The elders must be prepared to stand up and reprove those who need it no matter what the consequences. This does not mean that they should embarrass someone who is morally or spiritually slipping. This can first be done in private. But more often it must be done!

"Authority" is a strong word that means "to command, give orders, direction." It is used of the orders given by authority from one in high rank. It is the word used when Christ forcibly and powerfully gave commands to the demons (Mark 1:27). It is used to speak of Paul's apostolic authority (2 Cor. 8:8). That same force is used here for the authority given Titus. "Speak with unhesitating confidence in the truth!" "The minister is an ambassador of the great King he represents. The truth inspires him with power."[99] "Do these things 'in the most authoritative manner possible.'"[100]

"Disregard" is a compound verb from *peri* ("around, beyond") and *phro-neō* ("to think, consider"). "Let no one *think around* you," or "Let no one *think beyond* you," in the sense of writing off your abilities, thoughts, or authority. "Let no one think around you (and so despise you). . . . [it] implies the possibility of one making mental circles around one and so 'out-thinking' him."[101] Those who have spent any time at all in the ministry know that there are some in the congregation who are always playing games. They plan and plot against the pastor. They are continually being contentious and bringing on strife. "There is jealousy and strife among you, are you not fleshly, and are you not walking like mere men?" (1 Cor. 3:3b). "Speak with decision, and rebuke and punish if need be with vigor, remembering the dark character of the people with whom you have to do."[102]

In conclusion, Paul ends the chapter with the command to teach in both doctrine and ethics. "Titus is not to communicate them objectively and diffidently as if they were mere cold facts."[103] Timothy must put heart and soul into what he says, and he must have godly and biblical reasons behind the commands he utters. It will be an awesome moment, when at the Bema, ministers will ask the Judge, "Did I lead your people correctly?"

Study Questions

1. Is there good interaction and instruction between the older and younger people at your church?

2. Verse 5 has two elements that tend to bother people. It says that wives are to be "workers at home" and are to be "subject to their own husbands." How do you understand these commands?

3. Why do you think Paul instructed slaves about their behavior (vv. 9–10) yet didn't speak out against slavery?

4. In what ways can Christians behave at work so "that they may adorn the doctrine of God our Savior in every respect" (v. 10)?

5. How do you understand the phrase "bringing salvation to all men" (v. 11)?

6. According to verses 12 and 13, what should motivate us to holy living? What motivates you?

7. Are you "zealous for good deeds" (v. 14)?

8. Does your pastor "reprove" (v. 15) when necessary?

CHAPTER 13

The Goal Is to Live Sound Doctrine
Titus 3:1-15

Preview:
People who are saved as adults sometimes have a difficult time figuring out how now to relate to the world. It was no different for the brand-new Christians of the Roman Empire. They may have asked themselves, "What am I to think of Caesar now that I know he isn't a god?" Am I required to obey the government? What about my friends and their false deities? Paul addresses these questions about the government and society in Titus 3.

Demonstrating Sound Doctrine (3:1-8)

From these and other passages, "it is evident that the Apostles had great difficulty in keeping the common people subject to the authority of magistrates and princes."[1] Indeed, Paul urges the believers not to rebel against the government, but instead to be cooperative and obey the authorities. He even urged them to be helpful whenever possible. They would have to maintain that delicate balance between being in the world but not of it (1 John 4:4-5).

Paul had addressed this issue in some detail in Romans 13:1-7. He adds in the 1 Timothy letter, "I urge that entreaties and prayers, petitions and thanksgivings, be made on behalf of all men, for kings and all who are in authority, so that we may lead a tranquil and quiet life in all godliness and dignity" (2:1-2). It seems as if Paul's ultimate motive is that he wants no problems to surface that would hinder the Gentile population from coming to Christ. He earlier wrote that God "desires all men to be saved and to come to the knowledge of the truth" (v. 4). Titus should continually remind those under his charge of this responsibility to government leaders when possible.

The apostle Peter writes virtually the same thing as Paul. "Submit yourselves for the Lord's sake to every human institution, whether to a king as the one in authority, or to governors as sent by him. . . . For such is the will of God that by doing right you may silence the ignorance of foolish men. Act as free men, and do not use your freedom as a covering for evil" (1 Pet. 2:13–16).

But what if the Roman authorities require the Christians to worship the emperor? Church history tells us this demand would come to pass soon. Then the issue of conscience and the worship of God alone would be put to the test. Daniel's three friends faced this issue (Dan. 3:1–30) when they refused to bow to Nebuchadnezzar's image. Following the miraculous deliverance of the young Hebrew men from the furnace, Nebuchadnezzar blessed God and testified how the three had trusted the Lord. Though the church will be raptured before the Tribulation, some will come to Christ in that horrible time. They will have to face the same decision about worshiping the image of the beast (Rev. 13:15–16). Martyrdom will carry many to glory during that period, such as the 144,000 who are "purchased from the earth . . . and purchased from among men as first fruits to God and to the Lamb" (14:3–4).

In the New Testament "obedience" is "used absolutely of the obedient behavior of believers . . . in personal relationships and before God."[2] But as has been mentioned, this obedience cannot be absolute if it touches on spiritual, moral, or conscience issues. No government has the right to quench what is true or what is spoken from the heart. This biblical principle was established by Peter and John as they were brought before the religious rulers in Jerusalem. They said to the Jewish Council, "Whether it is right in the sight of God to give heed to you rather than to God, you be the judge; for we cannot stop speaking what we have seen and heard" (Acts 4:19b–20).

The expression "be ready" is used of soldiers who are ready and eager to move into combat. A similar idea is found in 2 Timothy 2:21, ". . . prepared for every good work." Paul's point is that the Christian may be asked to carry out a specific task assigned by the leadership or governors of the town. No matter what, the task, unless it is immoral, should be cheerfully executed. "Whenever the need presents itself—think of epidemics, wars, conflagrations, etc.—believers must be ready to show their good spirit, in thorough cooperation with the government which protects them."[3]

Believers in Christ must watch their attitudes and words (v. 2). They must never defame or slander anyone. They are never to utter anything false or color their words in any way that would do harm. They should never injure another or practice injustice. For any human being to follow these guidelines in a perfect way is a miracle because human nature wants to strike out and put others down. Only those who have been born again have the inner power to make positive conduct a part of their actions. What a change will take place in society when Christians strive to do what is right!

"Malign" is the Greek word *blasphēmeō*, "to slander, wrongly accuse." The human spirit often wants to put others down in order to lift up self. "We should not make the bad traits of [another's] character prominent, and pass over all that is good."[4] The Greek word for "peaceable" literally means "non-fighter." Paul is not referring to warfare or defense of family and home. He is speaking about human behavior and personal relationships. The broad context may still touch on how to treat government leaders, but it certainly refers also to neighbors and fellow citizens. A "gentle" person is someone who is kind and humble.

The Christian cannot simply talk a good line, but has to reveal an attitude of genuine consideration for everyone ("showing every consideration"). Is it possible to fake honest consideration? Certainly. In Greek secular life, consideration was often laughed at and seen as feigned, hypocritical, and false concern for someone else, driven by self-interest. In the New Testament it must be genuine.[5] When someone has sinned, it is easy to judge that person and to cast stones. The "religious" can then become judgmental and critical without thinking about their own weaknesses. Paul knew this when he wrote, "If a man is caught in any trespass, you who are spiritual, restore such a one in a spirit of gentleness; each one looking to yourself, lest you too be tempted" (Gal. 6:1). "The Christian spirit is forbearing and kindly, not urging its rights to the uttermost, lest by doing so it should stir up wrath and bitterness. Instead of indulging a passionate severity, it disarms opposition by meekly enduring wrong. . . . If God is so kind and beneficent to all, we ought to be meek and gentle towards each other."[6]

Interestingly, the apostle includes himself in this emotional indictment of verse 3. He too once lived like this, but God rescued him spiritually and also morally. He received inner peace and no longer had to pretend that he was sinless or a faithful law keeper. We often fail to see Paul in this light. It is a reminder of how even the most humanly righteous can be imperfect, but, too, it shows the richness of the grace found in the Lord Jesus Christ, that one could be so transformed in the way the apostle Paul was.

"Foolish" describes one who has made a choice not to use their intellect and understanding, and consequently falls into foolish behavior. Christ used the same Greek word when he confronted the travelers on the road to Emmaus: "O foolish men and slow of heart to believe in all that the prophets have spoken! Was it not necessary for the Christ to suffer these things and to enter into His glory?" (Luke 24:25–26). In Galatians 3:1–3, Paul also used the word to confront the Galatian believers, who had been presented with the truth, but chose not to obey it.

"Disobedient" carries the idea to be unconvinced about, to be unpersuaded. The disobedient do not fully trust or depend on those in authority over them, thus leading to a rebellious spirit or to balking at doing what is right. "Unwilling to be persuaded, contemptuous of God's will, spurning belief, hardened heart."[7]

The lost are also "deceived," continually fooled or seduced by lies and error. It could even be said they were misled by self-deception. "All who are estranged from God must therefore wander and go astray during their whole life."[8]

As unbelievers, our nature was once set only on sinning; we were enslaved. "Although the unsaved, natural man willfully chooses to sin, he does so because his very constitution is sinful, and he has neither the desire nor the ability to be anything but sinful. He is therefore both willingly and inevitably enslaved to sin in its many and various forms."[9] Paul spells out this "total depravity" in many of his letters: "God gave them over in the lusts of their hearts" (Rom. 1:24); "God gave them over to degrading passions" (v. 26); "God gave them over to a depraved mind" (v. 28); "There is none who seeks for God; all have turned aside" (3:11b–12a).

"Spending our life" actually comes from one verb. This word can be used to describe drawing a straight line. From this, the word came to mean "to continue to stay in a certain state or path, to keep going in the same direction."[10] The lost make no change of direction toward God. They stay in their sins and continue on in the same course. Lost people remain in the natural state unless touched by God (Eph. 4:31; Col. 3:8).

"Malice" is the simple Greek word *kakos* with the basic meaning of "evil." "Envy" has the common meaning of "jealousy, spite" (Rom. 1:29; Gal. 5:21, 26; 1 Tim. 6:4; 1 Pet. 2:1). "Hateful" is used only here in the New Testament. It is a very emotional word that can be translated "detestable, abhorrent." It means to show hatred not simply feel it.[11] One may be hateful just so long. The results will come forth in the personality.

In the phrase "hating one another," the apostle uses the more common Greek word for hate (*miseō*). It is written as a present tense participle and thus could be rendered "The ones who are continually hating one another." It is used to indicate the cause of all of the sins he has just listed. "It was our natural hatefulness which begot mutual hatred."[12] The hate and wrath in the heart is powerful, boiling over to a desire of revenge against others. We all once lived with seething tensions between our neighbors. Since we have been there, there should now be pity and sympathy for those still trapped in such sin.[13] The Lord desires to bring peace to the heart and soul of the child of God. He stated emphatically, "Peace I leave with you; My peace I give to you; not as the world gives, do I give to you" (John 14:27). Paul added, "Now may the Lord of peace Himself continually grant you peace in every circumstance. The Lord be with you all!" (2 Thess. 3:16).

With the "but" (v. 4), Paul sets forth a contrast from what the past life was like. God makes a change in the believer's position by "the washing of regeneration and renewing by the Holy Spirit" (v. 5). A new person and a new outlook are created. With this transformation, the apostle urges believers to "be careful to engage in good deeds" (v. 8) in contrast to what they practiced before. Christianity is both a belief and a walk; it teaches a new position in Christ and a new experience with Christ! It cannot simply be a dead belief system. All of this begins with the "kindness" or "essential goodness" of God. In this verse "the contrast is startling. In verse 3 man is the actor, but in verses 4–7 man is . . . the recipient, and God becomes the actor."[14] He is the One who reaches out to His lost subjects. "How unsearchable are His judgments and unfathomable His ways!" (Rom. 11:33).

As already pointed out, "God our Savior" is a common term used by Paul and other apostles (1 Tim. 1:1; 2:3; 4:10; Titus 1:3; 2:10, 13; 2 Pet. 1:1; Jude 1:25). In the New Testament it was first used by Mary in Luke 1:47: "And my spirit has rejoiced in God my Savior." God is first called the Savior in Psalm 17:7, with twelve other references that say the same. On two occasions in the Old Testament, the Lord makes it clear that "there is no savior besides Me" (Isa. 43:11; Hosea 13:4). In Titus 2:11 Paul seems to reach back into the Old Testament to confirm the work of God as Savior. "For the grace of God has appeared, bringing salvation to all men." This, of course, was the provision of salvation found only in the Lord Jesus. He is also our Savior!

Since God makes it clear that there is no Savior besides Him, to say that Jesus was also a Savior would be a mistake, unless He is also God. This truth throws further light on the doctrine of the Trinity. Jesus is very God, and very Man!

Because God cares for people ("His love for mankind"), He sent His Son Jesus to die for the sins of humanity. Does this verse teach that Jesus died for everyone, or did He die for the elect? This is a discussion that will likely continue until the Lord returns. The Bible seems clearly to teach that Christ's work at the cross was sufficient for all but applied only to the elect. But there are also verses that speak to the issue of unconditional election and predestination. Without contradiction, both emphases are biblical. These passages indicate that Christ died for all: 2 Corinthians 5:19; Colossians 1:26–29; 1 Timothy 2:4, 6; 4:10; Titus 3:4; Hebrews 2:9; 2 Peter 2:1; 3:9; 1 John 2:2; 4:14.

"Appeared" means to "display the revelation, the manifestation" of the grace of God in Christ (see 2:11). It is the "shining of the light" of God's love for His creatures. The word is singular in number, but it refers to both the Lord's "kindness" and His "love for mankind." And Jesus is coming again. In fact, believers are urged to be careful of how they walk "until the appearing of our Lord Jesus Christ" (1 Tim. 6:14).

Verse 5 is one of the most important and profound verses on the doctrine of salvation in all of Paul's letters. It is packed with important concepts that help us understand the nature of our redemption. In verse 4 the apostle tells us *why* God saved us, here he explains *how* He accomplished our regeneration.

"He saved us" means God rescued, delivered, and spared us from judgment. What God set out to do, He effectively accomplished. The salvation process is finished, though final redemption remains, either by the Rapture or by the death of the believer. The past tense of the verb signifies "that this salvation has already taken place and that it has delivered the Christians from what they were."[15] "We now possess his salvation, although it is still incomplete, awaiting its consummation at Christ's return."[16]

"In his act of saving us God could not take and did not in any way take into consideration any works that had been done by us."[17] Here in this passage, Paul is using righteousness in a broad sense. Our righteousness in no way measures up to please the Lord. How we evaluate righteousness is not even close to His standard. "The order eliminates any thought of salvation due to personal merit and magnifies God's sovereign grace."[18] The "we" is emphatic, pointing to the fact that we were helpless and totally unable to please God. "The implication is: there were no such works. Neither Paul nor anyone else had ever performed such a work, for before God and his holy law *all*—both Jews and pagans—are by nature 'under sin' (Rom. 3:9)."[19]

"The basis for our salvation is stated both negatively and positively. Negatively, He saved us 'not by works of righteousness which we have done.' God could never deal with us on this principle since all our works, apart from conversion, are unrighteous."[20] As Isaiah writes, "All our righteous deeds are like a filthy garment; and all of us wither like a leaf, and our iniquities, like the wind, take us away" (Isa. 64:6).

The "His" is emphatic in the expression "but according to His mercy." Paul is powerfully stressing the truth that we could not save ourselves, but by His mercy *He* did. Mercy is the pity of the Lord for His helpless and sinful creatures. There is nothing in us that can generate or cause the Lord to be merciful. Showing mercy is something He does because of who He is. He is all merciful. This mercy is the basis of our salvation. "God has mercy and pities our miserable condition and delivers us from it."[21]

How did He do it? "By the washing of regeneration and renewing by the Holy Spirit." One might have expected "baptism," but "washing" carries the stronger meaning of ritual or religious cleansing. This washing by the Holy Spirit accomplishes two things—both "regeneration" and "renewing." Notice that the washing is performed by the Holy Spirit and thus is a metaphor for spiritual cleansing, not the actual application of physical water. Water in itself cannot create a new person as the words "regeneration" and "renewing" imply.

Kenneth Wuest argues that regeneration has to do with the cleansing of the sinner by the blood of Christ, and renewing has to do with the cleansing for the daily walk. Or, the first effects justification and the second sanctification. However, it is not impossible that the grammar allows for the two words to be synonymous: "The washing of regeneration *that is* the renewing by the Holy Spirit." "Both 'rebirth' and 'renewal' may be regarded as dependent on 'washing' to form one concept. Then the washing of rebirth is further described as a renewal wrought by the Spirit."[22]

This may explain Jesus' words to Nicodemus in John 3. During the conversation, the Lord made it clear that the washing of water was the work of the Spirit (v. 5). This verse should read, "unless one is born of water, even the Spirit, he cannot enter into the kingdom of God." Later in the book of John, Christ emphasizes the washing of the Spirit again. He says of the believer, "'From his innermost being will flow rivers of living water.' But this He spoke of the Spirit, whom those who believed in Him were to receive; for the Spirit was not yet given, because Jesus was not yet glorified" (7:38–39a).

This laver washing by the Holy Spirit was promised in the new covenant. The new covenant was first prophesied for Israel in Jeremiah 31:31 and would be a covenant that would replace the Mosaic Law covenant (vv. 32–37). It would provide a washing (Ezek. 36:25) and a new heart and a new spirit within (v. 26), which would probably be the Holy Spirit of God (v. 27). Like a new birth, God's Spirit placed within would bring the Jewish people alive spiritually (37:14). The sacrifice of Christ would ratify this new covenant. At the Last Supper with His disciples, the Lord said, "This cup which is poured out for you is the new covenant in My blood" (Luke 22:20). Though this new covenant was predicted first for Israel, the church now benefits from it. Now believers in Christ have been "made . . . adequate as servants of a new covenant, not of the letter but of the Spirit; for the letter kills, but the Spirit gives life" (2 Cor. 3:6). And, all believers have been placed into the spiritual body of Christ, by which we are washed and through which we are given spiritual gifts (1 Cor. 12:12–13).

The pronoun "whom" in verse 6 references back to the Spirit, affirming His deity and personality. Paul then describes the giving forth of the Holy Spirit at Pentecost (Acts 2), the agent of the new birth, regeneration, and renewal. In Acts, Luke says the believing disciples were "all filled with the Holy Spirit" at that time (2:4), but he also writes that Peter quoted Joel 2:28–30 where the Lord said, "I will pour forth of My Spirit upon all mankind" (Acts 2:17). The disciples were filled (or controlled) by the Holy Spirit, but later Peter adds that they were also baptized by the same Spirit (11:15–17).[23] Though the disciples were "saved" in Old Testament terminology, they had not been placed into the union with the risen Christ, which would be a particular work in the dispensation of the church.

When the Holy Spirit was poured out, it was done so "richly"—that is, "abundantly, fully, without restriction, without reservation." There is no holding back the work of the Holy Spirit with the believer. The child of God receives the immeasurable and unlimited involvement of the grace of the Spirit. Spiritually speaking, the Spirit makes believers wealthy by His activities in their lives. "'Richly' means in abundant measure so as to effect the results that God, our Savior, desires."[24]

The Spirit "is represented, not simply as given, but as poured out,—nay, poured out richly—in order to convey some idea of the plenteous beneficence of the gift. This rich bestowal is peculiar to New Testament times; and here, as elsewhere, it is expressly connected with the mediation of Christ, who as Savior has opened the way for it, and Himself sends forth the Spirit as the fruit of His work on earth."[25]

Paul further explains that all this took place "through Jesus Christ our Lord." Note how in this passage God the Father, God the Spirit, and God the Son are beautifully combined.[26]

Verse 7 seems to tie back to the "kindness of God" (v. 4) who "saved us" (v. 5). "His mercy" tells us on what basis He saved us, and the work of the Holy Spirit tells us by what means He employed. Now here in verse 7 Paul puts it all together.

This is the only place in the Pastoral Epistles that Paul writes of justification of the believer. He uses the word in 1 Timothy 3:16 to describe how the Spirit *justified* the life of Christ. But the New American Standard Bible rightly translates the word as "vindication" in that context. "Being justified" means that we were "declared righteous" or "legally acquitted" before the bar of justice of the holy God. What an awesome sight! We used to be sinful and unrighteous and enemies of God, but now, because of the work of Christ on the cross, we are set free and have the righteousness of Jesus applied to our account. We were given "even the righteousness of God through faith in Jesus Christ for all those who believe; . . . being justified as a gift by His grace through the redemption which is in Christ Jesus" (Rom. 3:22, 24).

How vital to keep in mind as well that we are saved "by His grace." The word "grace" was used as a common greeting, such as in 1:4: "Grace and peace from God the Father and Christ Jesus our Savior." But there is also the doctrine of grace by which we are saved and even blessed on a continuing basis. The Lord saved us according "to His own purpose and grace which was granted us in Christ Jesus from all eternity" (2 Tim. 1:9). Hence, saving grace originates from God the Son and from God the Father (1 Tim. 1:14; Titus 2:11; 3:7).

After being saved we are not left to our own devices ("we would be made heirs"). An heir is one who is rightfully and legally declared to receive an inheritance. Being made an heir is one of Paul's favorite ideas.[27] Elsewhere Paul writes of the guarantee or "pledge of our inheritance" (Eph. 1:14) and of "the riches of the glory of His inheritance in the saints" (v. 18). This inheritance is an eternal promise (Heb. 9:15). It is incorruptible (1 Pet. 1:4), and it is not the result of law keeping (Gal. 3:18). Rather, it is described as a reward not earned, but given as a gift from the Lord (Col. 3:24).

The Inheritance of the Saints

By faith believers inherit salvation (Eph. 1:14).

The inheritance, from the new covenant, is eternal in nature (Heb. 9:15).

To be an heir of salvation comes by a promise not by works (Gal. 3:29).

Believers are heirs of God through Christ (Gal. 4:7).

Justification by grace makes one an heir of eternal life (Titus 3:7).

The inheritance for believers is incorruptible (1 Pet. 1:4).

Furthermore, we know these things are true and we are not simply speculating or wishing that eternal life was real. We have these spiritual blessings "according to the hope of eternal life." Hope in the New Testament carries the thought of anticipation. We are absolutely certain God will open the door of eternity to us.

Our salvation is as yet hidden; and therefore Paul now says that we are heirs of life, not because we have arrived at the present possession of it, but because hope brings to us full and complete certainty of it.[28]

Beginning in verse 8, Titus is urged to speak out boldly in order to fortify the believers in Christ so that they will produce fruit that will result in blessing to others. Paul adds importance and solemnity to his words by this now familiar expression: "This is a trustworthy statement."

What all the apostle has said ("concerning these things"), he desires Titus to repeat and continue in regard to the Cretans. "Good deeds" must follow the proclamation and declaration that the Christians say they hold to. They cannot live as hypocrites. In God's mysterious providence, He has ordained good works. We are "created in Christ Jesus *for* good works, which God prepared beforehand, that we should walk in them" (Eph. 2:10, italics added). "In a forceful manner Titus is to exhort the people in their service for Christ. ["Be careful"] denotes the application of earnest and continued thought, a careful striving of soul in this direction, that the belief in the doctrines of the gospel should be substantiated by a steady performance of its commanded duties."[29]

"Good deeds" substantiate the care the Lord has for others, but they also show that the love of Christ is being expressed through the giving and charity of the believers ("These things are good and profitable for men"). One can imagine that the Cretans had some time to make up. After the evangelism on the island, the small assemblies seemed to have floundered in carnality and lack of leadership.

This is why Titus was commissioned by Paul with a very difficult task—to mature the churches so that they may become beacons of Christ and so that they may be a blessing to the lost. James asks, "What use is it . . . if a man says he has faith, but he has no works?" (James 2:14). Without being profound, Paul says in a very simple way that these works are good. He could not get anymore basic than that! But he also adds profitable. "These good works are for the believers themselves and, even more significantly as far as the emphasis of this passage is concerned, for the unsaved sinners around them who are drawn to Christ by the exemplary lives of those He has graciously transformed."[30]

Avoiding Those Who Oppose Sound Doctrine (3:9–11)

In this paragraph Paul does not want Titus to become embroiled in wrangling and arguing about Judaistic beliefs and issues over the Law. He warns Titus that he will have to face factious and perverted men who have evil intentions. He could be snared into verbal debates with some of the Jews who despise the simple gospel, which in their minds, subverts the requirements of Moses. There always seems to be around those who wish to destroy, and who cannot tolerate deep yet plain truth.

Christians are to engage in good deeds "but" (v. 9) "avoid foolish contro-versies." Paul is saying, "Do not get yourself trapped in their arguments, but turn away from them" (see 2 Tim. 2:16, 23).

"Foolish controversies" may also here be translated as "foolish investiga-tions, stupid discussions." Paul deals with the same problem in 1 Timothy 6:4 and 2 Timothy 2:3. In 2 Timothy 6:4, Timothy is encouraged by the apostle not to get trapped in senseless and "unnecessary investigations." Here in Titus the thought probably means senseless debates.

The apostle is describing an all out assault, or war, instigated by the Jewish extremists on Crete. In fact, the Greek word for "disputes" has the same root as does the word for "sword." They will do and say anything to destroy the message of the gospel. The apostle wrote more in detail about this problem when he told Timothy not "to pay attention to myths and endless genealogies, which give rise to mere speculation rather than furthering the administration of God which is by faith" (1 Tim. 1:4).

Here in his letter to Titus, Paul adds that such arguments "are unprofitable and worthless." The Greek word for "unprofitable" is used only here and in Hebrews 7:18 and means "useless, unsuitable." "Worthless" can be translated "vain, futile." The apostle is not mincing words. He is using emotionally descriptive words to paint a picture of the subversion attempted by some in the Jewish community. Those bringing on such opposition were probably highly intelligent and learned scholars who hope to destroy the message of Christ. These men "disturb and embitter the feelings; they lead to the indul-gence of a bad spirit; they are often difficult to be settled, and are of no prac-tical importance if they could be determined."[31]

The reference to genealogies is probably a reference to the recorded names in Numbers, to which wild allegorical interpretations had been assigned. Such fanciful meanings had already been assigned by Philo, whose religious writ-ings were becoming known at this time, and were popular in many Jewish schools. Paul wished to put a stop to this influence. He saw it as separating the Jewish and Gentile converts in the churches. A life and death struggle seems to have developed between the apostle, the other apostles, and the rabbinical schools. Paul felt that if these heresies entered the teaching going on in the churches, the truth would be diminished and the congregations would shrink to narrow Jewish sects promoting unbiblical and incomplete Judaism. This is why he wrote that such teachings were "worthless."

"Reject" (v. 10) means "avoid, refuse." "Factious" is the Greek word *hairetikos*, from which we get *heretic*. The word comes from *haireō*, meaning "to take, to take for one's self, to choose, prefer." "The noun means, 'fitted or able to take or choose, schismatic, factious.' A heretic is one therefore who refuses to accept true doctrine as it is revealed in the Bible, and prefers to choose for himself what he is to believe."[32]

The "warning" (*nouthesia*) is actually "an admonition, an exhortation." *Nouthesia* is related to the Greek word for "mind." Thus, Paul is saying, "Strongly place in their minds that what they are saying is wrong and rejected."

Interacting with Unbelievers

Unbelievers may come into the assembly to hear the gospel (1 Cor. 14:23).

God desires the unbeliever to be saved (1 Tim. 2:4).

Believers should not be ashamed of the gospel before unbelievers (2 Tim. 1:8).

The believer needs to share the "hope of heaven," found only in the gospel (Col. 1:4–6).

Believers are to proclaim Christ to the lost (Col. 1:28).

Believers are to conduct themselves with wisdom toward those who are "outsiders" (Col. 4:5).

"A heretic is a man . . . self-willed, and contending for his own theories, though they are opposed and contradictory to the universally received doctrines. . . . if he refuses to be advised and continues recalcitrant, leave him to himself—have nothing more to do with him, either in admonition or intercourse."[33] Paul is urging that the man be given a chance to change his mind and to think over his false teachings ("first and second warning"). But then if he continues, he must be rejected. Paul is placing before young pastors such as Titus the directive that they should act with firmness and authority. Some pastors cower down when being challenged doctrinally. They are afraid of the sheep. Possibly they are trying to avoid being a bully to the congregation, but there is a time when those who are wrong must be silenced.

Verse 11 is couched in extremely strong language.[34] "Perverted" has the force of "to twist, to distort." "Argument with a man whose basal mental convictions differ from your own, or whose mind has had a twist, is mere waste of breath."[35] Paul uses the present tense to emphasize their ongoing wickedness ("is sinning"). "The factious person, who is twisted by his constant sinning, will manifest his wicked condition by his own words and actions, therefore by becoming self-condemned."[36] His own course, in attempting a division or schisms in the church, shows him that it is right that he should be separated from the communion of Christians. He who attempts to rend the church, without a good reason, should himself be separated from it.[37]

Paul's Salutation (3:12–15)

Paul's final words are to the point and without much elaboration. He reveals very little of his final plans, though he mentions four fellow disciples who are part of his support in the service of Christ. As he closes this letter, he is more than likely somewhere in Macedonia. Whether this is Philippi or not is uncertain. We can be fairly certain he is not in Nicopolis since he writes in verse 12 that he plans to winter there later.

Nicopolis was probably chosen because it was the most famous of what is called the "Victory Cities." The metropolis was so named because of the victory of Augustus over Antony in the fall of 31 BC. Augustus was encamped on the northern promontory and Antony on the southern. The decisive battle was actually fought at sea.

Verse 12 is the only New Testament reference to Nicopolis, though from this one mention, many scholars believe that the apostle planned to use it as a center for further evangelism. This key center would have been perfect for reaching the entire western region of this part of the larger territory know as Achaia. The circumstances by which Paul resolved to go to Nicopolis, and his reason for communicating this to Titus, are unknown. It is even more unclear whether he actually made it to the city.

From Rome, sometime later, Paul wrote to Timothy that he had recently gone through Miletus and Corinth (2 Tim. 4:20). It is possible that he would have passed through Corinth to Nicopolis. Some conjecture that he actually reached that city, and that he was arrested there while carrying out his witness and taken to Rome.

Little is known about Artemas (v. 12), who is mentioned in church history and tradition as the bishop of the city of Lystra. The name seems to be a shortened form of Artemidoros, meaning "a gift of Artemis." This designation may be an indeication that his parents worshiped the Greek goddess Artemis who was the protector of both humans and animals. Here in this verse, it appears as if Paul is planning on both Artemas and Tychicus taking the place of Titus on the island of Crete.

Tychicus is well known as a companion and helper to the apostle Paul, and he is mentioned in Acts 20:4; Ephesians 6:21–22; Colossians 4:7; and 2 Timothy 4:12. Tychicus, whose name means "fortunate," originally resided in Asia Minor (Acts 20:4). As a loyal worker, he traveled with Paul on his third missionary journey. Along with Onesimus, he carried the apostle's letter to the church at Colosse (Col. 4:7–9) and related to the believers there the personal condition of this great servant of the Lord. Paul also sent Tychicus to Ephesus on at least one occasion and possibly to Crete on another. Church tradition says that he died a martyr's death.

One can sense the urgency in Paul's words ("make every effort to come to me at Nicopolis"). The apostle probably understood that his world was closing in on him. He knew his time was short, and he wanted to see Titus one more time. Both men coming to Nicopolis would have to travel about the same distance. This city was an ideal location and suitable meeting place.

The winters could be harsh, and Nicopolis provided a little warmer weather from the cold blowing down from the north. Since Paul did not know how much longer he could minister, he may have planned for Titus to launch from here further west, say to Spain, with the gospel. "It seems probable that Titus actually reached Nicopolis, and performed some evangelistic work in Dalmatia, to which he returned at a later time."[38]

"Diligently" (v. 13) is related to the words "make every effort" of the previous verse. It has the connotation of doing something hurriedly, eagerly, and earnestly.[39] Again, it is as if Paul senses the storm clouds on the horizon. He seems concerned about his fellow workers as if the task before him must be finished quickly.

"Help" is from the verb *propempō*, a compound of *pro* ("before") and *pempō* ("to send, equip"). The word is translated "to send forth as one equipped for a journey."[40] Paul wishes for these two men to be thoroughly supplied with all they need for the task before them. The aorist tense and the imperative mood of command may well indicate the sense of urgency the apostle has in mind. The first part of this verse may carry the thought, "Quickly and hurriedly equip these men and send them on their way."

Zenas the lawyer is mentioned only here in the New Testament. His name seems to be a contraction of Zenodorus. Some feel the term lawyer **that** indicates he was a Jew who was learned in the Old Testament Law. But more than likely his Greek name indicates that he was a jurist in the Roman courts. Hippolytus cites a tradition that he became the bishop of the city of Diospolis.

Apollos is better known in the New Testament. His name means *destroyer*. Apollos was an Alexandrian Jew who came to Ephesus after Paul's first visit. He was taught by Priscilla and Aquila. Well educated in the Old Testament Scriptures, he was a forceful speaker, though he needed to better understand the new revelation of Christian doctrine. He is mentioned in Acts 18–19; 1 Corinthians 1:12; 3:4–6, 22; 4:6; and 16:12. He greatly strengthened the believing brothers by using the Word of God to demonstrate that Jesus was the Messiah (Acts 18:28). Though no one can say for certain, he may have been the author of the book of Hebrews.

These men were to be expedited and outfitted with clothing, money, and baggage "so that nothing is lacking." We cannot assume these men were with Titus now, for Paul would then have sent them salutations and would have stated where they were to travel. "They were with Paul, had received their directions from him, and carried this letter to Titus who was to help in sending them on. We have no means of knowing their ultimate destination, not even whether both were bound for the same place."[41]

Paul's instructions about good deeds in verse 13 must have taken his thoughts back to 2:7, 14, and 3:8, which he highlights a final time here in verse 14. In no way is Christianity to be a passive faith. The world changes when they see our passion for helping others. The support and care among believers, though never lived out in perfect form, mark in a distinctive way those who love Jesus.

"Our people" is an unusual and rare possessive pronoun that simply means "ours" but with the expanded thought of "those who belong to us." It is adequately translated "our people," but the thought really conveys closeness, relationship, and intimacy. The apostle adds "also," or "ours also." Though he has the Cretans in mind, by the "also" the command is applicable for believers everywhere. "If Titus was not to forget fellow-laborers, how incumbent it was upon the saints generally. The whole weight was not to fall alone upon the shoulders of Titus; others were to share the responsibility. Too often the practical side of the work of the assembly is left to a minority."[42]

"Must learn" is a very unusual Greek verb that means "to learn by doing, by practice." The apostle is saying, "Our own must learn how to perform good deeds by continually doing them." "The thought is that of learning by use and practice, to acquire the habit of, . . . This injunction needs to be heeded in a day when believers give so much of their time and energies to their own things and seem indifferent not only to lost sinners, but also to needy saints."[43]

"To engage" means "to devote themselves to," as it does in verse 8. Believers are to so carry out good works "to glorify God, testify their subjection to him and gratitude for mercies received; to show forth their faith to men; to adorn the doctrine of Christ, and a profession of it; to recommend religion to others: to stop the mouths of gainsayers, and put to silence the ignorance of foolish men."[44]

We forget that Christians must be trained in righteousness and in righteous acts. "Throughout the Pastorals ["good works"] consistently means 'good works' in the widest sense of fine actions or righteous deeds, so that it probably means the same here as well. 'Our people' must demonstrate that they are such, that they truly belong to Paul's following by giving themselves to good works."[45]

The word "pressing" is related to a verb that is often translated with the sense of "compelling." Another form of the word carries the thought of troubles and tribulations. The apostle's point is that people are suffering under duress and need relief. In this "distressful" and pressured environment, in which believers were being persecuted, the church should not stand by in idleness.

Christians who are not helping others are living unfruitful lives. Jesus said, "By this is My Father glorified, that you bear much fruit, and so prove to be My disciples" (John 15:8).

Paul closes his letter with an exchange of greetings and blessings (v. 15). His concluding benediction about grace ties in with how he began the letter, with God's grace (1:4). The apostle continually teaches that grace alone brings salvation (2:11) and brings out godly living (v. 12).

Study Questions

1. Are you subjecting yourself to rulers and authorities (v. 1)?

2. How can we tell when a discussion is worth pursuing and when it is foolish (v. 3)?

3. Some believe people are basically good. How does verse 3 refute that belief?

4. What does verse 5 say about our role in salvation? God's role?

5. What good deeds do you engage in (vv. 1, 8, 14)?

6. In verse 10, Paul tells us to "reject a factious man after a first and second warning." What does that look like?

Section IV

Philemon

CHAPTER 14

Background of Philemon

Philemon is one of four New Testament books called collectively the Prison Epistles. The others are Ephesians, Philippians, and Colossians. They are so named because the author was in jail when he wrote them. That the writer of Philemon was incarcerated at the time is evidenced by verses 13 ("in my imprisonment") and 23 ("my fellow prisoner").

It is impossible to study the book of Philemon without also examining Colossians. Colossians 4 especially links these books and provides us with some background information. There we are told that Tychicus is the one who bears the letter to the Colossians, and that Onesimus, Philemon's slave, travels with him. That knowledge, combined with the fact that Onesimus is from Colossae (Col. 4:9), causes one to conclude that (a) Tychicus carried both letters, and (b) Philemon lived in or near Colossae.

Coming chronologically before the Pastoral Epistles, the book of Philemon is the shortest of Paul's epistles. With only about 335 words in the original Greek text, some say this is more of a postcard than a letter.

Canonicity

It is impossible to accept Colossians without the book of Philemon. They are so basic to each other that to reject one is to deny the other. Since almost no liberal scholar denies Colossians, Philemon stands with it. Because this letter is so short and of a very personal nature, it could not be expected that it was noticed in the early apostolic literature. However, there are many proofs of its early existence and acceptance as authentic. Ignatius appears to allude to verse 20 in his works *Ephesians* (chapter 2) and *Magnesians* (chapter 12). Tertullian knew about Philemon, and Origen quotes verse 14 as ascribed to the apostle Paul.

Canonicity is also confirmed by the fact that three times the author calls himself Paul (vv. 1, 9, 19). Furthermore, the thoughts and wording express the mind of the apostle as known from his other writings. And again, because of the linkage with Colossians, the Pauline authorship is confirmed, making the epistle acceptable as part of the inspired Word of God. In the fourth and fifth centuries, some critics attacked the book, but its genuineness and value were defended by the church fathers Jerome and Chrysostom. Most scholars agree that Philemon's acceptance is recognized by almost all Bible historians.

Authorship and Occasion

As already stated, the Pauline authorship of Philemon has rarely been challenged. Few scholars today teach that someone besides Paul wrote this little book. Its writing was prompted by a visit from Onesimus (a runaway slave) to Paul while Paul was in prison. After Onesimus was saved under Paul's ministry, the apostle deemed it necessary to send a note to Onesimus's owner, Philemon, asking him to warmly welcome back his new brother in the faith.

Certain other elements indicate that Paul is the author, such as his greeting (v. 1) and salutation (v. 25). He calls himself "the prisoner of Christ" (v. 1), mentions Timothy (v. 1), and uses the Pauline expression "I thank my God always, making mention of you in my prayers" (v. 4; Rom. 1:8–9). He uses the Pauline expression of the believer's spiritual relationship: "in Christ" (vv. 8, 20, 23).

Place and Date of Writing

Where and when Paul composed this epistle depends on which imprisonment is in view here. The three most likely possibilities are Ephesus, Caesarea, and Rome. All three choices have a common weakness: speculation is involved to some degree or another. We are helped by the (safe) assumption that all four Prison Epistles were composed at about the same time, and thus we can garner evidence from a number of passages, not just those in Philemon.

The choice for Ephesus depends upon the most guesswork. There is no direct statement in Scripture placing the apostle in an Ephesian jail. Caesarea is a more logical choice. Paul was imprisoned there for two years (Acts 24:27), more than enough time to write four letters. However, a reading of the book of Acts indicates that he was very restricted and inactive during this incarceration.

Rome is the best choice if for no other reason than that was the consensus of the early church. In addition, Acts 28 tells us that the apostle had a measure of freedom while in Rome even though he was still under arrest

(28:30–31). That same passage informs us that he spent two years under this "house arrest." The mention of Caesar's household in Philippians 4:22 likewise points to Rome.

If indeed Paul was in Rome at the time of writing, then Philemon (and the other Prison Epistles) was composed about AD 61 or 62.

The Issue of Slavery

Estimates as to how many slaves resided in the Roman Empire range from one-third to one-half of the population. Whatever the correct figure is, they existed in substantial numbers. Some were indentured to pay off a debt, but most were part of the spoils of war. Rome conquered huge areas of land, and the captured peoples greatly swelled the labor force.

Slavery in the Roman Empire
Many people were born into slavery.
Those captured in war were either killed or placed into slavery.
People could become slaves by debt, default, or as criminals.
Children could be sold into slavery.
People could place themselves into slavery voluntarily.
There were few laws governing the treatment of slaves.
Though it rarely happened, some slaves could purchase their freedom.
Household slaves had some freedom to travel or negotiate financial matters for their masters.
Christianity taught that slaves should be treated kindly and with dignity.

The treatment of slaves varied widely from household to household. No doubt more than a few had brutal masters; others were given some responsibility within the home. An example is Joseph in Potiphar's house (Gen. 39:1–4). Greeks were well educated and thus were highly sought after. Legally, servants were at the mercy of their owners. Especially during the early years of the empire, masters could beat, torture, and even kill a slave with no fear of reprisal from the government. However, it was unwise to treat them so because even an uneducated slave was a fairly large investment for all but the very wealthy.[1]

It has long puzzled Christians as to why the New Testament doesn't speak out more forcefully against the institution of slavery. One would think such a wicked practice would be condemned on every page. Even in the Old

Testament there are many verses regulating the treatment of slaves but few that speak against slavery itself.[2]

The following paragraphs are not a defense of slavery (because it should not be defended), but are given to explain why slavery isn't prominently denounced in the New Testament. First, the political system of the ancient Roman Empire was such that the populace had no significant influence on those who made the laws. Hence, it would have been futile for Christians (who were rather few in number anyway) to publicly speak against slavery. It would have been more profitable to go about abolishing it by other means.

Second, it would have been an economic disaster if the slaves had been released all in one day. Most of them would be destitute with no way to support their families. Although some were educated, thousands probably would have died.

Finally, it should be noted that the writers of the New Testament were primarily concerned with proper doctrine, personal righteousness, and true holiness. They didn't speak out against slavery, not because it was an integral part of the fabric of society, but because it had more to do with the workings of Roman society than holiness. Idolatry was also a major part of the culture, but the Bible clearly condemns it.[3]

Therefore, the strategy of the New Testament is to make the best of a bad situation (see Eph. 6:9; Col. 4:1) with the ultimate goal of abolishing it. The reader is reminded that slavery in the Bible has virtually nothing to do with race. In the United States, slavery was founded on the sin of racism, but that is not the nature of slavery relative to the Scriptures. Allowing the gospel to work in the hearts of the people would eventually result in the removal of the institution of slavery from society.

Themes

This epistle is permeated with forgiveness, reconciliation, and hope. Onesimus, a slave, had runaway from his owner, Philemon, and possibly stole some things on the way out (v. 18). As a result, there was a very good chance Philemon was going to punish him severely. But this is where Paul steps in.

He writes to Philemon, telling him of Onesimus's conversion (v. 10) and asking him not to be harsh with his new brother in Christ. "Don't continue to think of him as a rebellious slave," the apostle is saying, "but think of him now as a fellow soldier in the Lord's service." What comfort and hope these words must have brought to Onesimus!

Some see a parallel between this story and Christ's relationship to us. In their sin, people are alienated from God, but through Christ's death, they can be reconciled to Him. The illustration breaks down in that Onesimus had to "clean up his act" before Philemon would consider taking him back. By contrast, Christ died for us "while we were yet sinners" (Rom. 5:8).

All Christians, at some point in their lives, can relate to both Onesimus and Philemon. We have either offended somebody or somebody has offended us. This epistle provides helpful instructions as to how a person should deal with reconciliation, regardless of which side of the matter he or she is on.

These themes of forgiveness, reconciliation, and hope may be the key to explaining why such a short and personal letter made it into the Bible. It is not only an example of reconciliation; it is the first step on the long journey to abolish slavery.

That this letter does have a place in the New Testament strongly suggests that Philemon heeded Paul's advice and welcomed Onesimus as a brother. If he hadn't, then (a) in God's providence, this epistle would not, in all likelihood, have made it into the canon, and (b) other Christian slave owners would have felt no compulsion to treat their slaves in a humane way either. In that sense, this situation was a test case for the church.[4]

One Old Testament book has a particular spiritual connection with Philemon. In the book of Proverbs, Solomon writes, "A gentle answer turns away wrath, but a harsh word stirs up anger" (15:1), and "The poor man utters supplications" (18:23). In the same way, Paul uses the attitude of the poor man and speaks softly to accomplish his goal of reconciliation. Another proverb may be applicable to Philemon. Reading this short letter brings the words of Solomon to mind. "The king's favor is toward a servant who acts wisely" (14:35). Poor Onesimus had caused terrible shame to his master and had even brought on his anger and disfavor. He could have been killed as a runaway slave. But after his conversion he returned and was seen as a faithful servant who would be blessed by his owner and master! The grace shown Onesimus was not unlike that showered upon Mephibosheth, the son of Jonathan (2 Sam. 9). As Onesimus was to be accepted back for the sake of Paul, Mephibosheth was received for Jonathan's sake. In both accounts the reception was to be continual, forming a new relationship. In one, a brother is accepted, and in another the son of the friend of the king is given a permanent place in the palace.

CHAPTER 15

The Goal Is Reconciliation
Philemon 1:1–25

Preview:
Even a superficial reading of Philemon leads one to realize that this is Paul's most personal letter. Some feel guilty for looking into its contents because it is as if they are reading someone else's mail. The apostle's love for the Lord and for others comes through with a warm glow. His purpose in writing it is to persuade one of his converts, Philemon, to welcome back one of his recent converts, Onesimus. Philemon is Onesimus's master, and Onesimus had escaped and sought out Paul. If Paul had not intervened on behalf of Onesimus, Philemon likely would have treated his disobedient slave harshly.

Paul Appreciates Philemon (1:1–7)

Paul describes himself as a prisoner of Christ Jesus from time to time (Eph. 3:1; 4:1; 2 Tim. 1:8; and twice more in Philemon, vv. 9, 23) but this is the only time he does so in a salutation. By this phrase he of course does not mean that Jesus is holding him captive, but he is being held because of his testimony about Christ. There is a slight difference between Paul saying here he is a "prisoner of Jesus Christ" and "prisoner of the Lord" (Eph. 4:1). Here in Philemon his imprisonment is directly from the Lord while in the latter it has to with an association with Christ and being in His fellowship. Paul draws on his humble circumstances with the final end not being in doubt. Paul adopts a lowly attitude toward his son in the faith. He calls himself a "fellow-worker" and puts himself on the same plane. Both men were engaged in the same ministry and worked together in the bonds of love.

209

Important Expressions In Philemon

Prisoner of Christ Jesus (vv. 1, 9, 10, 13, 23)

Brother (vv. 1, 7, 16, 20)

Fellow worker (v. 1)

Fellow soldier (v. 2)

Fellowship (v. 6)

Fellow prisoner (v. 23)

Fellow workers (v. 24)

Confidence in Christ (v. 8)

Refresh my heart in Christ (v. 20)

Prisoner in Christ Jesus (v. 23)

I hear of your love (v. 5)

Comfort in your love (v. 7)

For love's sake (v. 9)

Philemon, the recipient of the letter, is described as "our beloved brother and fellow worker." Although this is a personal letter, it is not altogether a private letter. At least three other people (besides Philemon) know about it. The first two verses mention Timothy, Apphia, and Archippus. Timothy is not under arrest but is there to give comfort and aid to his mentor and friend. We are not told much about the relationship between Philemon, Apphia, and Archippus, but some have speculated that Apphia is Philemon's wife and Archippus is their son or possibly a servant. However, since the "your" at the end of verse 2 is singular, it seems that Philemon is the only one who lives in this house. Too, because Archippus is called "our fellow soldier," he may be the head elder or pastor of the assembly.

Just like Prisca and Aquila before, Philemon had opened the door of his house for a church. Everyone knew of the troubles with Onesimus and his defection from the family. Meeting in a home proves that the early churches were not meeting in church buildings. This was not a problem, because the early assemblies were small. Though their witness in the community was strong, not having a designated official church structure kept their meetings out of the limelight. Those who offered their homes for meetings were probably wealthy or had businesses. They were more than likely well respected and helped draw new converts to the church congregations. The epistle suggests that Philemon was wealthy and had a home large enough for a weekly gathering. Having a number of slaves would also indicate this.

The word *church* comes from *ek* and *kaleō* and means the "out-called ones." Sometimes it is translated as "assembly," or often it can even refer to the Jewish assemblies, the synagogues. The first mention of church in the New Testament sense is in Matthew 16:18; 18:17. Here Christ is predicting that there is coming a new dispensation of the church age. Paul mentions the word church in all of his epistles except 2 Timothy. The word is not found in Peter's epistles or in 1 and 2 John. The old English word *church* comes from the word *kuriakos* and means "belonging to the Lord." Its main reference is to the building, although a true local church is really about the gathering of believers. The spiritual church is the body of Christ.

Verses 3 and following are more typical of the apostle's opening words (benediction and thanksgiving) except that he switches from the plural to the singular. He asks the Lord to bless *them* with grace and peace in verse 3 but then focuses exclusively on Philemon beginning in verse 4.[1] What a man of prayer Paul must have been. The greeting "Grace to you, and peace" is a common address in the letters of that day, though with Paul, the greeting is spiritually significant and truly implies a blessing from the Lord. In all of the Bible, "peace" includes all that is blessed and good and not just emotional security and an absence of chaos. The source of grace and peace is from both God the Father and the Lord Jesus Christ. In this linkage, Paul is giving the clear doctrine of their coequality!

In verse 4, in common with most of the apostle's letters (except Galatians), he reminds Philemon of his continual thanksgiving and prayers on his behalf (vv. 4–6). Without question, it was blessed comfort for him to know that, in spite of the apostle's many urgent commitments and even in spite of being cut off from his follower and convert for so long, he took this time to mention him on an ongoing basis before the Lord.

Paul is grateful for Philemon because he doesn't just talk about his love for Jesus (v. 5), he exhibits it in his relationships with other Christians. To love others is not a natural inclination, and to develop it means we have to deepen our faith in, and love for, Christ. A true and intense love for Jesus will overflow in a love for others.

The foundation of Paul's gratitude was that he had heard of Philemon's love and faith as far away as Rome. It might be suspected that "love" and "faith" would be in a different order, because normally in the Christian experience faith precedes love. But here love takes the lead because it is one of the major themes of this letter. It is quite obvious that there is a difference between "faith toward the Lord" and "faith toward all saints." When faith is at work toward God, it has a deep spiritual connotation, but when exercised toward the saints, it is more practical but is also imperfect. People can disappoint, but the Lord can't! The point of verse 5 seems to be that Philemon lived by a strong principle of faith that governed him. It affected his way of life toward the Lord and toward the believers in Christ. Therefore, his trust was practical and living, and motivating as well.

Paul continues to talk about Philemon's faith and love in verses 6 and 7 respectively. To properly translate and interpret verse 6 is a challenge. It seems to be saying that Philemon is to consider all the wonderful blessings he has in Christ ("knowledge of every good thing") and let that influence the living out of his faith. How he responded to Onesimus was being carefully watched by the church. Receiving this new brother in warm fellowship would be a great testimony of Christianity in action. Paul's desire is for Philemon to make the right choice.

The particular object of the prayer here was so Philemon's trust would be shared by all of the saints in order that they, as well as he, could have a complete and mature knowledge of the good qualities that was in them. Where genuine faith and trust are at work, good has to follow. No good can be discovered where evil rules. The flesh cannot of itself produce that which is spiritual and good.

Verse 7 implies that it is highly probable Philemon carried out Paul's instructions. He has already been a tremendous blessing to many others. These may not only be those in his house church, but also those Christians who passed through Colossae. This godly and loving man had refreshed their hearts. Hearing of this brought "much joy and comfort" to the apostle during his "house arrest" (Acts 28:30). Therefore, he is proud to call Philemon his brother.

Paul's point in the wish or prayer of verse 7 is to exemplify with thanksgiving Philemon's great love and faith for which he was known. This brought great peace, comfort, and joy to Paul and also caused a measure of relief in the burdens of the saints. Philemon's virtue is mentioned intentionally because it would be put to the test in a specific way by the request that Paul would now make. The hearts ("bowels," *splanchna*) of the saints had been refreshed. This word is used ten times in the New Testament, but only in Acts 1:18 does it mean literal bowels. The intestines were seen as the seat of the emotions and the affections. When people are dramatically moved in an emotional way, the intestines often churn and stir. Thus, they became the organs of emotion and feeling. The Greek word for "refreshed" is translated "rest" in Matthew 11:28

and has a reference to relief from work that allows a renewal of strength. It is used again in verse 20 of Philemon and is joined again with the word "heart."

Paul Appeals to Philemon (1:8–19)

It would be easy to see verses 1 through 7 as Paul "buttering up" Philemon, but that is not the case. What he is doing is urging Philemon to treat his runaway slave in the same way he treats other believers. Yes, Onesimus has done some bad things, but he is a follower of Christ now, so extend him a little mercy.

The "therefore" in verse 8 means that the author is drawing to a conclusion those things he has been writing about in the previous verses. The essence of verses 8–10 is this: Paul has the authority to command Philemon to respond to Onesimus properly, and he is willing to do that ("confidence in Christ," v. 8), but instead he is just going to appeal to Philemon. "For love's sake" (v. 9) he will ask a favor instead of issuing a demand. Seven reasons are suggested in verses 9–12 as to why Philemon should consider bringing Onesimus back to the fold. (1) Paul's request was asked on the basis of Christian love. (2) The request came from an older man and a respected apostle. (3) The request came from someone who was helpless and in prison. (4) The request was for a child in the faith. (5) The request was about one born into bondage. (6) The request was about one who had come to God and dramatically changed his life. (7) It would be like receiving Paul himself!

This strategy is both wise and appropriate. Orders may get something done, but the person receiving the orders may resent being given a directive for something that requires a mere request. An appeal will cause Philemon to receive Onesimus back with a suitable attitude. He will not feel that he has to do it.

Two of Paul's reasons would be most compelling. Now in his sixties, the apostle describes himself as "the aged" (v. 9). In the ancient Near East, elderly men were respected. They were viewed as wise and thus authoritative. Therefore, even if Paul were not an apostle, Philemon should honor his request. Why did Paul then remind Philemon that he was in chains? Perhaps to gain a little sympathy, but more importantly to suggest that Paul's ability to help Onesimus was very limited.

In verse 10, Paul finally reveals the specifics of what he has in mind. He has been writing about Onesimus, Philemon's missing slave, who is now a fellow believer since the apostle preached the gospel to him. We do not know how Onesimus knew about Paul or how he found him, but they now had a close and wonderful relationship. Paul tenderly calls him "my child."

Verse 11 speaks of the power of the gospel to change lives. Onesimus may or may not have been a particularly good servant before, but now Paul is convinced that he will be a valuable servant of Christ. The apostle has a play on words here. The name "Onesimus" means "profitable" or "useful." Though endowed with a good name, Onesimus had failed to live up to the expectation implied in the name given him. He had proved to be the direct opposite. Now that he had come to Christ, he could live up to his name designation. He could be relied upon to be a blessing, no matter what he might do or where he might go. He was a great example of the power of the gospel of Christ, for it alone could change the simple slave into someone useful.

There are other places in the Word of God where there is a play on the meaning of names. Jacob means "the supplanter." He supplanted his brother twice and cheated Esau out of his birthright (Gen. 27:36). In contrast we have the story of Jabez whose name means "sorrow." He prayed that he could be kept from the evil that might bring sorrow and troubles upon him (1 Chron. 4:10).

By examining carefully the names God often bestows in His providence, it is obvious that He wishes to impart certain truths. For example, the "sons of God" implies a relationship with God the Father. "Saints" gives the idea of holiness in the nature of those who are saved. "Christian" shows that the believer must reflect the image of Christ. "Brothers" are encouraged to treat each other as brethren. Such names and designations should reflect what a believer is to be and what he or she is to do. Quite often believers in Christ fail to live up to the holy standards given in such names.

To further demonstrate his trust of Philemon, Paul sends Onesimus back to his owner (v. 12). It seems logical that he would have traveled with Tychicus.[2] All along the journey Onesimus must have wondered if his master would welcome him with open arms or clenched fists. We are not informed about their reunion, but one can imagine that Philemon was glad to have his servant back. This verse likewise shows how dear Onesimus had become to Paul, who declares that sending him away was like "sending my very heart." We are not told how Paul contacted Onesimus in prison. Maybe Onesimus was put there as a prisoner and somehow gained his freedom even before Paul. The apostle was mature in his own faith and certainly would not have been envious of the fact that his son in the faith may have gotten out before him. Paul never complains about the difficult situation he is in for the sake of the gospel.

The apostle exhibits restraint in verses 13–14 as he did in verses 8–9. He really wanted to keep Onesimus with him but thought it better not to. No pressure was put upon Philemon to follow through with Paul's request; however, because of his Christian character, we would expect him to willingly respond. The thought in verse 13 is that if Onesimus stayed in Rome, he would in fact be representing his master, so that the service he gave to the apostle would be like that which he would be giving to Philemon. "In your behalf" would indicate this, and it would happen only if Philemon consented. "In your behalf" is from the preposition *huper* with the meaning of "for you," though sometimes it can mean the opposite, "instead of." But that would not be the case here. Onesimus would be in Rome not merely in the place of his master, but actually "for him," representing him. Some have compared this with a soldier who is on the front line not only in place of those who are at home but there on their behalf.

He did belong to Philemon, and besides, if the Roman authorities had discovered this runaway slave, his trip back home may have been unpleasant,[3] and Paul could have been punished for harboring a fugitive. Furthermore, Paul hinted that it was God's will for Philemon to "have him back forever" (v. 15). Having told Philemon why he was sending Onesimus back home with the sacrifice that this entailed (vv. 13-14), Paul now shows that the slave's leaving had proven to be a blessing in disguise, because it fostered a new relationship that now would remain always.

Slavery in the New Testament

Paul, Peter, and James considered themselves to be slaves of the Lord (Rom. 1:1; James 1:1; 2 Pet. 1:1).

Believers are enslaved to God (Rom. 6:22).

Believers should not judge another's servant (Rom. 14:4).

Though a believer is free, he is still a slave of Christ (1 Cor. 7:22).

Believers are not the servants of men (1 Cor. 7:23).

The gospel of Christ is for both slave and free (Col. 3:11).

Slaves should honor their masters (1 Tim. 6:1).

Servants of Christ are not to strive with each other (2 Tim. 2:24).

Submissive slaves find favor with God (1 Pet. 2:18–19).

To understand why Paul even thought about retaining Onesimus, we must look at verses 13 and 19. Philemon, too, was lead to the Lord by Paul (v. 19). A way to "recompense" the apostle would be to give him his slave. This is not to imply that Paul was in the ministry "for the money," for he was not.

Another reason Paul thought it unwise to hang on to Onesimus was that he didn't have Philemon's permission (v. 14). He did not want to take advantage of Philemon's goodness by forcing him to hand Onesimus over. In fact, Paul may have been out of God's will by keeping Onesimus (as noted above).

What's more, Onesimus was returning a better person (v. 16). He was now "more than a slave"; he was "a beloved brother," "especially to me," Paul adds. He would be a more trustworthy and efficient worker for Philemon. Too, Philemon should no longer think of Onesimus as a piece of property, but "as a man" (NIV; "in the flesh," NASB). Their relationship has been elevated from that of slave-master to man-to-man because they are now both "in the Lord."

Paul amplifies this thought in verse 17. The word "partner" is from the same Greek root that is often translated "fellowship" (*koinonos*). He is urging Philemon to welcome his anxiety-ridden slave into Christian fellowship.[4] This receiving should match Philemon's esteem and regard for the apostle and be done in the same manner he would adopt if his own spiritual father would suddenly appear. This welcome was to be joyous and open and should not in any way be spoiled by recriminations, spite, or malice.

Verse 18 insinuates that Onesimus may have stolen something besides time from his master. He may have fled with some of his master's belongings. In the interest of what is right, it was only fitting that this problem should be addressed and cleared up. It was bad enough to run away and cheat his master of his services, but it was worse to steal from him in the doing.

Paul handles the issue like an accountant by telling Philemon that there are two sets of books, one in the name of Onesimus and the other in the name of Paul. What is owned by the former, no matter what the amount, is to be transferred to the account of the latter, who now gives a promissory note for what is owed. By Paul's argument the account should be closed. When he writes that he has penned this with his own hand, he may be saying in so many words that he is signing a statement in a legal manner, and his signature is his guarantee.

It is a logical assumption to say that Onesimus needed money for the long trip to Rome. Whatever the case, Paul is willing to make up for any losses incurred by Philemon,[5] hopefully causing him to receive Onesimus back more readily. Any unresolved problems among God's people will lead only to bigger problems. Ephesians 4:32 commands us to "be kind to one another, tender-hearted, forgiving each other, just as God in Christ also has forgiven you."

But could Paul, a prisoner, be in any position to pay off someone's debt? Apparently he did have some means of support, because Felix was hoping Paul would bribe him (Acts 24:26), and Luke also reports that the apostle rented his own place in Rome (Acts 28:30).[6] As a Pharisee he would have been rather wealthy, and he may have had some money still remaining, or he could have had generous friends sustaining him in his ministry.

To convince Philemon of his sincerity, Paul writes an IOU (v. 19a). Paul sometimes had someone else actually write his letter while he dictated it (cf. Rom. 16:22). Here it is as if he grabs the stylus himself and puts down his legal signature (cf. 1 Cor. 16:21; Gal. 6:11; Col. 4:18; 2 Thess. 3:17). This passage (vv. 18–19) indirectly teaches that it is the duty of every Christian to make every effort to reconcile two feuding parties. This talk of being in debt provides an occasion for Paul to remind Philemon that he was lead to the Lord by Paul.

Paul Adjures Philemon (1:20–25)

The author has used some accounting terms in the last few verses ("owes," "charge," "account," "repay"), and he uses another one in verse 20: "benefit." Paul will "profit" and have his heart refreshed if Philemon will do what is right by forgiving Onesimus. This is not a monetary profit (in fact he may even lose money!), but a profit "in the Lord."

Lessons in Grace and Compassion

To act with compassion is based on the principle of Christian love (Philem. 1:9).

Christian compassion comes from the heart (Philem. 1:12).

Kindness and grace should be freely given and not by compulsion (Philem. 1:14).

Compassion should be shown to believers based on Christian brotherhood (Philem. 1:16)

Compassion should sometimes cause one to be willing to forgive a debt (Philem. 1:17).

Compassion can often have positive consequences for others (Philem. 1:18–21).

To be gracious often means that one goes beyond what is asked or required (Philem. 1:18)

Paul is very certain that Philemon will take heed to this letter (v. 21). It is his duty as a godly man to do so, even going beyond what Paul asks (cf. Phil. 2:12; 2 Thess. 3:14).[7] One wonders if this little epistle would have been placed in the Bible if Philemon had not taken the appropriate action.

What is this "more" Paul expects Philemon to do? I don't think Paul is asking him to free Onesimus, for verse 15 states, "you should have him back forever." It could be that Philemon is to treat all of his slaves better now, or that he is to occasionally give Onesimus time off to exercise his young faith.[8]

That Paul expected to be released from his chains is clear from verse 22. When he says, "I hope," he isn't merely expressing wishful thinking; he has a certain anticipation. He, in fact, is planning to pay a visit to Philemon. (By the way, the apostle is not inviting himself over. Hospitality was the social norm of that day. Philemon's house was certainly big enough to accommodate Paul if that is indeed where he stayed.) At the beginning of this letter, Paul makes mention of his own prayers, but now he refers to theirs. He was looking forward to the time he would possibly be in their house, for that would prove that God had answered in a positive way, though in His providence, He does what He pleases and what is right for the sake of the gospel.

Notice as well Paul's attitude about prayer. It would not be the Roman government's sudden change of heart toward Paul that would get him released, but an act of God—to His glory.[9] Nor would Paul's freedom be the result of Philemon's prayers alone. The whole church was interceding on his behalf as the plurals ("your prayers," "you") show.

A handful of friends send their greetings to Philemon in verses 23 and 24. All five of these men (and a sixth) are named in Colossians 4, from which we learn more about them. One of them, Epaphras, a "fellow prisoner," is a native of Colossae and prays fervently for those in Colossae and the surrounding region (the Lycus valley). Mark, also known as John Mark, the writer of the second gospel, is Barnabas's cousin. Aristarchus was Paul's fellow prisoner at the time Colossians was written. Luke is called the beloved physician. Demas is the sad case. He later deserted the apostle "having loved this present world" (2 Tim. 4:10).

By mentioning Mark along with the others, though Mark had been somewhat strong minded before, Paul was showing how the grace of restoration works. Sometimes even great men, such as Paul, are slow to restore the fallen, particularly if they have caused problems and emotional pain for others. No one can deny that Mark had been at the center of the dispute that divided Paul and Barnabas, yet in spite of that, the apostle now mentions his value and service, while restoring fellowship. To mention Demas, who had devoted service to Paul for some time, had to be painful, though the apostle seems reconciled that people can turn against others and bring on personal grief. Demas was lured away from the gospel by the world. The sad feelings of Paul's heart can scarcely be imagined. Demas's desertion of Paul as a close friend and companion had to sting (2 Tim. 4:10).

This epistle ends in verse 25 the way it began, with Paul beseeching the Lord to bless Philemon and his house, and the church at Colossae meeting there, with grace.[10] That is where the emphasis should be, because we would not exist or be able to accomplish anything for God without His marvelous grace. He uses almost the same language that he uses in the closing of the book of Galatians except that he adds the word "brethren" there (6:18). The expression "with your spirit" is used at the end of both letters. This shows that the gift of grace would influence their spirit, one of the highest faculties of the believer (1 Thess. 5:23). The possessive plural "you" in Philemon 25 could include the aristocrat Philemon, his believing household and other slaves, and probably also for certain the church that was meeting on a regular basis in his house. All of them were in need of God's grace in their spirits.

Finally, it must be recognized that the Philemon letter is more than simply a document giving the church a lesson against slavery. It is a practical illustration of how kindness and grace should come to play in the treatment of others. Slavery in the Christian world did not cease instantly, though godly truths were put into place that would end this practice in time. Philemon is also about forgiveness, proper restitution, acceptance, and the ability to get up and go forward in the face of wrongs. It is also about Christian brotherhood no matter what the economic or social status is between fellow believers. The epistle of James also addresses this issue of prejudice and mistreatment as practiced under the glaring light of forgiveness exemplified in the gospel. Though Philemon is a small letter, it carries with it huge implications about how to practice Christian kindness and grace!

Study Questions

1. What does the book of Philemon tell us about Paul's view of slavery?

2. What have you learned about forgiveness?

3. Has this epistle influenced your view of people who are from a lower socioeconomic class?

4. Is there someone who has wronged you, but you have not forgiven that person yet?

5. What steps are you willing to take to reconcile two feuding Christians?

6. Do you believe in the effectiveness of prayer as Paul did (v. 22)?

Bibliography

Barrett, C. K. *The Pastoral Epistles*. Oxford: Clarendon, 1963.

Fee, Gordon. *1 and 2 Timothy, Titus*. NIBC. Peabody, MA: Hendrickson, 1988.

Guthrie, Donald. *The Pastoral Epistles*. TNTC. Rev. ed. Downers Grove, IL: InterVarsity, 1990.

Hendriksen, William. *Exposition of the Pastoral Epistles*. Grand Rapids: Baker, 1979.

Hiebert, D. Edmond. *Titus and Philemon*. Chicago: Moody, 1957.

Hughes, R. Kent. *1 and 2 Timothy and Titus*. Wheaton: Crossway, 2000.

Johnson, Luke Timothy. *The First and Second Letters to Timothy*. New York: Doubleday, 2001.

Kent, Homer. *The Pastoral Epistles*. Chicago: Moody, 1986.

_____. *Treasures of Wisdom: Studies in Colossians and Philemon*. Grand Rapids: Baker, 1978.

Knight, George W. *Commentary on the Pastoral Epistles*. NIGTC. Grand Rapids: Eerdmans, 1992.

Litfin, A. Duane. "1 Timothy." "2 Timothy." "Titus." *The Bible Knowledge Commentary*. John F. Walvoord and Roy B. Zuck, eds. Wheaton: Victor, 1983.

Marshall, I. Howard. *The Pastoral Epistles*. ICC. Edinburgh: T. and T. Clark, 1999.

Mounce, William. *Pastoral Epistles*. WBC. Nashville: Nelson, 2000.

Phillips, John. *Exploring the Pastoral Epistles*. Grand Rapids: Kregel, 2004.

Stott, John R. W. *The Message of 1 Timothy and Titus*. BST. Downers Grove, IL: InterVarsity, 1996.

_____. *The Message of 2 Timothy*. BST. Downers Grove, IL: InterVarsity, 1993.

NOTES

Introduction—Background of Pastoral Epistles

1. Donald Guthrie, *New Testament Introduction* (Downers Grove, IL: InterVarsity, 1990), 607.
2. William Hendriksen, *Exposition of the Pastoral Epistles* (Grand Rapids: Baker, 1979), 3.
3. Ibid.
4. Ibid.
5. The reader is urged to examine Homer Kent, *The Pastoral Epistles* (Chicago: Moody, 1986), 13–68 and Henry Thiessen, *Introduction to the New Testament* (Grand Rapids: Eerdmans, 1943), 253–260, from which most of this material is taken.
6. Polycarp, *Epistle to the Philippians*, sec. 4
7. Clement of Alexandria, *Stromata*, 2.11.
8. Tertullian, *On Prescription against Heretics*, chap. 25.
9. Clement of Rome, *First Epistle to the Corinthians*, chap. 5.
10. Samuel Cartledge, "Timothy, First Letter to," *Baker Encyclopedia of the Bible* (Grand Rapids: Baker, 1988), 2064.
11. Kent, *Pastoral Epistles*, offers a reasonable itinerary of Paul's journeys (pp. 47–50).
12. The word *deacon* comes from *diakonia*, seen three times in Acts 6 (in one form or another) to describe the work done by the men chosen by the congregation.
13. The reader should consult Mal Couch, ed., *A Biblical Theology of the Church* (Grand Rapids: Kregel, 1999), for more information.
14. Besides, that would be adding more deception.
15. Kent, *Pastoral Epistles*, 66.
16. Read P. N. Harrison, *The Problem of the Pastoral Epistles* (London: Oxford University Prress, 1921), appendix 4, and E. K. Simpson *The Pastoral Epistles* (Grand Rapids: Eerdmans, 1950), 18–21, for more details and lists.
17. The specifics may be found in George W. Knight, *Commentary on the Pastoral Epistles*, NIGTC, (Grand Rapids: Eerdmans, 1992), and Guthrie, *New Testament Introduction*, 1001–1010.
18. Eusebius, *Ecclesiastical History* 2.25.5, quoted in Knight, *Pastoral Epistles*, 54.
19. In fact, some commentaries on the Pastoral Epistles address them in that order.
20. Kent, *Pastoral Epistles*, 14.
21. D. Edmond Hiebert, *An Introduction to the New Testament*, Vol. 2 (Winona Lake, IN: BMH Books, 1999), 329.
22. Ibid., 328.
23. Ibid., 355–356.

24. Knight, *Pastoral Epistles,* 6.
25. The information in this paragraph is taken from ibid., 7.
26. Knight, *Pastoral Epistles,* 9.

Chapter 1—The Goal Is Love

1. Paul includes "mercy" in 2 Timothy 1:2 also.
2. William Hendriksen, *Exposition of the Pastoral Epistles* (Grand Rapids: Baker, 1979), 51n19.
3. Daniel Arichea and Howard Hatton, *Paul's Letters to Timothy and to Titus* (New York: United Bible Societies, 1995), 9.
4. The Septuagint, or LXX, is a Greek translation of the Old Testament written about 250–200 BC. Because it was composed about the same time as the New Testament, it is often helpful in determining the usages of Greek terms.
5. William Mounce, *Pastoral Epistles,* WBC (Nashville: Nelson, 2000), 6.
6. Ibid.
7. Homer Kent, *The Pastoral Epistles* (Chicago: Moody, 1986), 73.
8. George W. Knight, *Commentary on the Pastoral Epistles,* NIGTC (Grand Rapids: Eerdmans, 1992), 6.
9. This trio of words is found in 2 John 3.
10. Kent, *Pastoral Epistles,* 75.
11. Arichea and Hatton, *Paul's Letters,* 11.
12. I believe this concept explains Jesus' cry from the cross of "My God, My God, why hast Thou forsaken Me?" Christ's relationship to the Father did not cease to exist for a time, but their fellowship was severed while our sin was on Him. Similarly, a husband and wife who have an argument are still married, but their fellowship has been damaged.
13. Keep in mind that most of Paul's epistles are written to the believers in a city or community meeting in house churches. There was no First Baptist Ephesus.
14. An apostate is one who has gone into apostasy, a denial of some or all biblical doctrine.
15. Note that Paul predicted this invasion in his speech to the Ephesian elders in Acts 20.
16. The New International Version translates it "devoted to." The New Revised Standard Version has "to occupy themselves."
17. Gnosticism (from the Greek word for "knowledge," *gnōsis*) was a heresy that became widespread in the second century. These people claimed to have "special knowledge," which in turn caused them to be more spiritually mature.
18. Christians should not base their beliefs on guesswork. The only stable platform on which to build our theology is Scripture.
19. Even today we call a male attendant on an airplane a steward. Dispensationalists get the idea of a dispensation (or stewardship) from the Greek word *oikonomia.* God "manages" humankind with a certain set of requirements in each dispensation (or "economy"). These are not different methods of salvation (for that is always by grace through faith) but are distinct procedures with which He deals with humans.
20. Paul makes this "love" command even broader in 1 Corinthians 16:14: "Let all that you do be done in love." More significantly, whatever we do in life should be done for the glory of God (1 Cor. 10:31).
21. Mounce, *Pastoral Epistles,* 23.
22. Ibid., 24.
23. By "positionally" I mean that in the sight of God our sins have been removed, but on a practical level we still sin.
24. Knight, *Pastoral Epistles,* 77.

25. It could be literally translated as "with knowledge" or "co-knowledge," which is the case in most major languages.

26. Mounce, *Pastoral Epistles*, 25.

27. Some could object to this expression, saying, "Insincere faith is no faith at all." But Paul is simply emphasizing one aspect of faith. See Ibid.

28. Ralph Earle, "1, 2 Timothy," *The Expositor's Bible Commentary*, Frank E. Gaebelein, gen. ed., vol. 11 (Grand Rapids: Zondervan, 1978), 351.

29. Mounce, *Pastoral Epistles*, 26.

30. J. D. Douglas et al, eds., *New Bible Dictionary* (Wheaton: Tyndale, 1982), 685. "Law" can also refer to a Mosaic administration (Rom. 5:13), and in its most general sense, to a principle ("law of faith" Rom. 3:27).

31. Walter Bauer, William F. Arndt, F. Wilbur Gingrich, and Frederick W. Danker, eds., *A Greek-English Lexicon of the New Testament and Other Early Christian Literature*, 2nd ed. (Chicago: University of Chicago Press, 1979), 400. Hereafter BAGD.

32. Arichea and Hatton, *Paul's Letters*, 21.

33. Some scholars advance the interpretation that because "law" here does not have an article ("the"), Paul has in mind only general principles, rules for governing society. However, the evidence favors the idea that it is to be understood as the Mosaic Law. At least three reasons affirm this conclusion. First, the previous verse does have "the" Law. Second, there are other passages where Paul does not write the article but there is no doubt he is referring to the Mosaic Law. Third, Paul's purpose in this passage is to elucidate the proper use of the Law over against the false teachers' misuse of it. It wouldn't make sense to say they were abusing general principles.

34. Knight, *Pastoral Epistles*, 82–83. Knight goes on to say that the would-be law-teachers are not Judaizers such as in Galatians. In other words, they are not teaching about salvation. Indeed, Paul subsequently writes about actions (murder, kidnapping, etc.) and not about salvation.

35. Mounce, *Pastoral Epistles*, 35.

36. Other such lists found in Paul include Romans 1:29–31 and Galatians 5:19–21.

37. I am indebted to Mounce, 36–42, *Pastoral Epistles*, and Knight, *Pastoral Epistles*, 83–89, for most of this material.

38. Interestingly, the origin of our English word *profane* means "outside the temple." In other words, it is not suitable to be in a sacred place. See Hendriksen, *Pastoral Epistles*, 67.

39. The good angels are pure, but they are not to be worshiped.

40. In the Septuagint, *bebaloi* is rendered "ordinary" in 1 Samuel 21:4, and in Leviticus 19:12 it refers to profaning the name of the Lord.

41. Arichea and Hatton, *Paul's Letters*, 23–24. Cf. Matthew 6:9, "Hallowed be Thy name."

42. The two words in question are *patroloas* and *metroloas*.

43. Hendriksen, *Pastoral Epistles*, 68 (emphasis his).

44. The English word *pornography* is based on this word.

45. Hendriksen, *Pastoral Epistles*, 70.

46. Mounce, *Pastoral Epistles*, 41.

47. Ibid., 42.

48. Ibid., 43.

49. Knight, *Pastoral Epistles*, 91.

50. Wayne Grudem, *Systematic Theology* (Grand Rapids: Zondervan, 1994), 218.

51. It may be of interest to note that *episteuthain* ("was entrusted") is a form of the word *pisteuō* ("to believe, have faith").

52. *Charis* ("thank") is usually translated "grace," but there are other passages where it expresses gratitude (Rom. 6:17; 2 Cor. 8:16).

53. Mounce, *Pastoral Epistles*, 49. "Strengthened" (*endunamoō*) is aorist, as are many of the other verbs in verses 12 –17. Paul seems to be looking back to one event and not to his entire ministry.

54. A simpler interpretation may be that Paul had already shown himself a fervent and faithful spiritual leader as a Pharisee, albeit misguided.

55. Ibid.

56. Blasphemy can also be occasioned by exercising prerogatives that belong exclusively to God (see Mark 2:1–12). Arichea and Hatton, *Paul's Letters*, 30.

57. Albert Barnes, "The First Epistle of Paul to Timothy," *Barnes' Notes on the Old and New Testaments*, 14 vols (Grand Rapids: Baker, 1998), 121.

58. Kent, *Pastoral Epistles*, 85–86.

59. John MacArthur, *First Timothy* (Chicago: Moody, 1995), 30.

60. The Old Testament recognized a difference between sin committed defiantly and that done ignorantly. Numbers 15 details the offering required for those who commit a transgression unknowingly.

61. Knight, *Pastoral Epistles*, 96.

62. Ibid., 55.

63. Hendriksen, *Pastoral Epistles*, 77.

64. ". . . a trustworthy statement . . ." is found five times in the pastoral epistles (1 Tim. 1:15; 3:1; 4:9; 2 Tim. 2:11; Titus 3:8) and nowhere else in the New Testament. "Acceptance" and "acceptable" appear four times, all in 1 Timothy (1:15, 2:3, 4:9, 5:4). Thus, only in 1 Timothy 1:15 and 4:9 did Paul use both of them. "Statement" translates *logos* ("saying" in NIV, KJV, NKJV, and NRSV).

65. See Knight, *Pastoral Epistles*, 100, for an interesting discussion of the formula "faithful sayings."

66. Some scholars deny that Paul ever said this about himself, feeling it was too harsh and unrealistic. However, there is no textual warrant for reaching such a conclusion. The spiritual "height" he achieved would further magnify the stark wickedness of his former days. If Romans 7 is referring to his present state, then there too he is very hard on himself.

67. Most of this paragraph comes from Mounce, *Pastoral Epistles*, 56.

68. In Luke 18:13 the tax collector calls himself "*the* sinner."

69. "Foremost" here could have a temporal sense in that Paul was the first of many whose salvation was quite unexpected (cf. "those who would believe in Him").

70. Mounce, *Pastoral Epistles*, 57.

71. Arichea and Hatton, *Paul's Letters*, 35.

72. Hendriksen, *Pastoral Epistles*, 84.

73. Mounce, *Pastoral Epistles*, 59. He goes on to point out the previous passage (vv. 8–11), also terminated with uplifting words.

74. Descriptions of God as King in the Old Testament are rare but can be found (Ps. 74:12, Jer. 10:10). Too, it is implied in the expression "kingdom of the LORD" (1 Chron. 28:5; 2 Chron. 13:8).

75. *Aphthartos* is used here in verse 17, whereas *athanasia* is found in 1 Timothy 6:16. The two words are closely related but are not complete synonyms. Mounce, *Pastoral Epistles*, 61.

76. Hendriksen, *Pastoral Epistles*, 84.

77. "Wise" is not found in the oldest manuscripts. It was likely inserted here by some scribes in an attempt to parallel Romans 16:27.

78. BAGD, 288, 289.

79. See Mounce, *Pastoral Epistles*, 70–72, for a thorough discussion. Paul and Barnabas, too, were called to the mission field by the voice of the Holy Spirit (Acts 13:2). Kent,

Pastoral Epistles, 91–92, suggests a third option. Paul is speaking of the Old Testament prophecies that led Timothy to and prepared him for this ministry (2 Tim. 3:15).

80. Another suggestion is that Timothy was given instruction on how to handle heretics. Luke Timothy Johnson, *The First and Second Letters to Timothy* (New York: Doubleday, 2001), 186.

81. Hendriksen, *Pastoral Epistles,* 85.

82. The *en* is instrumental.

83. The word "which" is singular, indicating its antecedent is "conscience," as opposed to "faith and conscience".

84. Hendriksen, *Pastoral Epistles,* 67–68. Kent (*Pastoral Epistles,* 93) believes the Alexanders of 1 Timothy 1:20 and 2 Timothy 4:14 are not the same man, because the man in 2 Timothy is distinguished by Paul's identification of him as "the coppersmith."

85. Arichea and Hatton, *Paul's Letters,* 43.

86. MacArthur, *First Timothy,* 47.

87. Parallels are seen in Job 2:6 where God hands Job over to Satan, and even though the devil is allowed to corrupt Job's flesh, he is not permitted to touch his soul.

88. Paul's presence was not necessary to judge and sentence these unrepentant sinners. In 1 Corinthians 5:4–5 he writes as if he were not in Corinth at the time of the discipline.

89. The heretics must have been believers, because the church is not to judge outsiders (1 Cor. 5:12; cf. Acts 5:1–11).

90. Hendriksen, *Pastoral Epistles,* 87 (italics his). He adds that since the apostles had the gift of healing, they also had the gift of suffering. See Acts 13:11.

91. Ibid., 68, 69. See 2 Corinthians 12:1–10.

92. Knight, *Pastoral Epistles,* 111.

93. Johnson, *Letters to Timothy,* 186.

94. It is, however, possible to construe 1 Corinthians 5:5 as indicating that the man is not saved.

95. MacArthur, *First Timothy,* 47.

Chapter 2—The Goal Is Worshipfulness

1. William Mounce, *Pastoral Epistles,* WBC (Nashville: Nelson, 2000), 76.

2. Mounce asserts that they are different types of prayers, because each word is an accusative plural (ibid., 79).

3. Almost all of this paragraph is based on James Swanson, *A Dictionary of Biblical Languages With Semantic Domains, Greek: New Testament* (Logos Version).

4. William Hendriksen, *Exposition of the Pastoral Epistles* (Grand Rapids: Baker, 1979), 92.

5. Mounce, *Pastoral Epistles,* 79. "Entreaties" as a verb sometimes has a person as the object (Acts 9:38).

6. I am indebted to Mounce (*Pastoral Epistles,* 79–80) for the material in this paragraph.

7. There is disagreement as to whether "all men" means every single person or all *kinds* of men. If Paul meant to say "kinds" (*genos*), he could have written that word as he did in 1 Corinthians 12:10, 28 and 14:10. Also at his disposal was "varieties" (*diairesis*). That salvation is made available to all, and Christ died for all is stressed in the next few verses (vv. 4, 6).

8. John MacArthur, *1 Timothy* (Chicago: Moody, 1995), 61.

9. This statement is not an endorsement of political involvement (2 Tim. 2:4). Is civil disobedience ever justified? Yes, whenever the government tells you to do something unbiblical (Acts 5:29).

10. George W. Knight, *Commentary on the Pastoral Epistles,* NIGTC (Grand Rapids: Eerdmans, 1992), 117.

11. Hendriksen, *Pastoral Epistles,* 95.

12. Knight, *Pastoral Epistles,* 117.

13. Mounce, *Pastoral Epistles,* 84.

14. Ibid., 82.

15. It is also true that God is pleased when our lives are characterized by godliness, but the "this" more probably has "prayers . . . on behalf of all men" (v. 1) as its antecedent. See Mounce, *Pastoral Epistles,* 85, for some reasons.

16. Some cursive manuscripts even have *gar* after *touto* in order to make the connection more explicit. Knight, *Pastoral Epistles,* 118.

17. As opposed to *agathos,* which is nuanced as morally good. Mounce, *Pastoral Epistles,* 85.

18. Walter Bauer, William F. Arndt, F. Wilbur Gingrich, and Frederick W. Danker, eds., *A Greek-English Lexicon of the New Testament and Other Early Christian Literature,* 2nd ed. (Chicago: University of Chicago Press, 1979), 270.

19. The expression "the knowledge of the truth" is Paul's term for the good news of the gospel. It is found three more times in the Pastoral Epistles (2 Tim. 2:25, 3:7; Titus 1:1).

20. A multitude of sources are available that cover this subject in detail, including *Evangelism and the Sovereignty of God* by J. I. Packer (Downers Grove, IL: InterVarsity, 1961) and *Divine Sovereignty and Human Responsibility* by D. A. Carson (Louisville: John Knox, 1981). I believe as well that the nature and function of God's will cannot be known in full detail by our finite minds.

21. Hendriksen, *Pastoral Epistles,* 98.

22. It is unfortunate that some have determined to translate *anthropos* as "human" or "person" and not as "man." There is no reason to start chipping away at the evidence affirming Jesus' masculinity.

23. Ibid.

24. Someone could point out that Jesus said He gave His life "a ransom for many" (Matt. 20:28; Mark 10:45), but this is no conflict, because He did not say *only* the many.

25. "Ransom" in 2:6 is not the normal Greek word for "ransom." The word here is *antilutron* (found nowhere else in the New Testament), and thus could be translated "substitute-ransom." This concept is further enforced by *huper* ("on behalf of," "for").

26. A testimony is the telling of what someone knows. For example, it may be a Christian testimony of what God has done in a person's life or the testimony of an eyewitness to a crime in court as to what he or she saw and heard.

27. Knight, *Pastoral Epistles,* 124.

28. Knight (ibid., 125) teaches that these are not three offices but that being an apostle automatically encompasses preaching and teaching. However, on the very next page (126), Knight says that Paul distinguishes between apostles and teachers in passages such as 1 Corinthians 12:28–29 and Ephesians 4:11.

29. Ibid., 126.

30. Mounce, *Pastoral Epistles,* 92.

31. Knight, *Pastoral Epistles,* 127.

32. Literally, "one through two." It is a literary term meaning the use of two words to express one concept.

33. Mounce, *Pastoral Epistles,* 92–93.

34. Hendriksen has a good discussion on the relationship between one's position and one's attitude (*Pastoral Epistles,* 103–4).

35. Homer Kent, *The Pastoral Epistles* (Chicago: Moody, 1986), 103.

36. Ibid., 105.

37. Kent, *Pastoral Epistles,* 106.

38. A few clarifying statements are necessary here. This passage is not teaching that men are superior to women; they aren't (cf. Gal. 3:28). Nor does this passage have any-

thing to do with intellect, character, or ability. God established this arrangement (men in leadership roles) to bring order out of the chaos caused by the Fall. Finally, verse 14 is not asserting that all women are gullible and men aren't.

39. Other passages to consider are Genesis 49:3–4; Numbers 8:17; and Luke 2:23.
40. This verse does not mean that godly women will always come safely through delivery of their children; godly women have died in childbirth.
41. Knight, *Pastoral Epistles*, 145.
42. See the bibliography for commentaries that give a fuller explanation.

Chapter 3—The Goal Is Character

1. I do not mean the man can never take the initiative. I had a man in my church who wanted to be a deacon and inquired as to which areas he needed to work on to be qualified. He sought the advice of godly men and soon achieved his goal.
2. From these two Greek words we get the English words *presbyter* and *episcopate* respectively.
3. It is rather difficult for a woman to be the "husband of one wife." This is not a degrading remark toward women. See comments on 2:12.
4. William Mounce, *Pastoral Epistles*, WBC (Nashville: Nelson, 2000), 170.
5. Albert Barnes, "The First Epistle of Paul to Timothy," *Barnes' Notes on the Old and New Testaments*, 14 vols (Grand Rapids: Baker, 1998), 143.
6. John MacArthur, *1 Timothy* (Chicago: Moody, 1995), 106.
7. Homer Kent, *The Pastoral Epistles* (Chicago: Moody, 1986), 128.
8. John MacArthur, *First Timothy*, (Chicago: Moody, 1995), 111.
9. This is another reason why a recently divorced man should not be placed in a leadership position.
10. George W. Knight, *Commentary on the Pastoral Epistles*, NIGTC (Grand Rapids: Eerdmans, 1992), 151.
11. William Hendriksen, *Exposition of the Pastoral Epistles* (Grand Rapids: Baker, 1979), 130.
12. Even though teaching is not an explicit requirement for a deacon, in 2 Timothy 2:24, Paul states that all Christians should be able to teach to some measure.
13. Kent, *Pastoral Epistles*, 134.
14. There is a third viewpoint that these are female assistants to the deacon but that, too, seems to be an unnatural disruption of the flow of the passage. Further, it is doubtful Paul would approve of a man working closely with a woman who is not his wife.
15. Knight has a good discussion on this verse (*Pastoral Epistles*, 170–72). Proponents of the "deaconess" view include Kent and MacArthur.
16. Those who favor the "deaconess" viewpoint argue against this point by correctly observing that there was no Greek word for "deaconess" in Paul's day. However, the apostle was not averse to creating new words to serve his purposes. Still another argument against the "wives" interpretation is that Paul could have written "their wives," but he did not.
17. Romans 16:1 is often set forth as proof that women were allowed to become deacons in the early church. However, the word "deacon" simply means "servant." Phoebe was not *necessarily* a deaconess.
18. If these women were female deacons, then there would be no reason for Paul to repeat here that they are to be dignified. He had already stated that in verse 8.
19. I am indebted to Hendriksen (*Pastoral Epistles*, 134–35) for most of this paragraph.
20. These incentives are not evil. Jesus said, "Lay up for yourselves treasures in heaven" (Matt. 6:20). Paul was looking forward to his rewards. He told Timothy, "I have fought the good fight, I have finished the course, I have kept the faith; in the future there is laid up for me the crown of righteousness, which the Lord, the righteous

Judge, will award to me on that day; and not only me, but also to all who have loved His appearing" (2 Tim. 4:7–8).

21. Church buildings per se did not exist until about two hundred years (or more) after Paul's death.

22. MacArthur, *First Timothy*, 135.

Chapter 4—The Goal Is Discipline

1. Apostasy means a denial of some or all biblical teaching.

2. The "teachers of the Law" mentioned in 1 Timothy 1:7 may be a prototype of the false teachers to come "in later times" (v. 1).

3. George W. Knight, *Commentary on the Pastoral Epistles*, NIGTC (Grand Rapids: Eerdmans, 1992), 190.

4. The antecedent of "which" (*ho*) may be just "foods" and not "marriage" and "foods," because their teachings against marriage are so patently wrong. See Ibid.

5. God does not create evil, but He does orchestrate our circumstances.

6. The congregation needs to keep themselves fed, but "nourish" here is in the singular, meaning Paul primarily had Timothy in mind.

7. Duane Litfin, "1 Timothy," *The Bible Knowledge Commentary*, John F. Walvoord and Roy B. Zuck, eds. (Wheaton: Victor, 1983), 740.

8. Knight, *Pastoral Epistles*, 199.

9. Ibid., 200.

10. As such, I believe He died for all people, not for the elect only, but as John 5:28–29 sadly teaches, not all will end up in heaven.

11. John MacArthur, *First Timothy* (Chicago: Moody, 1995), 179.

12. Nowhere in the New Testament does a "board of deacons" function in an authoritative way.

13. MacArthur, *First Timothy*, 180.

14. William Mounce, *Pastoral Epistles*, WBC (Nashville: Nelson, 2000), 264.

15. Ibid., 263.

16. Much of this discussion comes from Knight, *Pastoral Epistles*, 211–212.

17. The New may have added some unnecessary confusion by inserting the word "insure." Almost all other English translations have something on the order of "you will save both yourself and your hearers" (so NIV).

Chapter 5—The Goal Is Respectfulness

1. A brief study of the word "appeal" ("exhort," NIV) is helpful for understanding verses 1 and 2. The Greek word is *parakalei*. It and "rebuke" are the lone verbs in all of these two verses. "Appeal" governs the manner in which Timothy is to approach each age group. The Greek word generally means "to call alongside." It is even used to describe the Holy Spirit as our Helper (John 16:7; "Counselor," NIV).

2. Homer Kent, *The Pastoral Epistles* (Chicago: Moody, 1986), 162.

3. S. M. Baugh, "1 Timothy," *Zondervan Illustrated Bible Backgrounds Commentary* (Grand Rapids: Zondervan, 2002), 3:467.

4. "Marriage, Marriage Customs," *Baker Encyclopedia of the Bible* (Grand Rapids: Baker, 1988), 1406.

5. In the original language, "learn" is a command.

6. "Fixed her hope" (*ēlpiken*) is in the perfect tense, suggesting she developed a firm trust in God some years back and still trusts Him.

7. George W. Knight, *Commentary on the Pastoral Epistles*, NIGTC (Grand Rapids: Eerdmans, 1992), 219.

8. Ibid., 219–220.

9. Furthermore, if Paul were addressing the congregation as a whole, what could they have done that could have caused them not to be above reproach? Nothing in these verses is that severe. Finally, verse 7 is connected to verse 4 by the presence of the words "prescribe" (or "instruct") and "learn" respectively. See ibid., 220. However, we cannot be too dogmatic here, because Paul is *primarily* writing about widows, not their families.

10. This is not to say a widow not on the list couldn't be helped temporarily. The list was probably for the regular and ongoing benevolence ministry of the church.

11. In Paul's day Ephesus had at least two hundred thousand people. Others estimate a population as high as five hundred thousand.

12. Even though these are things for which the widow has already shown a propensity, Paul is not necessarily expecting them to serve the church in exchange for support. But if she ever were called upon to help out, it is good to know she is able to care for children, willing to do menial tasks, etc. Knight, *Pastoral Epistles*, 225.

13. That Paul mentions foot washing shows that it was not an expected and regular ordinance as are Communion and baptism. Ibid., 224.

14. I suppose one could argue that if this vow were *to God*, then it is indeed a very serious matter. On the other hand, it is strange that the church would make a widow take any kind of a pledge before the church would help her.

15. Deacons are not specifically assigned these duties. In Acts 6 the responsibilities of the elders and deacons are contrasted. The elders were to spend their time in prayer and ministry of the Word (6:2, 4). The deacons were to distribute food. This is not to say deacons do *only* those kinds of jobs, but the authority of the church is with the elders.

16. One could say this is not a shocking revelation since the words are from the Lord Himself, yet not everything He said made it into the New Testament (John 21:25). Knight (*Pastoral Epistles*, 234) has a good discussion of whether or not Paul actually is saying that Luke 10:7 is canonical, asking such questions as: How is Paul using *kai* here? Was Luke written before 1 Timothy was? Finally, Luke 10:7 itself is a loose paraphrase of Leviticus 19:13 and Deuteronomy 24:15.

17. These are not two or three witnesses to the sin, but witnesses that the accused has been confronted.

18. Never in the New Testament is an elder voted into office. Elders are appointed by an apostle or the apostle's representative. The verbs in verse 22 are all singular, intimating that Timothy alone laid hands on them. Titus 1:5 affirms this conclusion. Of course, because there are no apostles today, it is wise to have the board of elders appoint the men (cf. Prov. 11:14; 15:22; 24:6).

19. Paul often interrupts his train of thought. Second Corinthians 2:16 with 3:5 is an example.

20. There is some debate as to what Paul meant by "lay hands upon." One suggestion is that it refers to a ceremony to restore the fallen brother of verse 20 or to a replacement for him. However, since the other two passages in the Pastoral Epistles that mention the laying on of hands (1 Tim. 4:14; 2 Tim. 1:6) are in the context of an ordination, it is safe to assume 1 Timothy 5:22 is as well. Of course, Timothy should not be hasty whether the man is a new elder or a repentant one.

21. I. Howard Marshall, *The Pastoral Epistles*, ICC (Edinburgh: T. and T, Clark, 1999), 622.

22. One could understand verse 22 as either past sins or future sins, but the emphasis appears to be on the latter.

23. It is possible that verses 24 and 25 are not parallel, and the latter half of verse 25 is actually repeating the message of verse 24, that sins ("those which are otherwise") cannot remain hidden forever. However, many scholars believe the "otherwise" has reference to "quite evident" and not to "good."

24. John R. W. Stott, *The Message of 1 Timothy and Titus,* BST (Downers Grove, IL: InterVarsity, 1996), 141.
25. The "judgment" spoken of in verse 24 refers to the process of evaluating candidates for the office of elder, not to judgment before God.
26. Other scholars have speculated that the reason Paul inserted this comment was so that Timothy would not give the appearance of following the false teachers' asceticism (cf. 4:3). What may be another interesting aspect to this verse is that Ephesus had a reputation of producing poor quality wine (Baugh, "1 Timothy," 3:469).

Chapter 6—The Goal Is Godliness

1. *The Ryrie Study Bible* (expanded ed.; Chicago: Moody, 1995), 1901. Many New Testament passages speak to slaves or slavery, but 1 Corinthians 7:20–24 and Colossians 3:22–24 are the most germane to 1 Timothy 6:1–2.
2. Many scholars believe the use of the word "household" in the New Testament (Matt. 24:25; John 4:53; Acts 16:15, 31; et al) would include slaves as well as children.
3. For example, it can refer to his reputation: "He has really made a name for himself."
4. Galatians 3:28 has been misapplied by many Christians. Paul was declaring that all persons, regardless of social status, can be a part of the family of God. The Lord doesn't save people because they are rich or because they are nice or because they are male. That is the apostle's point. The verse has everything to do with a person's standing before the Lord and nothing to do with that person's roles in society and in the church.
5. This is the more literal meaning of the Greek word translated "benefit" (*euergesia*). The only other place this word is found in the New Testament is in Acts 4:9.
6. George W. Knight, *Commentary on the Pastoral Epistles,* NIGTC (Grand Rapids: Eerdmans, 1992), 247.
7. Thomas D. Lea and Hayne P. Griffin, *1, 2 Timothy/Titus,* NAC (Nashville: Broadman and Holman, 1992), 165.
8. William Hendriksen, *Exposition of the Pastoral Epistles* (Grand Rapids: Baker, 1979), 194 (emphasis in original).
9. The only exception in the Pastoral Epistles is in 1 Timothy 4:6 where "sound" is actually the Greek word *kalos,* "good" (so KJV, ASV, NIV).
10. R. Kent Hughes, *1 and 2 Timothy and Titus* (Wheaton: Crossway, 2000), 174.
11. Matthew 8:17; Luke 9:1; and Acts 19:12.
12. Warren W. Wiersbe, *Be Faithful,* The Bible Exposition Commentary: New Testament (Wheaton: Victor, 1989; Logos version).
13. Knight, *Pastoral Epistles,* 256. Emphasis his.
14. That the article could have been written here but wasn't is significant.
15. Homer A. Kent, *The Pastoral Epistles* (Chicago: Moody, 1986), 191.
16. Second Timothy 3:1ff. lists a number of character traits that will be evident in those horrible last days. The first one disclosed is "lovers of self" (v. 2).
17. The two words are *praus* ("gentle") and *paschō* ("to suffer").
18. First, keep in mind that people who confessed Jesus as Savior were usually baptized right away, and so those two events can be considered as one incident. Next, notice that the "take hold of eternal life" clause and the "made the good confession" clause are joined by "and," which suggests they took place at (about) the same time. When would Timothy have realized he was called to eternal life? When he was saved and baptized.
19. Gordon Fee, *1 and 2 Timothy, Titus,* NIBC (Peabody, MA: Hendrickson, 1988), 151–152.
20. If Paul had believed that the Tribulation was the Lord's next major event, then what he just said wouldn't make much sense. He is telling Timothy (and, by extension, all Christians) to be spiritually ready to meet the Lord. He does not tell him to brace for

the Tribulation. Other Pauline passages state the same concept (1 Cor. 1:7; 4:5; 15:51–52; 16:22; Phil. 3:20; 4:5; 1 Thess. 1:10; 2 Thess. 3:10–12; Titus 2:13).

21. See comments on 1 Timothy 1:11 for a discussion of the word "blessed."
22. Of course, Paul is not teaching that a person can buy his or her way into heaven. He is addressing believers here. Salvation is always by grace through faith.
23. Hendriksen, *Pastoral Epistles*, 210.

Chapter 7—The Goal Is Endurance

1. The same Greek word (*teknon*) lies behind both "child" and "son."
2. First Timothy is more official sounding and doctrinal. For more information on this opening salutation, see the commentary on 1 Timothy 1.
3. The same can be said of Jesus' remarks in John 1:47 about Nathanael. Describing him as having "no guile" does not mean that he has reached sinless perfection, but that he is a man of good character.
4. The Greek text literally has "from [my] forebears."
5. George W. Knight, *Commentary on the Pastoral Epistles*, NIGTC (Grand Rapids: Eerdmans, 1992), 370.
6. We should not draw any conclusions about spiritual gifts and how they are distributed from verse 6. Not enough information is given to support a certain deduction. In addition, the office of apostle ceased when the last of Jesus' apostles died (probably the apostle John).
7. It should also be pointed out that "do not be ashamed" (v. 8) is not an imperative but a subjunctive. That is, Timothy had not become ashamed, but Paul thought he might go in that direction. Homer Kent, *The Pastoral Epistles* (Chicago: Moody, 1986), 251.
8. Some scholars teach that this dative (*klasei*, "calling") is a dative of interest and thus should be translated "to a holy calling."
9. I. Howard Marshall, *The Pastoral Epistles*, ICC (Edinburgh: T. and T. Clark, 1999), 706.
10. John Stott, *The Message of 1 Timothy and Titus*, BST (Downers Grove, IL: InterVarsity, 1996), 36.
11. Warren W. Wiersbe, *The Bible Exposition Commentary* (Wheaton: Victor, 1989), 242.
12. William Hendriksen, *Exposition of the Pastoral Epistles* (Grand Rapids: Baker, 1979), 235.
13. William Mounce, *Pastoral Epistles*, WBC (Nashville: Nelson, 2000), 486.
14. Hendriksen, *Pastoral Epistles*, 237.
15. The verb "turned away" here (Greek, *apestraphēsan*) can mean turn away from the gospel, or turn away from Paul. I prefer the latter.
16. Ibid., 238. Others believe these were Asian Christians who lived in Rome, but Paul doesn't say they are *from* Asia, he says they are *in* Asia.
17. Stott, *1 Timothy and Titus*, 45.
18. In the New Testament, "Asia" refers to a Roman province. It was located in the present-day country of Turkey. Don't think Paul visited China or Korea. Ephesus was the capital of Asia.
19. What I mean by that parenthetical statement has to do with how one defines a "major" doctrine of Scripture. The most logical definition of a major doctrine is that it is one that is clearly taught in the Bible. By "clearly," I mean that there are at least two passages of Scripture whose literal or normal understanding teaches a particular concept or doctrine. In other words, if there is some principle that is important to God, He is not going to present it in a vague way in His Word. Now concerning 2 Timothy 1:15, Paul would not have written specific names ("Phygelus and Hermogenes") if the disagreement were over a minor doctrine.
20. Onesiphorus was, in all likelihood, from Ephesus. Verse 18 talks about his work there, and in 4:19 his household is among those to whom Paul sends greetings. Recall that Timothy was in Ephesus (1 Tim. 1:3).

21. Hendriksen, *Pastoral Epistles*, 257.

Chapter 8—The Goal Is Diligence

1. George W. Knight, *Commentary on the Pastoral Epistles*, NIGTC (Grand Rapids: Eerdmans, 1992), 389.
2. This verse does not lend credence to the idea of apostolic succession. See William Mounce, *Pastoral Epistles*, WBC (Nashville: Nelson, 2000), 504.
3. Knight, *Pastoral Epistles*, 391.
4. A. Duane Litfin, "2 Timothy," *The Bible Knowledge Commentary*, John F. Walvoord and Roy B. Zuck, eds. (Wheaton: Victor, 1983), 752.
5. A pastor told me one time that "taking every thought captive for Christ" (2 Cor. 10:5) was likely the most difficult command in the Bible. I would have to agree.
6. Mounce, *Pastoral Epistles*, 510.
7. Knight, *Pastoral Epistles*, 394. On the other hand, one could argue that the soldier's reward is "pleas[ing]" the one who enlisted him" (v. 4).
8. Litfin, "2 Timothy," 753.
9. John Stott, *The Message of 2 Timothy*, BST (Downers Grove, IL: InterVarsity, 1973), 62.
10. This is a rather literal translation.
11. Litfin, "2 Timothy," 753.
12. This passage is much more difficult and complex than it first appears. Why does Paul begin the statement with the word "For"? Who are "we"? Who is "He"? The word "Him" is inserted by the English translators; it's not in the Greek text. Who is this "Him"? There is a very high probability it is Christ (so also with the "He"), but again that is just assumed from the context. In what sense have we "died"? and died to what? Sin? Self? Was Paul thinking of Romans 6 when he penned these words? What does "He will deny us" mean? You get the idea.
13. William Hendriksen, *Exposition of the Pastoral Epistles* (Grand Rapids: Baker, 1979), 255–56.
14. These clauses are called first-class conditional statements. At times, "since" is not the appropriate translation, though. First Corinthians 15:13 is an example. Rendering this first-class conditional as "since" is heresy. One would have "Since there is no resurrection . . . ." Whether "if" or "since" should be used depends on the protasis's (the "if" clause) correspondence to reality.
15. "Or do you not know that all of us who have been baptized into Christ Jesus have been baptized into His death? Therefore we have been buried with Him through baptism into death, in order that as Christ was raised from the dead through the glory of the Father, so we too might walk in newness of life. For if we have become united with Him in the likeness of His death, certainly we shall be also in the likeness of His resurrection" (vv. 3–5). Verse 8 is nearly identical to 2:11, "Now if we have died with Christ, we believe that we shall also live with Him." See also 1 Corinthians 15:31; 2 Corinthians 4:10; Galatians 2:20; Colossians 2:12, 20.
16. If this interpretation is correct, then this passage (vv. 11–13) may have been part of a baptismal formula.
17. It must also be kept in mind that Peter did not have the fullness of the Holy Spirit until Pentecost (Acts 2).
18. The KJV translation, "Study to shew thyself approved unto God," is somewhat misleading. Paul is not so much exhorting Timothy to study hard as he is to conduct his ministry well and in accordance with the Bible ("the word of truth," v. 15)
19. Litfin, "2 Timothy," 754.
20. Since Paul was a tent-maker (Acts 18:3), this word may have been very familiar to him. Yet, this is the only place in the New Testament where this term occurs.
21. See www.bible.org/docs/nt/books/2ti/2tim-de.htm.

22. Walter L. Liefeld, *1 and 2 Timothy/Titus*, NIVAC (Grand Rapids: Zondervan, 1999), 258.

23. This is one of the few places where we are told some specifics about the heresy. Cf. Mounce, *Pastoral Epistles*, 527.

24. Homer A. Kent, *The Pastoral Epistles* (Chicago: Moody, 1986), 268.

25. By this I do not mean, for example, that a pastor who admits to immorality can just go right back in the pulpit the next Sunday. The New Testament holds leaders to a stricter standard (1 Tim. 3). Nor do I want to give the impression that I have solved every problem associated with interpreting this passage. I haven't. Conservative scholars do not all agree on exactly how Paul is using this illustration.

26. Liefeld, *1 and 2 Timothy/Titus*, 260, 261. Other commentators understand "these" to be the vessels of dishonor (backsliding Christians), and thus this is a call to separate from them to keep oneself pure.

27. John MacArthur, *2 Timothy* (Chicago: Moody, 1995), 90, italics in original.

28. Of course God *can* make use of people whose testimony is not all that great (such as Samson's), but by and large He utilizes those who desire to have a close walk with Him.

29. John Stott, *The Message of Second Timothy*, BST (Downers Grove, IL: InterVarsity, 1973), 72.

30. Thomas D. Lea and Hayne P. Griffin, *1, 2 Timothy/Titus*, NAC (Nashville: Broadman and Holman, 1992), 220. Other scholars put a slightly different spin on this passage. They believe that "with those who call on the Lord" is connected with "peace" only and not with "righteousness, faith, and love." Still others hold the opinion that "those who call on the Lord" refers not to all Christians but to those who are faithful in prayer. A third viewpoint contends that "from a pure heart" limits verse 22 to sincere believers. I think these three suggestions are too restrictive. Lea and Griffin's statement is closest to the truth.

31. Knight, *Pastoral Epistles*, 424, 425.

32. Litfin, "2 Timothy," 755.

33. As I mentioned in my comments on 1 Timothy 1:20, I do believe these false teachers are saved.

34. I do not believe a Christian can be demon possessed.

Chapter 9—The Goal Is to Expose Sin

1. See 1 Timothy 4:1–3 for a similar sentiment.

2. Within a New Testament context, the "last days" refers to the entire period from the ascension of Christ until His second coming. Primarily, though, it concerns the years leading up to the end of the world as we know it. The expression can be found as far back as Isaiah 2:2.

3. Those who hold to postmillennialism assert that society will improve as the influence of the gospel spreads. This and other passages contradict that line of reasoning.

4. This vice list should serve as a warning to those who promote "self-love" and "self-esteem." How we *feel* about ourselves is irrelevant to the Christian life. What we *know* about ourselves is what's important—we are sinners. See Romans 12:3.

5. Walter L. Liefeld, *1 and 2 Timothy/Titus*, NIVAC (Grand Rapids: Zondervan, 1999), 270.

6. I. Howard Marshall, *The Pastoral Epistles*, ICC (Edinburgh: T. and T. Clark, 1999), 482.

7. Some others are 1 Corinthians 15:33; 2 Corinthians 6:17; and Titus 3:10.

8. This susceptibility to deception may have been a motivating factor for Paul to pen 1 Timothy 2:11–14. William Mounce, *Pastoral Epistles*, WBC (Nashville: Nelson, 2000), 548–49, has some other good comments on this section.

9. A. Duane Litfin, "2 Timothy," *The Bible Knowledge Commentary*, John F. Walvoord and Roy B. Zuck, eds. (Wheaton: Victor, 1983), 756.

10. See Mounce, *Pastoral Epistles,* 550, for a list of ancient documents that mention Jannes and Jambres.
11. Homer Kent, *The Pastoral Epistles* (Chicago: Moody, 1986), 277.
12. *BibleWorks,* CD-ROM, ver. 6.0.1 (Norfolk, VA: BibleWorks, 2003).
13. Gordon Fee, *1 and 2 Timothy, Titus,* NIBC (Peabody, MA: Hendrickson, 1988), 276.
14. Mounce, *Pastoral Epistles,* 557.
15. Ibid.
16. Thomas D. Lea and Hayne P. Griffin, *1, 2 Timothy/Titus,* NAC (Nashville: Broadman and Holman, 1992), 231n37, quoting Luther.
17. Thus there is no contradiction between verse 9 and verse 13. In the former, the "ministry" of the heretics will eventually come to an end. Verse 13 is speaking in more general terms.
18. Of course, for Timothy the "sacred writings" would be the Old Testament.
19. When Bible students talk about the inerrancy of the Scriptures, they are talking about the original writings. Scholars refer to these original documents as the autographs. Christians who hold to inerrancy admit that slight human errors have crept in as the documents were being copied throughout the ages, but these are insignificant, and certainly no major doctrine is in question.

Chapter 10—The Goal Is to Keep the Faith

1. William Mounce, *Pastoral Epistles,* WBC (Nashville: Nelson, 2000), 571.
2. Rebuking is not for the pastor alone. All followers of Christ bear the responsibility of dealing with sin. We don't need to run to the pastor first thing when we are made aware of someone's iniquity. We must follow the steps outlined in Matthew 18.
3. In fact, Paul earlier told him to "use a little wine" (1 Tim. 5:23).
4. Some scholars see this phrase as a reference to Timothy's spiritual gift of evangelism, indicated in 2 Timothy 1:6. See George W. Knight, *Commentary on the Pastoral Epistles,* NIGTC (Grand Rapids: Eerdmans, 1992), 457.
5. A. Duane Litfin, "2 Timothy," *The Bible Knowledge Commentary,* John F. Walvoord and Roy B. Zuck, eds. (Wheaton: Victor, 1983), 758. Others take this imagery a step further and see this as a reference to Paul pouring out his blood as a martyr.
6. Paul didn't expect to be released from this imprisonment as he did from his first one (1 Tim. 4:13; Philem. 1:22). What he did expect was his "departure" to come about in the next few weeks. Verses 13 and 21 suggest, however, he considered it at least a possibility that he could live to see one more winter.
7. This thought lends support to the belief that Christians cannot lose their salvation. It would not make sense for Paul to tell us our crown is on reserve if there was a possibility we would not receive it. Peter expressed a similar idea in 1 Peter 1:4, "to obtain an inheritance which is imperishable and undefiled and will not fade away, reserved in heaven for you." See also 2 Peter 2:4; 3:7; Jude 1:13.
8. "That day" refers to Judgment Day, which for Christians is the judgment seat of Christ (Rom. 14:10; 2 Cor. 5:10). The Great White Throne Judgment is for unbelievers (Rev. 20:11).
9. John R. W. Stott, *The Message of 2 Timothy* (Downers Grove, IL: InterVarsity, 1973), 115.
10. It makes for an interesting study to compare and contrast verses 9–22 with Psalm 22.
11. In Philemon 1:24 Demas is associated with Aristarchus, a Thessalonian (Acts 20:4, 27:2; Knight, *Pastoral Epistles,* 464).
12. He was also probably the one who "escaped naked" at Jesus' arrest (Mark 14:51–52).
13. It is certainly possible that Paul had purchased these things before his conversion since he was a wealthy Pharisee (Phil. 3:5).
14. See Mounce, *Pastoral Epistles,* 591–94, for a good discussion of the possibilities.
15. Gordon Fee, *1 and 2 Timothy, Titus,* NIBC (Peabody, MA: Hendrickson, 1988), 296.

16. Litfin, "2 Timothy," 760.
17. Fee, *1 and 2 Timothy, Titus,* 297.
18. The Erastus of Romans 16:23 may be the same person. If so, then he was a high-ranking official.
19. Hence, they are sometimes called "signs," pointing out the way to God.
20. Knight, *Pastoral Epistles,* 478.

Chapter 11—The Goal Is Elder Leadership

1. Colin Brown, ed., *Dictionary of New Testament Theology* (Grand Rapids: Zondervan, 1975), 1:127.
2. Albert Barnes, *Notes on the New Testament* (Grand Rapids: Baker, 1885), 12:265.
3. T. Wilson and K. Stapley, *What the Bible Teaches: Titus* (Kilmarnock, Scotland: John Ritchie, 1983), 407.
4. Patrick Fairbairn, *Commentary on the Pastoral Epistles* (Grand Rapids: Zondervan, 1956), 257.
5. Archibald Thomas Robertson, *Word Pictures in the New Testament* (Nashville: Broadman, 1931), 4:597.
6. Ibid., 2:90.
7. A. Duane Litfin, "Titus," *The Bible Knowledge Commentary* (Wheaton: Victor, 1983), 761.
8. John Stott, *The Message of 1 Timothy and Titus* (Downers Grove, IL: InterVarsity, 1996), 169–170.
9. Wilson and Stapley, *Titus,* 409–410.
10. Horst Balz and Gerhard Schneider, eds., *Exegetical Dictionary of the New Testament* (Grand Rapids: Eerdmans, 1993), 3:326.
11. In 2 Corinthians Titus is mentioned nine times and always with much confidence and trust by the apostle Paul. Paul entrusted Titus with the second diplomatic mission to Corinth where he was responsible for the collecting of goods and funds for poorer believers in Jerusalem
12. John Calvin, *Calvin's Commentaries* (Grand Rapids: Baker, 1989), 21:287.
13. George W. Knight, *Commentary on the Pastoral Epistles,* NIGTC (Grand Rapids: Eerdmans, 1992), 287–288.
14. With the middle voice the responsibility really comes down on Titus, "This you must do yourself."
15. Litfin, "Titus," 762.
16. William Hendriksen, *Exposition of the Pastoral Epistles* (Grand Rapids: Baker, 1979), 345.
17. Balz and Schneider, *Exegetical Dictionary,* 2:36 (italics in original).
18. Homer Kent, *The Pastoral Epistles* (Chicago: Moody, 1986), 212.
19. Henry G. Liddell and Robert Scott, *A Greek-English Lexicon* (Cambridge: Oxford University Press, 1990), 127.
20. Ibid., 83.
21. In Ephesians 4:11 "the shepherds" are also called "the teachers." Thus, there are four important nouns used to describe the key spiritual leaders of the church: elder, overseer, pastor (shepherd), and teacher. In almost all New Testament passages, these men are seen as a plurality serving in each individual church. In other words, there should be a body of elders for each assembly. The four words above describe their roles and functions.
22. W. Robertson Nicoll, *The Expositor's Greek Testament* (Grand Rapids: Eerdmans, 1990), 4:187.
23. Calvin, *Calvin's Commentaries,* 21:291.
24. Barnes, *Notes,* 12:268.

25. Knight, *Pastoral Epistles*, 291.
26. Mal Couch, gen. ed., *A Biblical Theology of the Church* (Grand Rapids: Kregel, 1999), 182.
27. Barnes, *Notes*, 12:268.
28. Charles John Ellicott, *Commentary on the Whole Bible* (Grand Rapids: Zondervan, 1959), 8:252.
29. Ibid., 8:183.
30. Barnes, *Notes*, 12:269.
31. D. Edmond Hiebert, "Titus," *The Expositor's Bible Commentary* (Grand Rapids: Zondervan, 1978), 11:431.
32. Stott, *1 Timothy and Titus*, 177.
33. Liddell and Scott, *Greek-English Lexicon*, 76.
34. Nicoll, *Expositor's Greek Testament*, 4:188.
35. Henry Alford, *The Greek Testament* (Chicago: Moody, 1958), 3:411.
36. Calvin, *Calvin's Commentaries*, 21:295.
37. R. C. H. Lenski, "Titus," *St. Paul's Epistles* (Minneapolis: Augsburg, 1961), 899.
38. Ibid.
39. Knight, *Pastoral Epistles*, 293.
40. Matthew Poole, *Commentary of the Holy Bible* (Peabody, MA: Hendrickson, n.d.), 3:799.
41. Exell, Joseph S., gen. ed., *The Preacher's Complete Homiletic Commentary* (Grand Rapids: Baker, n.d.), 29:90.
42. Wilson and Stapley, *Titus*, 417–418.
43. Balz and Schneider, *Exegetical Dictionary*, 1:427.
44. Ibid.
45. Hendriksen, *Pastoral Epistles*, 351.
46. Hiebert, "Titus," 11:431.
47. Calvin, *Calvin's Commentaries*, 21:296.
48. Walter Bauer, William F. Arndt, F. Wilbur Gingrich, and Frederick W. Danker, eds., *A Greek-English Lexicon of the New Testament and Other Early Christian Literature*, 2nd ed. (Chicago: University of Chicago Press, 1979), 495.
49. Barnes, *Notes*, 12:269.
50. Robertson, *Word Pictures*, 4:600.
51. Ibid.
52. Nicoll, *Expositor's Greek Testament*, 4:188.
53. Ellicott, *Commentary on the Whole Bible*, 8:253.
54. Calvin, *Calvin's Commentaries*, 21:299.
55. R. C. H. Lenski, "Titus," *St. Paul's Epistles* (Minneapolis: Augsburg, 1961), 902.
56. Fairbairn, *Pastoral Epistles*, 266.
57. Ibid.
58. Stott, *1 Timothy and Titus*, 181.
59. Hiebert, "Titus," 11:433.
60. Alford, *Greek Testament*, 3:413.
61. Robertson, *Word Pictures*, 4:601.
62. Stott, *1 Timothy and Titus*, 182.
63. Wilson and Stapley, *Titus*, 421–22.
64. Kenneth S. Wuest, *Wuest's Word Studies* (Grand Rapids: Eerdmans, 1973), 2:188.
65. Nicoll, *Expositor's Greek Testament*, 4:190.
66. Lenski, "Titus," 907-8.
67. Liddell and Scott, *Greek-English Lexicon*, 149.

Chapter 12—The Goal Is Defending Sound Doctrine

1. Kenneth S. Wuest, *Wuest's Word Studies* (Grand Rapids: Eerdmans, 1973), 2:190.
2. W. Robertson Nicoll, *The Expositor's Greek Testament* (Grand Rapids: Eerdmans, 1990), 4:191.
3. Wuest, *Word Studies,* 2:190.
4. Horst Balz and Gerhard Schneider, *Exegetical Dictionary of the New Testament* (Grand Rapids: Eerdmans, 1981), 3:380.
5. Henry G. Liddell and Robert Scott, *A Greek-English Lexicon* (Cambridge: Oxford University Press, 1990), 322.
6. John MacArthur, *Titus* (Chicago: Moody, 1996), 73.
7. Balz and Schneider, *Exegetical Dictionary,* 3:238.
8. Ibid., 3:329–30.
9. Charles John Ellicott, *Commentary on the Whole Bible* (Grand Rapids: Zondervan, 1959), 8:255.
10. Joseph H. Thayer, *Thayer's Greek-English Lexicon of the New Testament* (Grand Rapids: Baker, 1977), 535.
11. Archibald Thomas Robertson, *Word Pictures in the New Testament* (Nashville: Broadman, 1931), 4:602.
12. Exell, Joseph S., gen. ed., *The Preacher's Complete Homiletic Commentary* (Grand Rapids: Baker, n.d.), 29:94.
13. D. Edmond Hiebert, "Titus," *The Expositor's Bible Commentary* (Grand Rapids: Zondervan, 1978), 11:436.
14. John Stott, *The Message of 1 Timothy and Titus,* (Downers Grove, IL: InterVarsity, 1996), 188.
15. George W. Knight, *Commentary on the Pastoral Epistles* (Grand Rapids: Eerdmans, 1992), 307.
16. Robertson, *Word Pictures,* 4:603.
17. Matthew Poole, *Commentary of the Holy Bible* (Peabody, MA: Hendrickson, n.d.), 3:802.
18. W. Robertson Nicoll, *The Expositor's Greek Testament* (Grand Rapids: Eerdmans, 1990), 4:192.
19. William Hendriksen, *Exposition of the Pastoral Epistles* (Grand Rapids: Baker, 1979), 365.
20. T. Wilson and K. Stapley, *What the Bible Teaches: Titus* (Kilmarnock, Scotland: John Ritchie, 1983), 430.
21. Wuest, *Word Studies,* 2:191.
22. Ellicott, *Commentary on the Whole Bible,* 8:258.
23. John Calvin, *Calvin's Commentaries* (Grand Rapids: Baker, 1989), 21:256.
24. MacArthur, *Titus,* 92.
25. Balz and Schneider, *Exegetical Dictionary,* 1:317.
26. Liddell and Scott, *Greek-English Lexicon,* 726.
27. Stott, *1 Timothy and Titus,* 191.
28. Patrick Fairbairn, *Commentary on the Pastoral Epistles* (Grand Rapids: Zondervan, 1956), 276.
29. A. Duane Litfin, "Titus," *The Bible Knowledge Commentary,* John F. Walvoord and Roy B. Zuck, eds. (Wheaton: Victor, 1983), 764.
30. Hiebert, "Titus," 11:438.
31. Hendriksen, *Pastoral Epistles,* 368.
32. Exell, *Preacher's Complete Homiletic Commentary,* 29:95.
33. John Gill, *Gill's Commentary* (Grand Rapids: Baker, 1980), 6:355.
34. Hiebert, "Titus," 11:438.
35. Knight, *Pastoral Epistles,* 314.

36. Patrick Fairbairn, *Commentary on the Pastoral Epistles* (Grand Rapids: Zondervan, 1956), 276.
37. Ibid.
38. Stott, *1 Timothy and Titus*, 191–92.
39. Exell, *Preacher's Complete Homiletic Commentary*, 29:97.
40. Joseph H. Thayer, *Greek-English Lexicon of the New Testament* (Grand Rapids: Baker, 1992), 429.
41. MacArthur, *Titus*, 102.
42. R. C. H. Lenski, "Titus," *St. Paul's Epistles* (Minneapolis: Augsburg, 1961), 917.
43. Walter Bauer, William F. Arndt, F. Wilbur Gingrich, and Frederick W. Danker, eds., *A Greek-English Lexicon of the New Testament and Other Early Christian Literature*, 2nd ed., (Chicago: University of Chicago Press, 1979), 445. Hereafter BAGD.
44. Calvin, *Calvin's Commentaries*, 21:316.
45. Henry Alford, *The Greek Testament* (Chicago: Moody, 1958), 2:417.
46. Poole, *Commentary of the Holy Bible*, 3:803.
47. Gill, *Gill's Commentary*, 6:355.
48. Wilson and Stapley, *Titus*, 434.
49. Lenski, "Titus," 918.
50. Wilson and Stapley, *Titus*, 435.
51. Nicoll, *Expositor's Greek Testament*, 4:194.
52. Kenneth S. Wuest, *Wuest's Word Studies* (Grand Rapids: Eerdmans, 1973), 2:193.
53. Albert Barnes, *Notes on the New Testament* (Grand Rapids: Baker, 1885), 12:278.
54. Ibid.
55. Wilson and Stapley, *Titus*, 435.
56. Calvin, *Calvin's Commentaries*, 21:318.
57. Fairbairn, *Pastoral Epistles*, 278.
58. Hendriksen, *Pastoral Epistles*, 371.
59. Gill, *Gill's Commentary*, 6:356.
60. Litfin, "Titus," 765.
61. MacArthur, *Titus*, 111.
62. Balz and Schneider, *Exegetical Dictionary*, 3:3.
63. Hiebert, "Titus," 11:440.
64. Knight, *Pastoral Epistles*, 319.
65. Liddell and Scott, *Greek-English Lexicon*, 118.
66. Poole, *Commentary on the Holy Bible*, 3:803.
67. Lenski, "Titus," 920.
68. Stott, *1 Timothy and Titus*, 193.
69. Exell, *Preacher's Complete Homiletic Commentary*, 29:97.
70. Fairbairn, *Pastoral Epistles*, 280.
71. Lenski, "Titus," 921.
72. Balz and Schneider, *Exegetical Dictionary*, 3:329–30.
73. Ibid., 3:330.
74. Wilson and Stapley, *Titus*, 437.
75. Hendriksen, *Pastoral Epistles*, 372.
76. Gill, *Gill's Commentary*, 6:356.
77. Ellicott, *Commentary on the Whole Bible*, 8:258.
78. Calvin, *Calvin's Commentaries*, 21:319.
79. Barnes, *Notes*, 12:279.
80. BAGD, 712.
81. Liddell and Scott, *Greek-English Lexicon*, 687.

82. Marvin R. Vincent, *Word Studies in the New Testament* (Peabody, MA: Hendrickson, n.d.), 4:344.
83. Nicoll, *Expositor's Greek Testament*, 4:195.
84. Most of this paragraph is taken from Hiebert, "Titus," 11:440.
85. Balz and Schneider, *Exegetical Dictionary*, 1:344–45.
86. Hiebert, "Titus," 11:441.
87. Lenski, "Titus," 923.
88. Barnes, *Notes*, 12:280.
89. Wuest, *Word Studies*, 2:195.
90. Balz and Schneider, *Exegetical Dictionary*, 2:365.
91. Knight, *Pastoral Epistles*, 328.
92. Balz and Schneider, *Exegetical Dictionary*, 3:75.
93. Lenski, "Titus," 924.
94. Fairbairn, *Pastoral Epistles*, 286.
95. Gill, *Gill's Commentary*, 6:358.
96. Hendriksen, *Pastoral Epistles*, 377.
97. Lenski, "Titus," 924.
98. Balz and Schneider, *Exegetical Dictionary*, 1:427.
99. Exell, *Preacher's Complete Homiletic Commentary*, 29:98.
100. Nicoll, *Expositor's Greek Testament*, 4:197.
101. Robertson, *Word Pictures*, 4:605.
102. Ellicott, *Commentary on the Whole Bible*, 8:259.
103. Stott, *1 Timothy and Titus*, 197.

Chapter 13—The Goal Is to Live Sound Doctrine

1. John Calvin, *Calvin's Commentaries* (Grand Rapids: Baker, 1989), 21:324.
2. Horst Balz and Gerhard Schneider, *Exegetical Dictionary of the New Testament* (Grand Rapids: Eerdmans, 1981), 3:62.
3. William Hendriksen, *Exposition of the Pastoral Epistles* (Grand Rapids: Baker, 1979), 386.
4. Albert Barnes, *Notes on the New Testament* (Grand Rapids: Baker, 1885), 12:282. See also Colossians 3:8; 1 Timothy 6:4.
5. John MacArthur, *Titus* (Chicago: Moody, 1996), 143–44.
6. Exell, Joseph S., gen. ed., *The Preacher's Complete Homiletic Commentary* (Grand Rapids: Baker, n.d.), 29:100.
7. T. Wilson and K. Stapley, *What the Bible Teaches: Titus* (Kilmarnock, Scotland: John Ritchie, 1983), 443.
8. Calvin, *Calvin's Commentaries*, 21:927.
9. MacArthur, *Titus*, 148.
10. Henry G. Liddell and Robert Scott, *A Greek-English Lexicon* (Cambridge; Oxford University Press, 1990), 186.
11. Ibid., 751.
12. Henry Alford, *The Greek Testament* (Chicago: Moody, 1958), 2:423.
13. Matthew Poole, *Commentary of the Holy Bible* (Peabody, MA: Hendrickson, n.d.), 3:804.
14. A. Duane Litfin, "Titus," *The Bible Knowledge Commentary*, John F. Walvoord and Roy B. Zuck, eds. (Wheaton: Victor, 1983), 766.
15. George W. Knight, *Commentary on the Pastoral Epistles* (Grand Rapids: Eerdmans, 1992), 341.
16. D. Edmond Hiebert, "Titus," *The Expositor's Bible Commentary* (Grand Rapids: Zondervan, 1978), 11:445.
17. R. C. H. Lenski, "Titus," *St. Paul's Epistles* (Minneapolis: Augsburg, 1961), 932.

18. Hiebert, "Titus," 11:445.

19. Hendriksen, *Pastoral Epistles,* 390.

20. Wilson and Stapley, *Titus,* 445.

21. Knight, *Pastoral Epistles,* 341.

22. Hiebert, "Titus," 11:445. But not all commentators agree. Ellicott translates it "the laver of regeneration but also of renovation by the Holy Spirit" (Charles John Ellicott, *Commentary on the Whole Bible* [Grand Rapids: Zondervan, 1959], 8:). In some ways, it may not matter. The picture seems to be clear that the Holy Spirit is doing a new inner work to bring about salvation. "Here 'washing' means 'laver' . . . , but a closer consideration of the word confirms that it refers to the act of washing rather than to the water in which the bath is taken" (Wilson and Stapley, *Titus*).

23. The filling and baptizing work of the Spirit are not the same functions. The baptismal work of the Spirit places the believer into the spiritual body of Christ.

24. Lenski, "Titus," 936.

25. Patrick Fairbairn, *Commentary on the Pastoral Epistles* (Grand Rapids: Zondervan, 1956), 298.

26. Hendriksen, *Pastoral Epistles,* 392.

27. Marvin R. Vincent, *Word Studies in the New Testament* (Peabody, MA: Hendrickson, n.d.), 4:350.

28. Calvin, *Calvin's Commentaries,* 21:336.

29. Fairbairn, *Pastoral Epistles,* 300.

30. MacArthur, *Titus,* 157.

31. Barnes, *Notes,* 12:286.

32. Kenneth S. Wuest, *Wuest's Word Studies* (Grand Rapids: Eerdmans, 1973), 2:201.

33. Exell, *Preacher's Complete Homiletic Commentary,* 29:103.

34. Fairbairn, *Pastoral Epistles,* 302.

35. W. Robertson Nicoll, *The Expositor's Greek Testament* (Grand Rapids: Eerdmans, 1990), 4:201.

36. MacArthur, *Titus,* 166.

37. Barnes, *Notes,* 12:288.

38. Hendriksen, *Pastoral Epistles,* 397.

39. Balz and Schneider, *Exegetical Dictionary,* 3:267.

40. Ibid., 3:160.

41. Lenski, "Titus," 946.

42. Wilson and Stapley, *Titus,* 453.

43. Ibid.

44. John Gill, *Gill's Commentary* (Grand Rapids: Baker, 1980), 6:364.

45. John Stott, *The Message of 1 Timothy and Titus* (Downers Grove, IL: InterVarsity, 1996), 212.

Chapter 14—Introduction to Philemon

1. Most of this paragraph comes from Richard R. Melick Jr., *Philippians, Colossians, and Philemon* (Nashville: Broadman, 1991), 341–43.

2. One such passage is Leviticus 25:42–43, and it seems to be addressing the problem of a Jew owning another Jew. Other passages to consider are Exodus 21:1–11; Deuteronomy 15:12–18; and Nehemiah 5:1–7.

3. Herbert M. Carson, *The Epistles to the Colossians and to Philemon* (Grand Rapids: Eerdmans, 1960), 22.

4. Melick, *Philippians, Colossians, and Philemon,* 343.

Chapter 15—The Goal Is Reconciliation

1. The "you" in "making mention of you" is singular and more than likely refers to the first named recipient, to wit Philemon.
2. As noted in the introduction, Tychicus seems to be the one who carried Colossians and Philemon back to Colossae.
3. Markus Barth and Helmut Blanke, *The Letter to Philemon*, ECC (Grand Rapids: Eerdmans, 2000), 363.
4. Actually, "accept" ("welcome," NIV) is an imperative.
5. Some see a parallel here with Christ. He paid a debt He didn't owe.
6. James D. G. Dunn, *The Epistles to the Colossians and to Philemon*, NIGTC (Grand Rapids: Eerdmans, 1996), 339n35.
7. William Hendriksen, *Exposition of Philippians, Colossians, and Philemon* (Grand Rapids: Baker, 1979), 224.
8. Ibid.
9. F. F. Bruce, *The Epistles to the Colossians, to Philemon, and to the Ephesians*, NICOT (Grand Rapids: Eerdmans, 1984), 223n102.
10. The "your" of Philemon 25 is plural.

About the Author

Charles Ray holds the Th.M. from Dallas Theological Seminary. He served for several years as professor at Tyndale Theological Seminary in Ft. Worth, TX, and as editor and writer for the Conservative Theological Society Journal. He was also the online editor for theological issues at the school. He and his wife Deborah and their children live near Dallas/Ft. Worth, where he works as an independent Bible researcher and writer.

About the General Editors

Mal Couch is founder and former president of Tyndale Theological Seminary and Biblical Institute in Fort Worth, Texas. He previously taught at Philadelphia College of the Bible, Moody Bible Institute, and Dallas Theological Seminary. His other publications include *The Hope of Christ's Return: A Premillennial Commentary on 1 and 2 Thessalonians, A Bible Handbook to Revelation, and Dictionary of Premillennial Theology.*

Edward Hindson is professor of religion, dean of the Institute of Biblical Studies, and assistant to the chancellor at Liberty University in Lynchburg, Virginia. He has authored more than twenty books, served as coeditor of several Bible projects, and was one of the translators for the New King James Version of the Bible. Dr. Hindson has served as a visiting lecturer at Oxford University and Harvard Divinity School as well as numerous evangelical seminaries. He has taught more than fifty thousand students in the past twenty-five years.